The *Authority* of
LANGUAGE

ALSO BY THE SAME AUTHOR:
Ethics Without Philosophy:
Wittgenstein and the Moral Life

The *Authority* of LANGUAGE

Heidegger, Wittgenstein, and the
Threat of Philosophical Nihilism

by James C. Edwards

University of South Florida Press
Tampa

B
823.3
.E38
1989

University of South Florida Press
© 1990 by the Board of Regents of the State of Florida
∞ Printed in the U.S.A. on acid-free paper.

The activities of the University of South Florida Press
are supported in part by the University of South Florida Research Council.

The University of South Florida Press is a member of University Presses of Florida, the scholarly publishing agency of
the State University System of Florida. Books are selected for
publication by faculty editorial committees at each of Florida's nine public universities: Florida A&M University (Tallahassee), Florida Atlantic University (Boca Raton), Florida
International University (Miami), Florida State University
(Tallahassee), University of Central Florida (Orlando), University of Florida (Gainesville), University of North Florida
(Jacksonville), University of South Florida (Tampa), University of West Florida (Pensacola).
    Orders for books published by all member presses should
be addressed to University Presses of Florida, 15 NW 15th
Street, Gainesville, Florida 32611.

Library of Congress Cataloging-in-Publication Data

Edwards, James C., b. 1943
    The authority of language : Heidegger, Wittgenstein, and the
threat of philosophical nihilism / James C. Edwards.
        p.   cm.
    Bibliography: p.
    Includes index.
    ISBN 0-8130-0942-1 (alk. paper)
    1. Nihilism (Philosophy)—History.   2. Heidegger, Martin,
1889-1976—Contributions in concept of nihilism.   3. Wittgenstein,
Ludwig, 1889-1951—Contributions in concept of nihilism.
4. Nietzsche, Friedrich Wilhelm, 1844-1900—Contributions in concept
of nihilism.   5. Languages—Philosophy—History.   I. Title.
B823.3.E38   1989
149'.8—dc20   89-34739
                                                              CIP

This book is for
Richard Rorty,
for Tom Turner,
and, most especially,
for Jane Chew

Contents

Acknowledgments

Although this is not a long book, it was long in the making, and it is important to me to acknowledge here some of the people who have helped make it possible. Work on it was begun in 1982–83 when, as a Woodrow Wilson Faculty Development Fellow, I was on leave from Furman University and living in Küsnacht, Switzerland, attending lectures there at the C. G. Jung Institute. I was supposed to be writing that year on Freud, Jung, and the imagination, but I found myself thinking hard about Nietzsche instead. The pages I scribbled upstairs at Florastrasse 20 were my first, and very primitive, attempts to understand the threat of philosophical nihilism. I am grateful to Furman for the leave, to the Woodrow Wilson Fellowship Foundation for the grant, and to Jacqueline Portenier, Erika-Ruth Brunotte, and especially Seth and Mary Rubin for making my year in Switzerland such a wonderful time.

Early drafts of parts of chapters 1 and 2 were written in 1984–85 for a Furman faculty seminar on literary theory, conceived and organized by Edgar V. McKnight and William E. Rogers and supported by the National Endowment for the Humanities. My thanks to the NEH and to Edgar, Bill, and all the other members of that stimulating seminar. It remains for me a model of what a college faculty ought to be doing. My thinking about Heidegger was helped by the chance to be a part of the tenth annual Collegium Phenomenologicum, held in Perugia, Italy, in the summer of 1985. I am especially grateful to Charles Scott, that year's director of the Collegium, for his provocative teaching and for his generous hospitality. I also benefited from conversations in Perugia with John Sallis, David Krell, and Reggie Lilly; but I am sure that none of them, including Scott, would endorse the reading of Heidegger presented in these pages.

x

Most of the book was written in Vienna in 1986–87, thanks both to a sabbatical leave from Furman University and to a fellowship from the American Council of Learned Societies. Without the generosity of the ACLS, a full year abroad would not have been possible, and I am deeply indebted to the Council for its support. I am grateful as well both to Furman's Committee on Research and Professional Growth and to John Crabtree, Vice-President for Academic Affairs and Dean, for approving the sabbatical. Crabtree has been steadfast in his support of scholarly activity at Furman, and I am glad to thank him here for his many efforts, extending over a decade, in my behalf. For their indispensable contributions toward making our year in Vienna such a good one, I wish to thank Herta Hirschler and Lonnie Johnson. Gratitude of another kind is felt for the Familie Jos. Schrammel, bakers, and to the staff of Shakespeare and Co. in the Sterngasse.

For the cheerful and efficient conversion of my scrawl into typescript I am indebted to Phyllis Watts, Dana Evans, Sue Collier, and Ann Helms. Both Claude Stulting and Darren Hutchinson read a nearly final draft of the book and made several useful suggestions for improvement. I continue, of course, to be grateful to the other members of the Department of Philosophy at Furman, Tom Buford, Doug MacDonald, and David Shaner, for their friendship and their aid.

This is the second book I have published with the University of South Florida Press, and I am grateful for their continuing interest in publishing philosophy. I would especially like to thank Professor Silvia Fiore, Chair of the Editorial Board at USF Press, for her cordial and helpful efforts in my behalf. I am also deeply in the debt of Teresa Saul of the Central Publishing Unit of the University Presses of Florida in Gainesville. Her editorial attentions to my typescript were timely and welcome.

It remains only to thank those acknowledged in the book's dedication. Richard Rorty's name rarely occurs in the book, but I hope that no one who reads it can fail to see there his comprehensive and beneficial influence. I hesitate to say such things, of course, not least because I am acutely aware of how awkward and shallow my efforts are in comparison to his own. Nevertheless it is true that without Rorty's example and encouragement, neither this book nor my earlier one would have seen the light of day. I wish they were both better indications of what I have learned from him. To Tom Turner and especially to Jane Chew my debts, both intellectual and otherwise, are too enormous and too personal properly to be recounted here; for them, in the spirit of *Tractatus* 7, the dedication itself will have to suffice.

Introduction

Like most works of philosophy, this book is motivated by questions rather than by theses. What I *don't* know is much more likely to direct the course of the argument than what I *do*. Thus it might be helpful to indicate to the reader the kinds of questions that are in play in these pages. Some of them are very general indeed; they are questions about our deepest philosophical and moral self-descriptions, questions about who we think we are, and why. As they present themselves to us today, these questions inevitably have their roots in that powerfully attractive self-image fashioned for us by the greatest Enlightenment thinkers: the image of a free and rational self-legislator deliberately mapping out an epistemic and ethical course through the world. Is that really who we are, or who we most want to be? Could we not agree upon a more edifying, or at least more plausible, form of self-description? But what would be the intellectual and moral costs of abandoning the Enlightenment conception? Is it possible to give up this philosophical view of who we are without at the same time undermining the liberal-democratic forms of political life that the view has nourished?

Some of the book's motivating questions are much more specific; they have to do directly with the work of those philosophers who have most provoked me: Nietzsche, Heidegger, and—above all—Wittgenstein. They are questions about what nihilism means, about the publicity and privacy of language, about rules and what it means to follow them, and about the dangers of sustained philosophical self-scrutiny. In one way or another, all these are questions about authority, in particular the authority of language: about its right to be trusted as it leads us to put to ourselves and one another various claims and questions. All these questions are shadowed by the threat of authority's collapse, or the threat of its reinvention in ever more horrifying forms. Perhaps it will come as no surprise that in writing the book I came to believe that my specific and my general questions must finally converge, that questions about the authority of language cannot be answered without also answering our most fundamental questions of self-identity.

My responses to these questions cannot be summarized here, but it may be useful at the outset to indicate the book's line of argument. In chapter 1 I give an extended account of the threat of philosophical nihilism, relying primarily on the work of Nietzsche and Heidegger. I locate the threat of such nihilism in the appeal of a particular philosophical representation of our lives, which construes our constitutive social practices as structures of rules to be followed by self-conscious agents. Such representation opens a philosophical space between us and our ordinary activities, a space into which philosophical nihilism easily insinuates its threat. I further argue that language is the fundamental test case of such representation: if language can be represented as a set of rules to be followed by speakers, then there is no good reason to doubt that *all* our constitutive social practices can be represented in a rule-referenced way. The question of philosophical nihilism, then, turns on the question of whether language can be so represented. I pursue this question about language in the work of this century's two great philosophers, Martin Heidegger and Ludwig Wittgenstein.

In chapter 2 I examine in detail later Heidegger's account of language. A close reading makes it clear that he successfully resists all rule-referenced explications of our linguistic competence and thus escapes the threat of philosophical nihilism. The authority of our practices is given by the primal authority of language itself: *die Sprache spricht*, says Heidegger, and all human thought and action is grounded in that speaking. But this account of language and its authority is not without deep problems. Heidegger's attack on the Enlightenment picture of the self, an attack founded in his radical experience of language as the primordially speaking *Logos*, threatens the moral and political heritage of the Western democracies. If language is made numinous and sovereign in this way, there seems nothing to protect us from the power of those who claim to speak with its voice. We and our institutions are delivered over to what Heidegger portentously calls our *Destiny*. Such quasi-religious rhetoric is disturbing, since it encourages in us both passivity and a yearning for eschatological transformation, the classic conditions for the rise of totalitarian moral and political structures. The threat of philosophical nihilism has been replaced by the threat of a kind of linguistic fascism, which elevates the *Logos* to the status of a god.

Looking to avoid that unhappy outcome, in chapter 3 I set out the essentials of Wittgenstein's investigation of the place of rules in language. As does Heidegger, Wittgenstein deconstructs any account of language that represents it as a calculus of rules to be followed by speakers. His discussion focuses on "the scene for our language-game," as he calls it, that is, those public circumstances of training and reaction that make possible our general agreement in what we say. Again like Heidegger, Wittgenstein's account of language turns out to be an attack on the Enlightenment picture of the self. At the bottom of our linguistic community is obedience, not free choice; appropriate reaction, not autonomous decision. Yet, I argue, Wittgenstein's views avoid any taint of authoritarianism; language for him is not the incipiently totalitarian *Logos* of Heidegger's account.

Chapter 4, the heart of the essay, develops the comparison between Wittgenstein's and Heidegger's accounts of language into a comparison of their deepest conceptions of authority per se. I argue that Wittgenstein's decentralized account of linguistic authority, an account that locates the source of our epistemic and ethical agreement in certain very general facts of nature, offers the best hope of an alternative to the Enlightenment conception of the autonomous self, while at the same time escaping the disturbing authoritarian implications of Heidegger's conception. Wittgenstein helps us to see that the necessary and sufficient conditions of the sense of language, and therefore of the sense of life as well, are certain brute facts about us, certain constellations of contingencies that make it possible for us to "go on in the same way," as he puts it. Nothing more (and nothing less) is "the scene for our language-game." The sense we make to ourselves and to one another is thus a grace of fate, a fortunate happenstance. There is no *reason* why sense is made. Yet this

Wittgensteinian insight fosters neither despair nor—more important—displaced worship. Language in his account is not the Heideggerian *Logos*; and its authority, grounded as it is on a manifold of accidents, cannot become the object of our religious fantasies. Language ceases to be the last stand of Spirit. In this way the threat of philosophical nihilism is avoided but not at the cost of a worse threat. The book concludes with a reading of the unusual spirituality (as I call it) present in Wittgenstein's later work: a spirituality without Spirit.

The book will, I hope, be of interest to philosophers working in both the Continental and the Anglo-American traditions. I have wanted to put Heidegger and Wittgenstein into genuine conversation with one another and to do so at a level deeper than just the comparison of whatever specific "philosophical views" they may hold. I have wanted to show that for each of them the center of gravity in their thinking is a kind of moral or religious vision, a deep conception of what gives sense to human language and life. That these visions are so powerful, and so very different, indicates our pressing need to come to terms with them. Not every philosopher will agree with my account, certainly. The aim of the book is not ready agreement, which is after all not so hard to achieve, but to provoke a more essential engagement with the work of these two great thinkers.

1

The Threat of Nihilism

I

Philosophers assure us that the unexamined life is not worth living, and so we are inclined to believe, at least until we begin to reflect that philosophy itself, the remedy philosophers prescribe, is apparently not without considerable dangers of its own. Some of these dangers are purely local, of course, and therefore inessential, such as the fatal trouble Socrates found with the reactionary citizens of Athens; but others seem attached to philosophical thinking itself, thus threatening us even where philosophy is most honored and encouraged. The most immediate of these essential risks are personal. Philosophy puts us in danger of discovering our self-deceptions and self-betrayals. When seen from a reflective point of view, one's life may fail to satisfy one's own best sense of what makes a life worthwhile to live. No doubt it is false that only one's firm belief in the worth of something allows one to pursue it with determination and vigor: most of us on occasion intently study baseball scores, or do crosswords, or invent palindromes, or even read airline magazines, without any illusion that these things matter very much, even to us. But these are only parts of a life, usually small parts at that. It would be different, and very painful, if *most* of what one loves and works at could not on examination hold one's respect. Reflection risks disillusionment, and disillusionment invites despair. Philosophy may force one either to despise one's life or to change it. Neither course is easy to run.

But such personal dangers are not the worst. The more general our philosophical reflection becomes, the more acute becomes its threat to us. At its zenith philosophical thinking threatens to produce a thoroughgoing *nihilism*, not just an individual despair. Here is how. Suppose that one were to try to extend to the utmost both the reach and the power of the sort of reflection already familiar to one from the personal case. One's aim in the first instance was merely to achieve a more perspicuous view of one's own practices in relation to one's highest ideals for oneself: to take the measure of one's own integrity, so to speak. The worth of one's life was to be judged by standards usefully sharpened and clarified by reflection but standards still internal to one's own particular point of view. Now, however, one has decided to set one's life in a much wider context of reflection, which will bring it into view alongside forms of human life very different from it, perhaps even antagonistic to it. One wants to judge its ideal worth in relation to these others. More, one does not want merely to employ one's own peculiar (and perhaps somehow objectionable) standards of worth in this comparison. (That might produce only a trivial act of self-congratulation.) Rather, one wants to judge the worth of one's form of life by appeal to standards themselves free of ideological or idiosyncratic taint, standards ideally acceptable across the whole range of lives to be judged. In this way, by giving philosophy its head, one hopes to measure the *fair value* of one's life.

To do so, one needs a reliable and appropriate way of comparing different forms of human life for the purpose of judging their relative worth, and one needs some acceptable criterion (or criteria) in terms of which such judgments of worth can be made. For the first, one can reasonably assume that the fundamental epistemic and ethical practices of these forms of life are the relevant considerations to be compared. There are, of course, any number of characteristic features of a way of life that could become someone's grounds for accepting or rejecting it. Someone could, for example, prefer a given life for the enthusiatic nature of its religious observances, or for its postmodern aesthetic sensibilities, or even for the wide variety of facile entertainments it offers. If a distinctively *philosophical* evaluation of forms of life is to be fair, however, it must take for granted as little as possible that is philosophically controversial, which means it must base its comparisons of worth on features of human excellence generally admitted (at least by philosophers) to be relevant to such comparisons. While many philosophical thinkers could be found to dispute the primary worth of (for example) religion or art or entertainment, and thus would reject evaluations of forms of life made on their basis, very few philosophers will deny that the distinctive excellence of human beings is our capacity for rational thought and action, and that our rationality shows itself most clearly in our self-conscious, self-critical attention to matters of knowledge and value, that is, in our most fundamental activities of epistemic and ethical judgment. Thus these activities, essentially definitive of our rationality, are for philosophers the appropriate characteristics to be compared and evaluated across the range of forms of life. If a given set of basic epistemic and ethical practices can stand up to our most intense critical scrutiny, then the form of life constituted by those practices can be considered essentially free of rational objection and, in that minimal sense at least, is a life worthy to be lived by human beings. (Of course, one might still find such a life not to one's taste. One might still deem a particular form of life, however unobjectionable from a rational point of view, unworthy to be lived *by oneself*. But that is not a *philosophical* objection to it, however strongly felt.)

What criterion of worth is appropriate for judging such practices from a distinctively philosophical point of view? It is not enough to say that our most basic rational practices should be rational. One wants to know what the rationality of epistemic and ethical practices specifically requires of them. What *shows* that they are indeed rational? Is there a distinctive and universal mark of rationality per se, and, if so, what is it? No nontrivial answers to these enormous questions can be essayed at this point. Nevertheless, we can at least recognize an important formal constraint any criterion of philosophical rationality must meet. This formal constraint derives from the fact that epistemic and ethical practices claim authority, not just power, over their participants. These practices claim the *right* to govern our truth claims and the *right* to guide our conduct; they are irreducibly normative. Such claims of epistemic and ethical authority, just because they are claims of right and not mere claims of power, must (we believe) be reflectively acceptable to any of the rational beings they claim to govern. Claims of genuine authority must (we believe) be able to demonstrate their right to be obeyed—and precisely to those persons against which that right is exercised. Otherwise such claims are tyrannical. So even if our philosophical intuitions cannot immediately specify a determinate and substantial criterion of rationality, at least our fundamental moral intuitions do specify a condition any such criterion would have to meet. A genuinely philosophically worthy form of life, one that is essentially free from rational objection, would have to be constituted by basic epistemic and ethical practices the authority of which is reflectively acceptable to *any* rational human being capable of living it. Any adequate criterion of philosophical rationality must be, in this sense, universal.

For the purpose, then, of judging the fair value of one's own life in a distinctively philosophical way, one needs to occupy an intellectual standpoint capable of specifying and clarifying the constitutive epistemic and ethical practices of *any* recognizably human form of life, not just one's own. Then, in reflecting from there on the philosophical worth of these various forms of life, one must employ only the most impersonal and impartial standards for judging the authority of the practices one has thus identified, that is, one must judge these practices against standards of authority that are not only reflectively acceptable to oneself from such a standpoint but also that would be reflectively acceptable for such a purpose to *anyone* capable of occupying that standpoint. (Call this philosophically defined and philosophically favored point of view, consisting of both the techniques of clarification and the standards of judgment, "the transcendental standpoint.")

Such a point of view is, of course, very much an ideal; and, so far as I can see, one would never be in a position to assert with certainty that one was actually in possession of it. The possibility of somehow improving the reach or accuracy of one's philosophical point of view could never be ruled out absolutely, no matter how improbable such improvement might seem at the time. Nevertheless, one *might* be able to make a closely related assertion. Perhaps (in the very distant future, to be sure, if we are to judge by present appearances) one might find oneself able to assert that, after the most extensive philosophical examination and cross-examination available, one had *no positive reason to doubt* that one now occupied the transcendental standpoint as just defined. (Call this "the apparently transcendental standpoint.") In such a philosophical Golden Age, one would have no positive reason to doubt the efficacy or the accuracy of one's techniques for revealing and clarifying the constitutive epistemic and ethical practices of the various forms of human life (that is, one would have an apparently general and reliable philosophical anthropology), and would equally have no reason to believe that the standards of authority used to judge the philosophical worth of these practices were in any respect unfair or unreliable for that purpose. One would thus have an apparently comprehensive and final epistemology and ethical theory.

Imagine, then, that one has achieved the apparently transcendental standpoint just defined. Apparently one is now in the best possible philosophical position fairly to judge the worth of one's life in relation to its alternatives. We can imagine a number of different outcomes to such a process of judgment carried out from this perspective. Three of these are especially significant. First, one might discover one's own form of life to be essentially unobjectionable from a philosophical point of view. That would be a satisfying result, of course: presuming that this life suits one, one can continue to live it with enthusiasm and good conscience. Second, one might discover that one's own form of life is philosophically objectionable (i.e., that some of its constitutive epistemic and ethical practices cannot be justified in terms of the best standards of authority available to one), but that there exist one or more alternative forms of life that are *not* objectionable in those terms. This is a less happy circumstance. Either one must continue to live a life now condemned by one's own philosophical reflection, or one must abandon that life in favor of another one. The latter choice may be easy to make, or it may not, depending on one's temperament and the extent to which the alternatives are distant, unfamiliar, or distasteful.

Finally, there seems a third imaginable outcome to such deliberations. It seems possible to imagine that, when examined individually from the apparently transcendental point of view, *all* the concrete epistemic and ethical practices one could see as actually possible for human beings (that is, all those particular practices that constitute other possible forms of life, as well as those constituting one's own, and including those practices that

were instrumental in bringing one to this philosophically favored standpoint in the first place) seem to be in some specific
way philosophically objectionable. That is, each one of them,
considered on its own, is apparently open to some particular objection (not necessarily the same in every case, of course) when
judged by the refined standards of epistemic and ethical authority available in the apparently transcendental standpoint.

In such a case, apparently, no epistemic or ethical practice
would have the worth it claims. And this first-order crisis of
epistemic and ethical authority would immediately provoke a
deeper one. If one's most philosophically favored standards of
authority, standards that from the apparently transcendental
point of view seemed unobjectionable as to fairness and reliability, now turn out apparently to condemn *all* the practices they
are meant to judge (and from which the standards themselves
were originally distilled), then one cannot help but doubt the
adequacy of those refined standards themselves. One seems in a
terrible bind, therefore: either one must give up all one's particular claims of epistemic and ethical authority, which seems impossible short of madness or death; or one must acknowledge
that, because they lead to this patently unacceptable outcome,
one's best standards for judging such authority are *themselves*
deeply flawed, thus admitting that one's own life cannot be
supported with any philosophical claims of worth made on their
basis.

This outcome to philosophical reflection would apparently
bring on a horrifying collapse in the worth of any life actually
open to us to live. Even if a worthwhile human life remains
conceivable as an abstract possibility (namely, as a life capable
of authoritatively answering every question of authority put to
it), it would now be clear that no such life could be lived by *us*.
Ex hypothesi, none of our actually discriminable epistemic and
ethical practices seem to stand up to our best philosophical reflection on them; what is worse, our very standards of philosophical worth are themselves fundamentally compromised by the
same course of reflection. Reflection *itself* is in question, therefore. We can no longer wholeheartedly trust a process that has
brought us to such a pass. Not only can we not see our way
clear to endorse any form of life we can now recognize, we can-

not even begin to formulate the standards of authority that could lead us to such endorsement in the future. Led by their own logic, our best efforts at philosophical self-examination have foundered. Thus we can no longer trust our own capacities for self-criticism and self-correction; the dream that nourished Socratic philosophy has become a nightmare. In action and in reflection we have been brought to a standstill. Because of the peculiar generality of both the objects and the nature of our reflection in this case, philosophy has (*ex hypothesi*) produced a genuine *nihilism*, not just a personal crisis.

Of course I am not claiming here that such a philosophical smash will ever actually occur. Both in its construction of an ideal situation for philosophical reflection and then in its imagination of an equally ideal destruction of it, what I have just described is patently a fantasy. In my view that is, as yet, no *criticism*. To understand the threat of nihilism, as I wish to, is first of all to recognize that it springs from some such fantasy of philosophical hubris as the one I have sketched above. Like any suicidal fantasy, and that is what this is, the threat of nihilism requires one to project the possibilities of one's present ambitions into their worst possible outcomes. Such a projection is bound to be imprecise at first, perhaps even somewhat incoherent. That does not mean it is not *serious*: a threat need not be actually justified, or even completely rational, in order to be effective, and therefore worth attention. (It is a dangerous prejudice of rationalism to maintain that the only real dangers are those that are rational.)

The pressing philosophical question about nihilism is not: Does the threat of nihilism exist? As a *threat*, and as a threat particularly intimate to the life of contemporary philosophical reflection, it certainly does. The pressing philosophical question about nihilism is: Does this threat have any genuinely philosophical basis, and if so, what is it? Is there anything in our practice of philosophical reflection that either, on the one hand, dooms us to the constant risk of the nihilist collapse of reflection itself or, on the other, insures that such a collapse could not occur, at least as the result of reflection's own powers?

In fact, of course, most professional philosophers today are not very much troubled by the possibility of nihilism. Questioned on the point, most would confidently deny that anything like the frightful circumstances I have just hypothesized could ever come about, either because they believe that transcendental reflection would eventually show that some of our practices *do* live up to the claims of authority made for them, or—more likely these days—because they believe that the transcendental standpoint for criticism of these practices is demonstrably illusory in the first place. Both sorts of responses, powerful as they are in the work of some philosophers, seem to me to be unsatisfactory. In their very different ways, both are trying to defeat the threat of nihilism outright, to show directly by force of philosophical argument that nihilism does not menace reflection in the way it seems to. But the threat of nihilism is a threat to these arguments too. Once the nihilist fantasy has insinuated itself, it is not clear that arguments of this sort can dislodge it. They may already have come too late, or too soon, to be effective. Besides, the history of such warfare in philosophy is not an encouraging one. Nihilism, skepticism, relativism, and so on, continue—as threats, at least—to survive the most energetic and ingenious assaults made on them. Perhaps, of course, we are still waiting for the right weapons, or the right generals; on the other hand, perhaps the war is unwinnable, and it is time to try for some sort of accommodation. Perhaps the fantasy of philosophical self-destruction has some genuinely philosophical basis after all. That is the possibility I want to investigate in this book.

II

In this connection it is interesting to glance at the recent work of two distinguished contemporary philosophers, Bernard Williams and Thomas Nagel.[1] Although neither is partial to the word 'nihilism', and neither openly trades in the sort of global skepticism I have just fantasized, both Williams and Nagel are willing to take seriously the various threats that philosophical reflection may pose to itself, and to the life it proposes to benefit. Both men are clearly trying to put themselves on a new foot-

---

1. Bernard Williams, *Ethics and the Limits of Philosophy*, and Thomas Nagel, *The View from Nowhere*.

ing in relation to these threats, one that concedes neither too much nor too little to the possibility of some sort of nihilist collapse.

Williams, whose book is specifically concerned with ethical theory in its diverse relations to ethical practice, argues persuasively that philosophical reflection of the very expansive sort we have been considering is likely to destroy substantial ethical knowledge, the sort of knowledge that shows itself in the ability to apply truthfully, and without hesitation or self-doubt, "thick" ethical concepts like *treachery, promise, brutality,* and *courage* (*Ethics and the Limits of Philosophy*, p. 129). Such knowledge is characteristic not only of societies more homogeneous and less self-critical than our own but also of the earlier stages of our own individual ethical development (pp. 148–49; 167–69). Williams recognizes that the destruction of such knowledge removes the traditional basis of ethical conviction, thus tending to undercut the motivation to act as ethical considerations require. Without the conviction that one's ethical beliefs are known to be *true,* that is, without a backing of ethical realism to justify their claims of authority, why would one continue to act in accordance with these beliefs, especially at the cost of one's own (or someone else's) comfort or pleasure?

It is just such substantial ethical truth claims that are, according to Williams, typically undermined by sustained philosophical activity. Socrates was wrong, says Williams: in fact reflection transmutes ethical knowledge into opinion, not vice versa. What is there, then, to stop the slide into a confusion of opinions and then into a resultant brutality? Won't philosophical investigations bring on a sort of ethical nihilism, a loss of trust that ethical considerations really matter?

Williams himself believes that ethical conviction grounded in substantial truth claims is now mostly impossible and must be replaced in reflective societies by what he calls ethical *confidence* (*Ethics,* p. 170); but, apart from noting that this is a social phenomenon and requires in a society a respect for the kind of reflective argument that brought about the need for such confidence in the first place, he says little about how it may be had. The book is better at portraying the threat of ethical nihilism than at taking its measure.

In his book Nagel addresses the threat of nihilism not just as the collapse of ethical authority but as an instance of the general philosophical difficulty of connecting the subjective standpoint of an individual (whether in reference to knowledge, value, or life's meaning) with a more objective understanding of reality. The further one submits a subjective view of oneself and one's practices to objective scrutiny, says Nagel, the less easy it is to maintain and to reconcile these two natural perspectives. A more and more objective view of things seems to *preclude* subjectivity, not incorporate it into a broader view and thus to explain it; yet neither perspective seems rationally dispensable for human beings. When one looks at the ordinary texture of any life, for instance, it is composed of subjective concerns that range from the ridiculous (fretting about one's haircut, to use Nagel's own example) to the sublime (trying to solve the four-color problem without computer help). To live a human life is to pursue, with an intensity that can astound or embarrass, some such set of particular interests of one's own.

> Yet there is a point of view from which none of it seems to matter. When you look at your struggles as if from a great height, in abstraction from the engagement you have with this life because it is yours—perhaps even in abstraction from your identification with the human race—you may feel a certain sympathy for the poor beggar, a pale pleasure in his triumphs and a mild concern for his disappointments. And of course given that this person exists, there is little he can do but keep going till he dies, and try to accomplish something by the standards internal to his form of life. But it wouldn't matter much if he failed, and it would matter perhaps even less if he didn't exist at all. The clash of [subjective and objective] standpoints is not absolute, but the disparity is very great. (Nagel, *The View from Nowhere*, pp. 215-16)

If the objective standpoint were to be sustained to the exclusion of the subjective, the threat of a sort of nihilism would be very real indeed, as Nagel himself points out.

If we push the claims of objective detachment to their logical conclusion, and survey the world from a standpoint completely detached from all interests, we discover that there is *nothing*—no values left of any kind: things can be said to matter at all only to individuals within the world. The result is objective nihilism. (P. 146)[2]

Although its source is different, Nagel's "objective nihilism" is identical in result to the sort of epistemic and ethical collapse sketched in the last section. Without effective epistemic and ethical values, the authority of such practices would disappear.

While I deeply admire what both Williams and Nagel have done in their books, I believe that it would be useful to take another run at the matter of nihilism. Subtle and suggestive as their responses to philosophical skepticism are, I am not convinced that either has given an account of this threat that is sufficiently differentiated—that is, an account that, first, locates precisely enough the presumption of modern philosophical reflection that opens our reflective lives to the possibility of a skeptical, perhaps ultimately nihilist, reduction (call this *understanding nihilism*) and, second, specifies the place of the threat of nihilism, once understood, within the entire economy of the examined life that philosophy honors (call this *appreciating nihilism*). To be sure, neither Williams nor Nagel has such an account as his major concern. Williams interests himself mostly with ethics, which is only one area of life threatened by philosophical reflection, and perhaps not even the central one, while Nagel discusses the threat of nihilism exclusively as it arises in the conflict between the subjective and objective viewpoints. I want to see whether the issue can be grasped in terms more exclusively its own.

For this purpose I propose an approach both historical and yet somewhat indirect. I propose attempting to understand and appreciate the threat of nihilism by looking first at its appearance in Nietzsche's work. This seems appropriate not only because it was Nietzsche who firmly established the term within

2. Nagel does not wholly endorse the point of view expressed in these sentences.

the vocabulary of philosophy but even more because he is the rare philosopher who actually *welcomes* nihilism, who can see it (in some of its forms at least) as "the highest degree of powerfulness of spirit, the over-richest life—partly destructive, partly ironic" (*The Will to Power*, sec. 14). While most philosophers naturally tend to fear a wholesale collapse of our common ethical and epistemic standards and thus try to prevent it, Nietzsche has designed his deepest philosophical reflections to *provoke* exactly that collapse, since it is (he believes) only out of the ruins of the oldest and highest of our values that radically new standards of choice can come. Painful as it may be, a philosophically induced nihilism is for him the necessary stage between the decadence of our present civilization and the brilliance of the one that we await. It seems likely that the nature of nihilism would be especially clear where epistemic and ethical reductionism is specifically intended as a *tool* of properly philosophical thinking, rather than just worried about as a hypothetical and accidental effect of it. Thus Nietzsche's work is the logical place, both historically and analytically, to begin my inquiry.

That is true, but only partly; thus the need for indirection. No great philosopher's work is transparent or all of a piece, of course, but Nietzsche's writings pose particularly acute difficulties for philosophical interpretation. Some of these are deliberately of his own making. His overheated rhetoric and his determinedly "literary" style are supposed to prevent a distant, and purely intellectual, contemplation of what he says. He wants his work to be a provocation, not just another barren philosophical construction. Thus he is apparently often willing to barter precision for effect. One can certainly understand, and even admire, such an intention on the part of a serious writer, but it does present significant problems for philosophical readers, who naturally tend to value clarity over engagement and argument over elegance.

But when it comes to understanding exactly what Nietzsche means by nihilism, some of the major problems are not his responsibility at all. The term 'nihilism' occurs in his work only in *The Will to Power*, and there mostly in the first two parts of Book 1, entitled "Nihilism" and "History of European Nihilism." That presents an immediate difficulty of an editorial sort, of course, since *The Will to Power* is only a collection of notes for a book, notes written at various times and in various states of mind, and never released for publication by Nietzsche himself.[3] These fragments were first published by Elizabeth Förster-Nietzsche in 1901, a year after her brother's death and twelve years after his complete mental collapse. The form of their publication, indeed the fact of their having been published at all, is highly controversial.

There are, therefore, two sorts of interpretive problems here. The first is the general hermeneutical question of how to read, understand, appreciate, and criticize philosophical writing so deliberately unphilosophical as Nietzche's. Second is the problem of whether to take *The Will to Power* as a genuinely Nietzschean text at all, and thus how to read the remarks on nihilism found there. Most philosophers have answered the first question largely by ignoring it. After some perfunctory comments on the glories of his language, his reliance on aphoristic exaggeration, his use of parables and narratives, and so on, they have continued to try to read Nietzsche as a philosopher among philosophers. They have assumed that he, like other philosophers, has a particular set of claims about knowledge, value, mind, and reality that he wants to present to the consideration of other thinkers, claims that he puts forth on the basis of some (explicit or implicit) argumentation intended to commend itself to the sort of philosophical intellect formed by the Western tradition of rational speculation and judgment. They have treated him, to put it shortly, as a *metaphysician*, even if, as is the case in Heidegger's famous analysis, he is a metaphysician who stands traditional metaphysics on its head.[4] Consistent with this hermeneutic, then, most philosophers have read *The Will to Power* as the bits and pieces of an unfinished metaphysical treatise, the preliminary drafts of the magnum opus that would set forth in all its philosophical detail the grand conception of reality Nietzsche had been working toward all his life. The remarks about nihilism are read in this metaphysical light.

I have already had to mention Heidegger, because he is responsible, curiously enough, both for the most impressive and thorough treatment of Nietzsche as the last great metaphysi-

3. For details, see Kaufmann's preface to his edition of *The Will to Power*.
4. A notable exception is Alexander Nehamas, *Nietzsche: Life as Literature*.

cian of the West and for the growing sense of dissatisfaction among philosophers with that sort of interpretation. No one could read Nietzsche as a metaphysician more deeply and intently than Heidegger does, but the overall effect of his powerful reading has been—at least in the last few years—that no one has much wanted to continue to do so. Thus his account is a kind of *reductio*. It renders Nietzsche both comprehensible and passé. (That may very well have been Heidegger's intention.) Nevertheless, in the next section of this chapter I will sketch the major features of Heidegger's account of Nietzsche's nihilism, not because I believe it to be the best philosophical account of Nietzsche per se (I most emphatically do *not*), but because it has the triple virtues of being historically influential, readily understandable, and capable of helping one see—in spite of its own inadequacies as Nietzsche-interpretation—where the threat of nihilism really lies.

III

There is certainly no possibility, and thankfully no need, of doing justice here to the full weight of Heidegger's reading of Nietzsche.[5] My intention is to try to understand what nihilism means, and so I will concentrate only on those parts of his analysis that are most useful to that end. The key to Heidegger's reading is, as I have noted, his assumption that Nietzsche is to be understood as a metaphysician, and in particular as a metaphysician who inverts the standard ideas of Western metaphysics. As Heidegger understands it, metaphysics is the essence of philosophy. Any philosopher worthy of the name tries first of all to offer a general ontology: to set out a comprehensive account of what being really is, in all its forms and manifestations. The history of philosophy, and thus (for Heidegger) the history of Western civilization, can be charted by reference to changes and refinements in these metaphysical conceptions.

5. This work is collected in Martin Heidegger, *Nietzsche* (Pfullingen: Verlag Gunther Neske, 1961). An English translation edited by David F. Krell, in four volumes, has been published in New York by Harper and Row.

The truth of being as a whole has been called *metaphysics*. Every era, every human epoch, is sustained by some metaphysics and is placed thereby in a definite relation to being as a whole and also to itself. (Heidegger, *Nietzsche*, 4:5)

If Nietzsche is truly a philosopher, thinks Heidegger, then the essence of his thinking will be found in some such enunciation of "the truth of being as a whole." All the other topics of his thinking—his perspectival epistemology, his nonegoistic philosophy of mind, his antimoralistic value theory—can be shown to derive from this fundamental conception. This conception Heidegger locates in Nietzsche's remarks about the will to power. To Heidegger's ear, these remarks promulgate a metaphysics that is antithetical to the Platonic metaphysics that had for so long dominated the West.

What exactly is the metaphysical Platonism that, according to Heidegger, Nietzsche opposes with his doctrine of the will to power? The essence of Platonism is its philosophical differentiation of what is into "two worlds," an idea that incorporates both an epistemological/ontological distinction and a distinction of worth. The world we ordinarily inhabit is a world of change, destruction, making and unmaking, attempt and failure, trial and error. Even our most forcible experiences of such a world apparently do not furnish us genuine *knowledge*—i.e., truth that does not alter with alterations in perceiver or environment—but only some degree of *opinion*. We find ourselves awash in a flux of images, unable to fasten upon anything that lasts. In his philosophy Plato certainly admits this apparent instability of the everyday world and of our understanding; indeed, he insists upon it. But he also insists upon a "world" outside the transient life we ordinarily experience: a world of things that exist in themselves and for themselves; a world that is supersensuous, immutable, eternal and perfect; a world that is truly knowable. This is the world of the Forms revealed in mathematical proof and philosophical dialectic, a world of pure "Being," not the messy and unpredictable "Becoming" we are accustomed to.

The most striking presentation of this Platonic doctrine is, of course, the Myth of the Cave in Book VII of the *Republic*. In that myth, probably the most familiar and influential of all philosophical narratives, some prisoners gradually and with difficulty make their way up from a subterranean world of smoky darkness and flickering shadows into the full light and air of day. There they see the actual objects of which they had in the cave seen only the images, and finally they are even able to look directly at the sun itself, which they recognize as the source of all light and thus of all vision. After this remarkable experience, they (unwillingly) return to the cave to tell the others still chained there of the reality—the "true world"—they have seen outside.

The story makes vividly clear the epistemological/ontological distinction between the "two worlds" of Becoming and Being. The choice of images also demonstrates that for Plato the *worth* of our ordinary life is deeply inferior to the worth of the world that lies above it. Cut off from the warm light and easy breath of the earth's surface, life in a cave is cold, oppressive, and dangerous; to remain in such a region could be satisfying to human beings only if they were deceived or otherwise degraded. This sharp distinction of value between the realms of Being and Becoming is crucial, and it prepares the way for Platonism to become "Christianized" and "moralized." For Nietzsche, Christianity is just "Platonism for the people" (Heidegger, *Nietzsche*, 4:46). With its emphasis on earthly life as a dark vale of tears to be passed through on one's way to the clear sight and permanent rewards of heaven, it preserves and extends the essential metaphysical and evaluative structures of Platonism. In both the Christian and the Platonic myths, ultimate human good is identified as the submission of human life and will to the transcendent ideals of the "true world." Both thereby encourage the human being to despise humanness itself. One's ordinary epistemic and ethical limitations are interpreted as corruption, as "sin"; finitude is turned into weakness, which can be overcome only by its sacrifice to something "higher." Human life can have genuine value only because it can be made to answer to something *more* than life.

These are not just the quaint superstitions of an earlier time, of course. The post-Christian idea of "morality" (whether Kantian or utilitarian) also depends upon positing the same sort of "true world" as ultimately valuable, although that world is now constituted by a priori standards of rightness or goodness rather than by mythological creatures like Forms or gods. "Morality" participates as well, therefore, in the radical devaluation of ordinary human life and will. However secular or demythologized its manner of presentation, says Nietzsche, "morality" is always an avatar of Platonism.

And not just "morality": epistemology belongs to the same family; it too is an attempt to make what we actually want and need to do (viz., to accept some truth claims about the world and to reject others) answer to something more than just our individual or collective desires and conventions. Just as the moralist requires that particular ethical traditions and individual ambitions answer to the demands of a universal "morality," so the epistemologist insists that particular epistemic practices be shown to mirror some a priori standards of reliability. In this way, according to Nietzsche, both the "good man" of the Western ethical and religious traditions and the "wise man" of the Western philosophical and scientific traditions have become slaves of the Platonic "true world" (Heidegger, *Nietzsche*, vol. 4, sec. 12).

On Heidegger's reading, Nietzsche's affirmation that reality is will to power is his absolute denial of the Platonic true world in all its forms. This, and not some trivial avowal of religious atheism, is also the force of the familiar Nietzschean claim that "God is dead."[6] To say these things is to claim that there is no transcendent, supersensuous world of any description, whether religious, philosophical, or scientific, to which human life and human will must conform in order to have their proper worth. *All* reality is will to power instead.

As Heidegger himself is quick to point out, however, exactly what Nietzsche means by will to power in this context is not so easy to see. Because it functions as a comprehensive metaphysical characterization, it is certainly a mistake to hear the phrase as meaning some sort of intentional, individual power-grubbing,

6. Martin Heidegger, "The Word of Nietzsche: 'God is Dead.' "

as if everything in reality consciously wanted to play the tyrant over everything else. That would be to interpret all will on the model of *human* will, which *is* of course often self-conscious and individually focused; what is wanted instead is to be able to see the individual human will to power (as expressed in the self-conscious drive toward tyranny over others, for instance) as a partial expression of something universal.

Heidegger interprets the basic nature of the Nietzschean will to power not as tyranny (not as power amassed for the sake of controlling others) but as *command*: power amassed for the sake of *self*-control, self-control that aims only at more self-control, thus requiring ever more power over oneself. Nietzschean will to power is not, in its essence, the particular desire to rule others, a desire that some beings have and some do not; rather, it is just his name for the *desire* of all life for more of its own life. A form of life wants, at bottom, only to live; will wants only to be able to continue to will. Will wants its particular "objects" (e.g., food, political power, Impressionist paintings) only as means to the end of its own continuance. In that way, all wills (and all lives) are the same.

> What the will wills it has already. For the will wills its will. Its will is what it has willed. The will wills itself. (Heidegger, "The Word of Nietzsche," p. 77)

What is required of life in order that it continue to live is *growth*: "To the essence of life belongs the will to grow, enhancement" (p. 73). Expressed in terms of the will to power this says: What is required of will in order that it continue to will is *self-commanding power*, that is, power that continually masters its own continual increase.

> For the essence of power lies in being master over the level of power attained at any time. Power is power only when and so long as it remains power-enhancement, and commands for itself "more power." Even a mere pause in power-enhancement, even the mere remaining at a standstill at a level of power, is already the beginning of a decline of power. (P. 78)

Nietzsche's metaphysical employment of the idea of the will to power is summarized by Heidegger in the following way:

> "Becoming" is, for Nietzsche, the "will to power." The "will to power" is thus the fundamental characteristic of "life," which word Nietzsche often uses also in the broad sense according to which, within metaphysics (cf. Hegel), it has been equated with "becoming." "Will to power," "becoming," "life," and "Being" in the broadest sense—these mean, in Nietzsche's language, the Same (*Will to Power*, Aph. 582, 1885–86, and Aph. 689, 1888). (Heidegger, "Word of Nietzsche," p. 74)

The Platonic "true world" does not exist; only "life" does.

But complex forms of "life" (e.g., human life) cannot exist without "value." Life that wants to preserve and enhance itself—and all life does, of course—must have a "point of view," a sense of direction capable of forming and containing its energies; otherwise it will dissipate its strength in confusion, declining in power until it finally dies. The more differentiated and complex a form of life is, the more conscious and "objective" its point of view needs to be. Algae doesn't depend upon consciousness and self-awareness to maintain and to extend itself; human beings do. In order to continue to live, therefore, human life must *consciously reckon* on something, and *value* is that upon which it reckons: "Value is value inasmuch as it counts (*gilt*)" (Heidegger, "Word of Nietzsche," p. 72). Value is what gets consciously counted on, reckoned with, by individuals and by cultures. It is the "objectification" of a "point of view."

Human civilization can thus be understood as a sequence of such values. Each form of human life uses a particular set of such structures of interpretation to define for itself both a range of goals and the appropriate means of pursuing them. Nietzsche's basic metaphysical doctrine now allows one to see for the first time exactly how such values arise.

> Here it is clear: values are the conditions of itself posited by the will to power. Only when the will to power, as the fundamental characteristic of everything real, comes to appearance, i.e., becomes true, and accordingly is

> grasped as the reality of everything real, does it become
> evident from whence values originate and through what
> all assessing of value is supported and directed. The
> principle of value-positing has now been recognized.
> (Heidegger, "Word of Nietzsche," p. 75)

That principle is, of course, the will to power: nothing more; nothing less.

Thus the values of a given form of life can in no way be claimed to mirror the structures of some religious or philosophical "true world." Values originate only in the fertility of a form of life working to preserve and enhance itself, and they survive (if they do) only because they perform that task of preservation/enhancement well, not because they represent some a priori realm of truth or goodness. One can now recognize that all values are (to use Heidegger's word) *posited*; truth and goodness are made, not discovered.

> "Truth" is therefore not something there, that might be
> found or discovered—but something that must be
> created and that gives a name to a process, or rather to a
> will to overcome that has in itself no end—introducing
> truth, as a *processus in infinitum*, an active
> determining—not a becoming-conscious of something
> that is in itself firm and determined. It is a word for the
> "will to power." (Nietzsche, *Will to Power*, sec. 512,
> p. 298)

It is now easy to see how the issue of nihilism assumes the focus of Nietzsche's attention. Our civilization rests upon metaphysical (i.e., Platonic/Jewish-Christian) underpinnings. To say that is not just to remark the tired historical fact that our civilization grew from ideas that Plato, the Yahwist, and Paul of Tarsus planted and fed; it is to say that our "highest values" *still* make essential reference to a "true world" beyond the everyday. Of course not every contemporary Western form of life is explicitly religious or philosophical. Various forms of secularism and positivism, usually supported by appeals to the natural and social sciences, have reduced for most of us the power and the charm of exuberant metaphysical speculation. Nevertheless, our

culture remains, on the whole, stoutly "idealistic" in its attitudes toward knowledge and morals. We are still a civilization
that feels the need to ground its most cherished epistemic and
ethical practices in something that endures, in something genuinely "truthful." We still want to believe that our moral values
and our scientific theories are "realistic," that is, that they accurately answer to something really there, not something that
we have merely hypothesized or otherwise conjured into being.
Indeed, the way the natural and social sciences are now treated
by popular culture as our fundamental sources of truth, inspiration, and comfort shows that they have largely assumed the
metaphysical place formerly occupied by religion and philosophy. The "true world" is now presumed to be inhabited by the
physicist, the political scientist, or the market researcher. In
this way, scientific "realism" is a scaled-down, latter-day version of Platonic "idealism."

But Nietzsche's metaphysics of the will to power cuts the root
of *any* such "idealism." If there is no "true world" to measure
our practices against, no truth at all except as "an active determining—not a becoming-conscious of something that is in itself
firm and determined," then both in science and in ethics the
idea of rational authority has lost its wonted force. Human
thought and action answer to nothing beyond their own absolute need to continue, by hook or by crook.

The Nietzschean recognition that every idea is a value, and
that all values—even our highest ones, such as truth, justice,
freedom, rationality, and the like—are posited by the will to
power, not grounded in some "true world," first of all brings
about the *devaluation* of such values. Because we can now see
that they do not have the "Platonic" authority that they claim,
they no longer have the effective power over our theoretical and
practical activities that they formerly did. We begin to question
their hold on us. This is the first stage of nihilism.

> What does nihilism mean? *That the highest values de-*
> *valuate themselves.* The aim is lacking; "why?" finds no
> answer. (Nietzsche, *Will to Power*, sec. 2)

But since complex forms of life must have effective values in
order to continue to live, this devaluation must be followed by a

revaluation. Such revaluation can take two forms, thus producing two kinds of nihilism, *incomplete* or *complete* (Heidegger, "Word of Nietzsche," pp. 66–70).

In incomplete nihilism the necessary revaluation replaces one's former "highest values" with new ones, while leaving the *structure* of one's values essentially unaltered: there remains, that is, the assumption (in some form) of a "true world" to which thought and action must somehow conform, although the particular values constituting that realm of authority are acknowledged to be different from those that went before. For a ready example of such incomplete nihilism, think of the nineteenth-century positivist critique of religion. Positivism strenuously and sometimes courageously attacked many of the particular epistemic and ethical practices characteristic of conventional religious life, and it tried to substitute some new values for those old exploded ones; but the hierarchical and Platonic structure of those new values remained essentially unchanged by the upheaval. The positivists feared intellectual anarchy at least as much as the theologians feared apostasy and licentiousness. Authority had to be preserved, therefore; there still must be some "highest values" to which all one's other values and interests must appropriately answer. There had to remain, that is, a set of epistemic and ethical practices assumed to have a final and demonstrable authority, a "truthfulness," that was grounded in something more than human convention, hypothesis, or interpretation. With positivism, of course, science and "the scientific method" were those "highest values." Everything answered to the demand that it be "scientific." The positivists were still looking to a "true world" as the source of authority; only now it was the "true world" revealed in the laboratory and in fossil strata, not in the Bible or in the teaching of the church. We still mostly live, according to Nietzsche, in the midst of such incomplete nihilism, and such temporizing only makes our sense of dislocation and fragility more acute (*Will to Power*, sec. 28). We are, he believes, fighting a losing battle when we try to maintain the "true world," even if only in a demythologized form like "scientific realism." Once the avalanche has begun, it is hopeless to stop it halfway down the slope.

Complete nihilism is possible only when there is a revaluation of the *structure* of value itself. Such revaluation requires, as Heidegger puts it, a new "principle" for the positing of value ("Word of Nietzsche," p. 70). The complete nihilist realizes that values have no source and no justification other than the will to power. There is no "true world" outside of "life" at all, and no *need* for it. The only "principle" of life and thought is the will to power itself: "An act or accomplishment is valid as such only to the extent that it serves to equip, nurture, and enhance will to power" (Heidegger, *Nietzsche*, 4:9). Epistemic and ethical practices have no "authority" other than this. The one who fully acknowledges this new "principle" of evaluation, and can rejoice in it, is a new creature: the Overman.

> From Nietzsche's point of view, the Overman is not meant to be a mere amplification of prior man, but the most unequivocally singular form of human existence that, as absolute will to power, is brought to power in every man to some degree and that thereby grants him his membership in being as a whole—and that shows him to be a true "being," close to reality and "life." The Overman simply leaves the man of traditional values behind, *overtakes* him, and transfers the justification for all laws and the positing of all values to the overpowering of power. (Heidegger, *Nietzsche*, 4:9)

In this way the Overman is, according to Heidegger, ready to embark upon "the absolute domination of the globe" (*Nietzsche*, 4:9). Unhampered in thought or action either by the imaginary constraints of a "true world" or by any sense of grief or nostalgia for the lost metaphysical constructions of "man," the Overman is the complete (or "classical") nihilist. The Overman has been able to cast off the stifling "authority" of his culture's constitutive epistemic and ethical practices by seeing through to their hidden mainspring (viz., the will to power). He has been able to make the wholesale collapse of all his standards into a *liberation*. He has moved "beyond" authority.

IV

Assuming (as we are here) that Heidegger is correct in his account so far, we can easily see what has made Nietzsche's kind of nihilism so unappealing—sometimes even so frightening—a prospect to most of his readers. In the first place, the initial "devaluation of the highest values" he foresees is bound to be both painful and dangerous to a civilization that has been built (as ours has) on the assumption of a "true world" ready to hand as both goal and limit of our ambitions. There is always the threat that in such a context that devaluation will be so severe that no effective revaluation can succeed it.

> The strength of the spirit may be worn out, exhausted, so that previous goals and values have become incommensurate and no longer are believed; so that the synthesis of values and goals (on which every strong culture rests) dissolves and the individual values war against one another: disintegration—and whatever refreshes, heals, calms, numbs, emerges into the foreground in various disguises, religious or moral, or political, or aesthetic, etc. (Nietzsche, *Will to Power*, sec. 23)

This is the sort of wholesale collapse imagined in the first section of this chapter: a complete loss of epistemic and ethical authority, brought about by sustained reflection. The philosophical search for a grounding "truth" has undermined one's hopes of ever attaining it in a form sufficient to meet one's original need, and the worth of life itself is therefore placed in question. But one cannot stand still forever. As Nietzsche astutely points out, this sort of reflective dead end makes one extremely vulnerable to the enemies of reflection itself. The self-lacerated intellect yearns for relief, and "whatever refreshes, heals, calms, numbs, emerges into the foreground." Philosophy makes way for some form of "faith." Thus reflection can destroy itself in the name of "life," but it is a life made of self-imposed insensibility and anti-intellectual *ressentiment*.

Such reactionary exhaustion of the spirit would be bad, no doubt; but the sort of revaluation Nietzsche hopes for could be considerably worse, at least if one takes him at his own account of it.

> From now on there will be more favorable precondi-
> tions for more comprehensive forms of dominion, whose
> like has never yet existed. And even this is not the most
> important thing; the possibility has been established for
> the production of international racial unions whose task
> will be to rear a master race, the future "masters of the
> earth;"—a new, tremendous aristocracy, based on the
> severest self-legislation, in which the will of philosophi-
> cal men of power and artist-tyrants will be made to en-
> dure for millennia—a higher kind of man who, thanks to
> their superiority in will, knowledge, riches, and influ-
> ence, employ democratic Europe as their most pliant and
> supple instrument for getting hold of the destinies of the
> earth, so as to work as artists upon "man" himself.
> Enough: the time is coming when politics will have a
> different meaning. (Nietzsche, *Will to Power*, sec. 960)

In trying to defend Nietzsche against the common slander that claims him as a proto-Nazi (a defense well worth making, of course), it has become the custom to play down such disturbing remarks as these by assuming that they (along with his vicious remarks about women) are readily separable from the main body of his philosophical work. One is assured—by silence if by nothing else—that Nietzsche's sketch here of the Overman as a member of an aggressive "master race" bent upon dominion of the earth is deceptive and inessential, too influenced by unfortunate fears and damages peculiar to its author. The Nietzschean idea is supposed to be better than his own understanding of it.

One wonders, however, whether such complacency is truly justified. Certainly it is a vulgar error to construe the Overman as some sort of ogre lusting to manipulate and consume those less savvy and less powerful than himself. The philosophical writer patiently and scrupulously working away on his books in his rented room in Sils Maria can be just as much an image of the Overman as is the political leader addressing a torchlight rally. Furthermore, there is no need to believe that the "complete" revaluation of his values will saddle the Overman with sadistic desires for despoiling and humiliating others. Quite the contrary, in fact: the revaluation should leave him entirely free of *ressentiment*, which according to Nietzsche is the root cause of such sadism.

Nevertheless, there remains something about this figure that is deeply unsettling to most of us. Part of our uneasiness derives from the fact that the Overman is the apex of "humanism," in the sense that he represents an absolutely unfettered pursuit of human interests to the exclusion of all others. All that there is lies open to the Overman's view as raw material to be used for good or ill in service of life's preservation and enhancement. Although there is no metaphysical requirement that he identify "life" with "human life" (any more than that he identify "human life" with "my life"), there is equally no effective reason for him *not* to do so. From a philosophical point of view, of course, life is life: there is no metaphysical reason why one biological form of it should be worth any more than another; there is no "true world" of value to grant such a distinction. All "worth" is posited by life itself, by the will to power. But the will to power the Overman knows is *human* will to power. The "complex form" of life that self-consciously posits values for human beings is *human* life. Thus the impetus of his action inevitably inclines toward human interests as paramount.

Such a one may, of course, decide ("posit") that the good of other forms of life is conducive to his own, and so he may decide to spare from destruction the whales or the Grand Canyon; but such actions will always have the form of condescension. There is, from the Overman's point of view, no value in whales or canyons "in themselves." They are valuable only insofar as they are, or may become, valuable to him. "Man is the measure of all things" (Heidegger, *Nietzsche*, 4:85–90). For some of us there is something decidedly ugly in this image of the Overman as a sophisticated consumer of the planet, with all reality set before him as a meal to be prepared and eaten according to his own taste and constitution. Even if the Overman is not a tyrant-in-training, as the vulgar reading supposes, he is—or will soon become—an imperialist of the human; and that can seem bad enough.

There is apparently another problem to be faced here as well, one more integral to the life of the Overman itself. It is, one might say, the problem of death. If life is just the quest for more life, then at some point that quest must finally be disappointed. If the Overman's life is self-consciously lived in order to preserve and enhance his own form of life, and lived for that reason only, as a full acknowledgment of the metaphysics of the will to power apparently demands, then sooner or later that life will have to be accounted a failure, since that form of life, like *all* forms of life, will eventually disappear.[7] In the long run, said Keynes, we're all dead. A life lived according to the "principle" of the will to power must be, therefore, inherently frustrating, or at least unsatisfying, once the very long view of it is taken. It all comes to nothing in the end. (Perhaps that is true of *any* life, but that is not the point. It is no defense of the life of the Overman to say that it shares in the absurdity of all life.) It is likely, of course, that the life of the Overman could still be lived in the face of this recognition—human beings show a remarkable ability to survive under adversity—but it is not easy to see how such a life could be joyous and self-overpowering in the way Nietzsche portrays it. Seen as the whole of life, the Dionysian dance can begin to look like a form of self-imposed, self-perpetuating hysteria.

Of course, that something seems ugly or frustrating or hysterical (*to us*) doesn't make it *false*. These objections to complete nihilism, even if they can be sustained against the charge of having misread Nietzsche, can always be dismissed as superficial and "moralistic." Not only do they depend for their force on values that could not survive the sort of revaluation that would produce the Overman (so that the carping about "humanism," for example, can be interpreted from the complete nihilist's perspective as an expression of "man's" neurotic self-distrust, soon

---

7. I am ignoring here the so-called doctrine of the eternal return. If this is interpreted as a kind of metaphysical cosmology, another—but equally painful—sort of frustration will beset the life of the Overman.

to be replaced with the Overman's confidence in his own nobility), they also fail to engage the essence of Nietzsche's position, namely, the metaphysics of the will to power, upon which rests (according to Heidegger) all his visionary claims. If this point is true, and for the moment we are content to restrict ourselves to Heidegger's reading, then the only legitimate critique of nihilism is some sort of metaphysical one: either one that internally argues against the Nietzschean metaphysics of the will to power on metaphysical grounds or one (like Heidegger's own) that tries to "overcome" metaphysics itself, thus "overcoming" the nihilism that is its alleged product.

But by this point it should have also become clear that, read metaphysically, Nietzsche's nihilism *deserves* no such critique. If Nietzsche's claims about nihilism rest essentially on his anti-Platonic metaphysics of the will to power, one has to wonder what the fuss has been about. Why have some substantial philosophers (Heidegger being the best example) thought it important to engage the issue of nihilism as it arises in Nietzsche's work? A moment's reflection is sufficient to convince one that this sort of "metaphysics" is open to crushing objections.

In the first place, there are substantial objections to this sort of metaphysical speculation itself. One need not owe allegiance to the Vienna circle to feel uncomfortable with philosophical attempts to characterize "the truth of being as a whole," especially when those attempts issue in pronouncements like Nietzsche's "All reality is will to power." Exactly what is supposed to be gained for us by such an abstract characterization of "reality"? And what could such a huge metaphysical claim (if that is indeed what it is) actually mean? Heidegger is very far from being a positivist, of course, but even he recognizes the difficulty one encounters here in interpreting in a sensible way Nietzsche's statements about the will to power. In Heidegger's commentary on this notion, in fact, one can see emerging precisely the pattern of conceptual inflation analyzed and damned by the positivist critics of metaphysics: in trying to save Nietzsche from the charge of having grossly anthropomorphized all reality (namely, by having understood all will, and thus all being, as *conscious* will), Heidegger expands the concept of will so much that it becomes vacuous ("Word of Nietzsche," pp. 77-78). Here the familiar Popperian question looks to be the right one: once the will to power is interpreted so broadly that a *rock* is will to power too, could any state of affairs be specified that would actually be acknowledged to falsify the Nietzschean metaphysical claim? And if not, then in what sense is it a *claim* at all?

But even if there *is* a point to a philosopher's trying to tell "the truth of being as a whole," and even if general metaphysical assertions of the form "All reality is . . . " can be shown to make some clear sense, there are particular problems with the sense of *this* one. One way or another, the Nietzschean claim that all reality is will to power seems to involve anyone who asserts it in philosophical problems of self-reference.

Nietzsche himself sees it as a clear implication of his doctrine of the will to power that no claim we make is an accurate "picture" of an antecedently determined reality. That is not because all our "pictures" are in some way *inaccurate*, or could just as well be thought so. (Nietzsche is not an epistemological skeptic of that sort.) Rather, they are not "pictures" at all. All our claims are "interpretations" of reality, not "representations" of it. Upon close examination, he believes, the traditional philosophical notion of representation falls to the ground; it is senseless. There is no *Ding-an-sich* out there to be described in a neutral, transparent medium of thought or language. "What there is" is always shorthand for "What there is *for us*." Thus *truth* for Nietzsche is an "active determining"; it is *made* by the will to power, not found and coolly noted by some disinterested intellect.

But what, then, is the status of *those* claims, and of the fundamental metaphysical claim about will to power upon which (according to Heidegger) they all depend? There is apparently no way to exempt them from their own characterizations; otherwise they would not have the metaphysical generality they so explicitly trade upon. Furthermore, if they somehow *could* be exempted, or if at least the fundamental one could, the result would be a disaster for Nietzschean metaphysics. If Nietzsche's claim about reality as will to power were itself a metaphysical representation, then it *must* be a *false* one, since if it were true, that would by implication rule out the possibility of such representation as it (*ex hypothesi*) itself is. Its sense *as a repre-sentation* would guarantee its falsity as such. Apparently, the only way to avoid such an unwelcome conclusion is for Nietzsche to admit that his basic metaphysical claim and its epistemolog-ical implications are themselves "interpretations" in service of the will to power. But at that point it is not clear what reason one actually has anymore for paying philosophical attention to them, at least in the way that Heidegger insists that we should. Once a metaphysics cuts itself loose from the claim to provide comprehensive and accurate representation of reality, it is not clear in what sense it remains a *metaphysics* at all.

At this point it must be clear that Heidegger's metaphysical reading of Nietzsche's philosophy is in some important sense a *reductio* of that philosophy. Heidegger's anti-Platonic interpre-tation of the will to power is an attempt to present as a meta-physics (i.e., as something comparable in intention and in sta-tus to Plato's doctrine of the "true world") a "doctrine" that would, if accepted as a metaphysics, make all such metaphysi-cal presentation, including its own, impossible. On this account, then, Nietzsche's metaphysics is either manifestly false, or else impossible to assert as a metaphysics. As a metaphysician, Nietzsche's only alternatives are egregious error or silence; and in either event, Heidegger's sort of commentary seems misplaced, not to say wrongheaded. If this metaphysics is the source of philosophical nihilism, then its threat is entirely negligible.

But now the question of my own procedure in this chapter must be faced: why have I focused on such a manifestly unsat-isfactory reading of Nietzsche and of what nihilism means? My purpose in this book is to understand and appreciate the threat of nihilism to philosophy: Does the specter of such wholesale collapse of epistemic and ethical authority have any genuine basis in philosphical reflection? Or is it just a fantasy that can be safely set aside? Heidegger's reading of Nietzsche may seem to have settled the question: the threat of nihilism rests, both historically and logically, on an incoherent "metaphysics," whether Nietzsche's own or some other's. Once that incoherence has been demonstrated, then the threat will disappear. But that is too fast, I believe. Curiously enough, Heidegger's metaphysi-cal account of Nietzsche, inadequate as it certainly is in its own terms, *does* help show where the threat of philosophical nihilsim really lies; and not only in Nietzsche's expression of it, but generally. Heidegger's fundamental and systematic error of interpretation, as is so often the case with philosophers, leads him to see something importantly and inconspicuously true. He is dead wrong about Nietzsche, I think, but he is right about philosophical nihilism, even if he doesn't quite understand why or how.

The key to Heidegger's insight is in this sentence from "The Word of Nietzsche": "But in its essence metaphysics is nihilism" (p. 110). By presenting Nietzsche's philosophical thinking as the articulation of an anti-Platonic metaphysics, and by setting the matter of his nihilism within the context of that metaphysics, both of which Heidegger (mistakenly) does, it can easily seem that the core of nihilism *is* the particular metaphysics of the will to power. It can seem, that is, that the threat of nihilist collapse and revaluation turns upon one's acceptance or rejection of *that particular* metaphysical account: if one accepts that account, then one must be a nihilist, happy or unhappy; if one rejects it, then one will escape or oppose the nihilist's claims by operating from the perspective of some other metaphysics.

But Heidegger himself finally realizes that this is not so. It is not a particular metaphysics that is responsible for the threat of nihilism; rather, it is *metaphysics itself*, in any form. "In its essence metaphysics is nihilism." The core of nihilism is the possibility of a certain sort of description of one's life: what we might call, without explanation for the moment, *metaphysical representation* of it. Nietzsche's "metaphysics" of the "will to power" (presuming for the moment that he had such) is just an extreme (and, as we have seen, philosophically problematic) form of such representation. Nietzsche's nihilism (considered metaphysically) is frightful not because we believe he is *right* in what he says (as we have seen, he *could not* be) but because we *understand what he is trying to do in saying it.* Put in terms of the metaphysics of the will to power, the threat of metaphysical nihilism may become peculiarly vivid to us; but it is not the idea of the will to power itself that constitutes the threat. It is *the possibility of metaphysical representation* that is so fearful, not Nietzsche's particular metaphysical vocabulary.

V

I have said, I hope provocatively, that the key to understanding the threat of nihilism to philosophy is to be found in Heidegger's assertion, "In its essence metaphysics is nihilism." Exactly what this tightly compressed claim means is not immediately clear, of course, since, like most of Heidegger's pronouncements, it assumes in the reader a quite particular resonance for its familiar words. To clarify it, therefore, it will first of all be necessary to unpack some of the idiosyncratic Heideggerian presuppositions hidden inside; that will be my aim in this section. Then we can approach the much more difficult task of trying to translate Heidegger's equation outside his own peculiar perspective.

I begin with an account of what Heidegger understands the essence of metaphysics to be. At the beginning of "The End of Philosophy and the Task of Thinking" there is the following dense description of the essence of metaphysical thinking:

> Philosophy is metaphysics. Metaphysics thinks beings as a whole—the world, man, God—with respect to Being, with respect to the belonging together of beings in Being. Metaphysics thinks beings as being in the manner of representational thinking which gives reasons. For since the beginning of philosophy and with that beginning, the Being of beings has showed itself as the ground (*archē, aition,* principle). The ground is that from which beings as such are what they are in their becoming, perishing, and persisting as something that can be known, handled, and worked upon. As the ground, Being brings beings to their actual presence. In accordance with the actual kind of presence, the ground has the character of grounding as the ontic causation of the real, as the transcendental making possible of the objectivity of objects, as the dialectical mediation of the movement of the absolute Spirit and of the historical process of production, as the will to power positing values.

What characterizes metaphysical thinking which grounds the ground for beings is the fact that metaphysical thinking, starting from what is present, represents it in its presence and thus exhibits it as grounded by its ground. (P. 374)

His account of metaphysics here comprises essentially four claims. First, and clearest, metaphysics is for Heidegger the essence of philosophy per se. The metaphysician's concern to characterize "being as a whole" (here called 'Being') is fundamental to all other philosophical interests, such as ethics, aesthetics, and epistemology (Heidegger, *Nietzsche*, 4:5). Without an account of what Being is, there is no genuine, living philosophy in these activities at all, only its disjointed members. This is why, as already noted, Heidegger feels compelled to present Nietzsche as a metaphysician: it's the only way, he thinks, to treat him as a real philosopher.

Second, in metaphysical thinking about Being, Being is always thought of as the Being of beings. Being cannot be thought of in itself, so to speak, as Being pure and simple; the metaphysical question of Being is always raised—indeed, *can only be* raised—in terms of the Being of all *beings*, taken together as a whole (world, man, and God, as he puts it). This is why Heidegger is so fond of saying that metaphysics is Platonism: it was Plato who made the philosophical/linguistic distinction between Being and beings in the first place, thereby making their relationship to one another philosophically questionable. So successful was he at setting the philosophical agenda that we have no idea of how to think of Being without thinking of it as the Being of all beings. It would be senseless, a pure and vacant abstraction, for us to try to think of "Being pure and simple." The metaphysical question can only be posed with all beings in the foreground; they are the inevitable data of metaphysical thinking. What is it for these beings to be? How can they be the beings that they are? Those are the only metaphysical questions we can ask.

Third, in metaphysical thinking the Being of beings is always thought as the *ground* of those beings. "For since the beginning of philosophy and with that beginning, the Being of beings has showed itself as the ground (*archē, aition,* principle)." Here is another way in which for Heidegger all metaphysics is a form of Platonism. Not only did Plato originally differentiate the whole of beings from Being, he distinguished them in such a way that the latter must appear to us as the ground of the former, that is, he construed them (*revealed* them, we might say) in such a way that the (explicit) present-ness of the former demanded as its precondition the (tacit) presence of the latter. Plato's world of "appearance" *logically,* not just causally, requires the "true world" as its "explanation" (*aition*). They cannot be separated, even in thought (Being is always the Being *of beings*); and their relationship *must* be that of grounded and ground.

For a comparison to this Platonic move, think of a visible figure appearing on a background, as in the experiments of Gestalt psychology: were there no (tacit) ground—"Being"—for it, there could be no (explicit) figure—"being"—in appearance. The 'could' in that sentence is a logical one. Once the distinction and relation between figure and ground has been noticed (revealed) in the characteristic Gestalt way, then to talk of such a figure appearing *without* a ground (as "pure figure" so to speak) is a senseless notion. So too for "beings" and "Being" after Plato's fundamental differentiation of them: the latter *must* be present as the ground of the former's appearance.

"The ground is that from which beings as such are what they are in their becoming, perishing, or persisting as something that can be known, handled, and worked upon." As we encounter the various beings that make up our world, those beings that are the data of philosophical/metaphysical speculation, they are present to us in various and determinate ways. In practical terms, a being is never just a being; it is a god, an object of the ego's consciousness, a value, a product of the class struggle, or whatever. In each case, different as these kinds of beings are, the metaphysical question is always the same. It is the question of *ground*: How did this actual being come to be what it is in the way that it is?

As the ground, Being brings beings to their actual presencing. The ground shows itself as presence. The present of presence consists in the fact that it brings what is present *each in its own way* to presence. (My emphasis)

For any kind of being actually present to us, there must be some "explanation" (*archē, aition*, principle) that can account for its being present to us in the way that it is. To revert to the Gestalt comparison, there must be some specific background that lets this particular figure be seen by us as it is, that brings this particular figure to its "actual presencing" before us. The ground is the presence that stands behind every actual presencing, the necessary background for the figure as it appears. For Heidegger, then, the metaphysical question is the question about the necessary presence/ground that stands behind *all* beings taken together as such. As that totality of beings has appeared to us differently at different times, so too have there been different answers to the metaphysical question of ground.

> In accordance with the actual kind of presence, the ground has the character of grounding as the ontic causation of the real [Galileo], as the transcendental making possible of the objectivity of objects [Kant], as the dialectical mediation of the movement of absolute spirit [Hegel] and of the historical process of production [Marx], as the will to power positing values [Nietzsche]. (Heidegger, "The End of Philosophy," p. 374)

Finally, we come to the most important (and perhaps most obscure) part of Heidegger's account of the essence of metaphysics. This has to do with the kind of thinking that is supposed to reveal the ground of presence upon which all the actual presentness of beings depends. "Metaphysics thinks beings as being in the manner of representational thinking [*vorstellendes Denken*] which gives reasons." The same point is made in this paragraph:

> What characterizes metaphysical thinking which grounds the ground for beings is the fact that metaphysical thinking, starting from what is present, represents it in its presence and thus exhibits it as grounded by its ground. (P. 374)

This needs a bit of commentary. It is clear that Heidegger believes that *vorstellendes Denken* is a particular *kind* of thinking, not (in spite of the intellectual imperialism of philosophy) to be identified with the essence of thinking itself. (That the identification finally cannot be made is why there remains for him a "task of thinking" even after the "end of philosophy.") But what particular kind of thinking is *vorstellendes Denken*, this representational thinking that gives reasons?

As a help in answering this question, let us look at the discussion of representation in Appendix 9 of "The Age of the World Picture."

> To represent means here: of oneself to set something before oneself and to make secure what has been set in place, as something set in place. . . . Representing is no longer the apprehending of that which presences, within whose unconcealment apprehending itself belongs, belongs indeed as a unique kind of presencing toward that which presences that is unconcealed. Representing is no longer a self-unconcealing for . . . , but is a laying hold and grasping of. . . . What presences does not hold sway, but rather assault rules. . . . That which is, is no longer that which presences; it is rather that which, in representing, is first set over against, that which stands fixedly over against, which has the character of object. Representing is making-stand-over-against, an objectifying that goes forward and masters. In this way representing drives everything together into the unity of that which is given the character of object. Representing is *coagitatio.* (Pp. 149–50)

As is typical with him, Heidegger relies heavily on the etymology of *vorstellen* in his account of it here. The German word comes apart naturally as *vor-stellen*: a setting-before; a standing-up-before [one] of [something]. Out of this root meaning Heidegger teases an entire philosophical conception. Several things in his discussion require specific comment. First, it is "of oneself" that one "set[s] something before oneself" in representation. Notice the aggressive activity insisted upon in this description. The representing subject is not a passive spectator to whom a revelation of some reality willy-nilly comes; the subject is not even one who patiently awaits and solicits such revelations and then opens up to them when they arrive. Rather, the representing subject is the one who actively sets up before oneself whatever appears there. "What presences does not hold sway, but rather assault rules."

Second, what one sets up before oneself in this active, aggressive way, one also *secures* as something set in place. Representation, says Heidegger, is always a matter of "making secure." Most obviously it is a making secure of what has been represented to oneself, the establishment of the epistemological "certainty" of the representation, for example; but it is at the same time a making secure of the representing subject as well. One sees both these aspects of security in the *Meditations* of Descartes, who is of course in the very front of Heidegger's mind throughout this discussion of *vorstellen*. In Descartes's philosophy, and for the first time, the security (i.e., the certainty) of the subject's representations becomes the key to the subject's *own* security; only if he can establish something "firm and lasting in the sciences," as he puts it in Meditation One, can Descartes be secure in the life he has committed himself to live. Representation seems to presuppose an essential *in*security, then. Only when the human being has lost the sense of being securely placed within Being's "Great Chain," a sense of metaphysical security characteristic both of Platonism and of medieval Christian theology, will representation become either necessary or possible. Disenchantment—philosophical disenchantment, at least—is its necessary condition. Representation is always an assertion *by* a subject that aims at the security of that subject. Thus representation is not only, or even fundamentally, an "epistemological" notion; its roots are ultimately metaphysical, according to Heidegger. Representation *as a possibility for epistemology* grows out of a particular (fractured) relationship of beings to their necessary ground.

Third, just as the activity of representation demands a particularly active subject, one that seeks to establish for itself this double security, it also demands a particularly passive object. Security, of either sort, demands such objectivity. In fact, it is only in the relationship of representation that a being truly becomes an "object" at all, according to Heidegger. *Vorstellen* is just that relationship that, for security considerations, *makes* beings into "objects." It is not easy to see exactly what Heidegger means by 'object' here. He says that the object is "no longer that which presences"; rather, it is "that which stands fixedly over against." Here is another etymological fact being treated by Heidegger as a philosophical insight. *Gegenstand* divides easily into *Gegen-stand*, that which stands over against. "Representing is making-stand-over-against, an objectifying that goes forward and masters." To be an "object," then, is to be something only acted upon, no longer something in any way essentially active (no longer active even to the extent of being "that which presences"). An "object" for Heidegger is something "mastered" by the subject who "sets it before"; to represent something is to have (in some sense) seized control of it, to have made it one's own. One has secured it as a means to one's own security. *Vorstellendes Denken* is a sort of conquest, then. When beings become the "objects" of one's "representations," one has made them subordinate to oneself. The representing subject has become a sort of god, setting up before itself the world it ordinarily inhabits.

Moreover, the "world" thus set up before one as a collection of "objects" is, to use the vocabulary of *Being and Time*, a world purely "present-to-hand" (*Vorhanden*). To be an "object" of a representation is to be seen and characterized outside any holistic, significance-giving, practical context of human activity and life. To be an "object" is not anymore to be seen as a hammer, for example, but as a bit of passive stuff with such-and-such "properties." "Objects," says Heidegger, do not "presence," that is, they do not disclose themselves to us as the things they are (e.g., hammers) in some context of our practical activity; rather, they "stand fixedly over against us," that is, they are isolated from their habitual significance and thus "fixed." One thinks here of the "fixing" of a specimen on a microscope slide: its removal from a living context in order that it be "seen" more clearly, seen "in itself." (Wordsworth: "We murder to dissect.")

After Descartes, according to Heidegger, all our thinking, philosophical and otherwise, has been determined as *vorstellendes Denken*. Philosophy has not stood still, of course; metaphysical system has succeeded metaphysical system. But all have remained essentially Cartesian, because all have kept in central place the attempt to "objectify" beings in order to understand them. All retain, in some form or other, the subject/object relationship that Descartes originally defined. The best evidence for this, he believes, is the dominance of technological/scientific modes of thought in our culture and the way in which even philosophy has increasingly conformed itself to them. Modern technology would not be possible without such objectification; and all our thinking, not exempting that in religion and art, is dominated by technology and its representations.[8]

But if representational thinking is so common, why does Heidegger characterize metaphysics in particular as *vorstellendes Denken*? It is because in metaphysics *vorstellendes Denken* is extended to its limit, and thus becomes itself in an essential sense. If in all technological/scientific thinking beings are thought (i.e., represented) as "objects," in metaphysical thinking there is the attempt to think (i.e., represent) the *ground* of such "objects." In metaphysics, that is, there is the attempt to "objectify" that which makes "objects" possible as such. What makes "objects" possible is *representation*, of course. So that means that metaphysical thinking is *vorstellendes Denken* that has become aware of itself *as vorstellendes Denken* and is thereby trying to make *itself* the "object" of its own particular awareness. In metaphysical thinking there is the attempt to represent that which makes representation itself possible; so metaphysics is representational thinking in an *essential* sense. This, I take it, is at least part of what Heidegger means when he says that metaphysical thinking is "representational thinking which gives reasons" ("The End of Philosophy," p. 374). Any form of technology requires *vorstellendes Denken*, but metaphysics attempts to be a *vorstellendes Denken* that "gives reasons" for itself as such. Metaphysics (*qua* representational thinking) tries to show how it is possible to think representationally *überhaupt*. And it tries to do that in a particular way by showing "objectively" what representational thinking is, by making representation its own "object." Thus Heidegger says, "In this way representing

8. See the essays in *The Question concerning Technology* for details and illustrations.

drives everything [*including itself*] together into the unity of that which is given the character of object."

Having understood in this way Heidegger's characterization of metaphysics as "representational thinking which gives reasons," we can now begin to understand its necessary connection to nihilism. If metaphysics were to succeed in its post-Cartesian attempt to drive everything together into objectivity, then it thereby would have made the ground of beings into just another being. That is, it would have successfully "objectified" the very conditions of objectivity itself. For Heidegger, the ground of beings is, as we have seen, that which allows beings to be present as the particular beings that they are. If all beings are "objects," as *vorstellendes Denken* insists, then metaphysics, as the attempt to reveal the ground of such beings, must concern itself with showing what makes "objectivity" possible as such. If metaphysics *itself* is *vorstellendes Denken*, as Heidegger says it is, then metaphysics is finally the attempt to make *metaphysics itself* its own "object," that is, to represent "objectively" its own grounding power of "objective" representation.

But if the ground of "objectivity" can be represented as just another "object," then it cannot (*qua* "object") be the *ground* of all "objects." To do so, it would have to be its *own* ground, and at that point one would have lost the Platonic distinction between Being and beings that gave rise to metaphysics—and thus to *vorstellendes Denken*—in the first place. Metaphysics would thus be denying its own founding insight. Therefore, if metaphysical *vorstellendes Denken* were somehow actually able to represent its own ground, which would mean somehow to represent *itself* as an "object" of its own representation, then *in that representation* (assuming it were possible) it would have *removed* (*qua* ground) the very ground it was seeking to reveal. By "succeeding," it would have left itself—and thus everything else—groundless. Metaphysical thinking would have destroyed itself.

In Heidegger's view, this is the force of the Madman's claims that "God is dead" and "We have killed him—you and I" (Nietzsche, *The Gay Science*, sec. 125, p. 95). Our own ambitions for absolute rational security for our lives, ambitions which—since Descartes, at least—are to be realized only by having an absolutely comprehensive and final ("certain") representation of all reality, have doomed themselves. And so Heidegger himself can say, in precisely the same vein as Nietzsche, that in its essence metaphysics—representational thinking that gives reasons—is nihilism. Our search to uncover the ground of beings, when that search is understood as *vorstellendes Denken* seeking to represent its own conditions of possibility, *must* lead either to anxiety or despair. Either it will turn out to be *impossible* to represent the conditions of representation itself, which will leave the ground of our lives as rational (i.e., representational) beings utterly mysterious, and therefore insecure; or that ground *will* somehow be capable of being represented as just another "object," and so we will lose it *as ground* in another way. In either event, the "highest values" of our lives as rational beings—i.e., our "representational" epistemic and ethical practices—will have devaluated themselves. We will have failed to secure both our representations and ourselves. The sense of life is thus in question in just the way Nietzsche foretold, but not because we have accepted his (so-called) metaphysics of the will to power. It is *metaphysics itself* that has brought us to this impasse. "In its essence metaphysics is nihilism."

VI

Not quite, one will say. Even if my exposition of Heidegger has been successful, all it shows is that his equation of metaphysics and nihilism makes a certain sense for Heidegger himself, not that it does for everyone. In fact, of course, my account has clearly demonstrated just how much the equation rests upon idiosyncratic (and largely unargued) Heideggerian claims about metaphysics as the essence of philosophy, about metaphysical thinking as *vorstellendes Denken* that gives reasons, and about what sort of thinking *vorstellendes Denken* is. Any one of these claims is mysterious and controversial enough; taken all together, they require something like the willing suspension of disbelief.

Can Heidegger's suggestive equation of metaphysics and nihilism be removed from the peculiar trappings of his own thinking? Can it be translated into an idiom less eccentric, so as to show us something important about the threat of nihilism and about the threat's philosophical basis, whether or not we are able to take Heidegger whole? I think so.

If it can, it will require a less quirky account of what metaphysical representation is. Let me try to generate one. We can accept, as a starting point at least, Heidegger's claim that metaphysics is *vorstellendes Denken* that gives reasons, especially if we resist giving 'metaphysics' any very special Heideggerian sense. The claim is just a claim about *philosophy*, and as such it seems perfectly acceptable. Certainly it is the case that (post-Socratic) philosophy has always tried to "give reasons" for its assertions. The connection between philosophical discourse and argument, however widely or narrowly that latter term might be interpreted by a given philosophical community, is not an inessential one. More, philosophy has always tried to "represent," to "set forth," its reasons, not simply to have them. Such representation is not just a matter of affecting a lawyerly style in its prose. Philosophy has always conceived itself to be a discourse not just reasonable, not just explicitly well argued, but a discourse self-consciously concerned to show what *makes* such a discourse as itself reasonable and well argued. Philosophy is always essentially self-reflective, and self-reflective all the way down. None of its presuppositions are out of bounds for its own challenge and defense. Philosophy is rational discourse that grants itself nothing absolutely, not even a firm sense of what such rational discourse as itself *is*. Not that philosophy is only, or even essentially, metadiscourse; rather, philosophy is discourse that, whatever its first-order topics, is always metadiscourse too. In that sense, then, it is always *representational* thinking that gives reasons. It is always trying to "represent," to "set before" one, its own conditions of authority in respect of one.

But there is a deeper sense in which philosophy can be understood as *vorstellendes Denken*. To see this, note the intimate connections of philosophy, especially modern philosophy, to various forms of epistemological and ethical skepticism. Heidegger himself touches upon these connections when he tries to link *vor-stellen* to "making secure," although there is no need for us here to claim, as he seems to, that there is some deep and essential linguistic/conceptual link between the idea of "representation" itself and the attempt to make something secure. It is enough for us to acknowledge the close *historical* relationship between philosophy (especially modern philosophy) and skepticism. Empson is probably right when he says that "it is not human to feel safely placed," and insofar as we have tried rationally and systematically to combat this inherent sense of frailty— to locate its precise sources, to trace its reach, to beat it back with the resources of consciousness and self-consciousness— philosophy has been a large and steady part of our arsenal. But what is crucial to note here is *how* philosophy has typically tried to do this. Characteristic of a distinctively philosophical defense of our lives has been a certain sort of *representation* of them. More precisely, the modern philosophical defense of our lives against the various threats of skepticism has largely accepted the peculiar sort of representation of those lives that allowed the skeptical threats to arise with such force in the first place. Let me show what I mean.

Skepticism is, most generally, the suspicion that (at least some of) our most fundamental epistemic and/or ethical practices are not what they claim to be, that they do not deliver the goods in the way that they say (and we typically believe) that they do. It is not necessary to our purposes here to try to specify all the various ways that epistemic and ethical practices can be suspected of failure, nor is it necessary for us to take a stand on whether these skeptical suspicions are ultimately justified. What matters to us right now is the typical way that the skeptic initially *conceives* the practices that are to be examined for their particular failings, whatever those may be.

Notice, first of all, that what the skeptic examines are ethical and/or epistemic *practices*. Nothing very technical or controversial is encompassed in my use of the word, but it is crucially important to note it nevertheless. The grist of the skeptic's mills are social practices, that is, *particular networks of human action*, particular ways of behaving (responding, acting) in relation to other human beings and to other features of our environment. A particular epistemic or ethical judgment, the immediate focus of the skeptic's attention, exists only as a part, a moment, of such a practice—nothing more and nothing less. An epistemic judgment, for example, is a matter of *taking something as true* (or taking it as false, or taking it as quite probable, or whatever): it is a *taking*; it is itself an *action*, actual or potential, set in a sense-giving context of other actions. Likewise, an ethical judgment is a matter of *taking something as courageous* (or taking it as deceitful, or taking it as obligatory, or whatever): it too, as an action, springs from some prior actions or events and will (*ceteris paribus*) issue in yet others.

To make a judgment, then, is to act in train with other actions; it is self-consciously to connect one set of one's actions to another set of actions or events: to let one's subsequent actions appropriately "follow from" the earlier set. A judgment, whether epistemic or ethical, is in this sense inescapably a part of a whole practice (or one might even say: *form of life*); and what the philosophical skeptic properly examines is that practice as a whole. Philosophical skepticism is of course not just the suspicion that one happens to be in error in making some particular judgment; to be such a skeptic is to suspect, perhaps even to be convinced, that no such claim (i.e., action) issuing from such a practice could but fail to be less than it says it is: that the practice itself is somehow inherently objectionable in respect of what it claims for itself.

It is not necessary to try to specify all the ways in which a philosophical skeptic might find a given epistemic or ethical practice objectionable. The important thing to see is the way in which the practice is held up to its philosophical examination in the first place. It is, I want to say, and using the term somewhat technically, held up to examination by being *represented*. This technique of presentation is now so familiar a philosophical way of describing human action that most of us do not recognize it to be controversial; indeed, most of us do not recognize such representation as *something in particular* at all. In this way the philosophical representation of our lives has become one of those things Wittgenstein described in section 129 of the *Philosophical Investigations*:

> The aspects of things that are most important for us
> are hidden because of their simplicity and familiarity.

(One is unable to notice something—because it is always before one's eyes.) The real foundations of his inquiry do not strike a man at all. Unless *that* fact has at some time struck him.—And this means: we fail to be struck by what, once seen, is most striking and most powerful.

To *represent* a practice in this distinctively philosophical way, either for the purpose of attacking it skeptically or for the purpose of defending it against such attacks, is to conceive in a quite particular fashion its constitutive actions in their relationship to one another. To put it most directly, if somewhat obscurely, it is to describe those actions in their relation to one another as being *governed by a rule*. A given social practice is, as I have indicated, a set of patterned expectations of human action and response. That is to say, in any practice, whether epistemic or ethical, particular actions (or events) are expected to lead to other actions (or events) in accordance with some fairly determinate pattern. It is not an accident, for example, that a mother's discovery that her child has told her a deliberate, gross, harmful lie will (*ceteris paribus*) lead her to certain sorts of remonstrances with the child, perhaps even to punish the child in some way. That sort of action (the lie) is unacceptable to us in this context; it is just "not done." Such is the nature of a moral practice, even of the simplest kind: it insists that certain sorts of actions follow from certain other sorts of actions. When these expectations are violated, steps of instruction or sanction are taken in response.

An epistemic or ethical practice is, in this sense, *regular*. It is not haphazard or anarchic; it connects actions to other actions and events in terms of some recognizable pattern. My description of this connection has intentionally been vague: I have spoken of "regularity," of a "fairly determinate pattern" connecting our actions to other actions and events, of a "patterned expectation" of action and response. One will surely want to protest that something more specific must be said; if not, then the notion of a social practice is largely empty. Exactly. My vagueness provokes, I hope, just the question that needs to be addressed here *as a specific question*. Granted that human epistemic and ethical life is constituted by various "practices," by various normative "patterns" of expectation in action and response—and who would oppose such a truism?—how are these "regularities" to be philosophically described? How are our social practices to be conceptualized as such? In what terms can we best examine, criticize, and correct them?

There is now a standard philosophical answer to these questions, although it is not usually noticed to be such. It assumes that in any given social practice one is *following a rule* (or a set of rules). To say that one is following a rule in doing what one does is to say more than just that some formula could be constructed that would, so to speak, accurately plot one's course as one moves from action to action. Such a description would show *regularity* in one's behavior but not yet *rule following* in one's action. The latter requires that one be doing what one is doing just *because* that action exemplifies what some rule requires of one, that is, just because one recognizes the *authority* of that rule in this situation. For example, it might be a rule that accurately describes my past behavior that I buy only suede shoes. Given that record of my purchases, I might even make the true prediction that in the future I will always—as a matter of fact— buy suede shoes. But just that is not enough to show that I am *following a rule* in buying such footwear. To show that would require showing that I buy suede shoes *because of* some rule. In that case I recognize the authority of the rule per se; I am truly *following* it.

Clearly, such recognition of authority requires a certain amount of consciousness (and self-consciousness) on the part of the rule follower, but not *full* self-consciousness, surely, since some such recognitions can be tacit and only later seen for what they were. Rule following is something that only human beings can do, and they do it just as they do (almost) everything else: sometimes consciously and carefully, sometimes not. A rule of a social practice is, then, something that can be *self-consciously followed* by someone; it is something that can be expressed and understood as a *direction*. It can be taught, learned, questioned, violated, mocked, worshipped, modified, or abandoned by those who follow it. A rule is a *principle*; it is a potential guide to self-conscious human action, not a simple regularity of movement. (These remarks are simply reminders of what rules are. They are of course in no sense a complete philosophical *analysis* of the concept of a rule.)

To say that a social practice is rule-governed, then, is to say that there is some structure of rules that the practice can be seen as (ideally) exemplifying; it is to say that the practice itself (in its ideal form, at least) can be fully described as *a set of rules to be followed,* as *a set of principles employed to guide the actions of those who are engaged in the practice.* As the participants in a social practice (so understood) move from action to action, they connect their actions to other actions or events in accordance with the rules that define (their idea of) the practice as such. From a philosophical point of view, then, the social practice just *is* a specific set of rules. That is what it means to *represent* a practice, in my particular sense of the term: it is to present the practice in its ideal as a structure of rules to be followed in action.

The philosophical possibility—indeed, attractiveness—of representing social practices in this way rests upon a very fundamental assumption about human action and its connection to rationality, and this assumption needs to be explicitly remarked. It is the assumption that the most appropriate description of rational human action is one that construes such action as essentially principled, as essentially rule-governed. Whatever we are doing whenever we are most clearly *doing* something, we are following, either tacitly or explicitly, a rule or set of rules. We are acting, tacitly or explicitly, so as to exemplify a set of principles we hold.

A key to this guiding assumption is *consistency.* "Doing the same thing" or "going on in the same way" are clear marks of rationality, whether in thought or in action; such consistency seems to be a necessary condition of rational action (certainly it is not sufficient). How can such consistency be plausibly accounted for? *Following a rule* seems a good answer; indeed, it can seem the only good answer, the only one consistent with our self-consciousness and freedom. Rules apparently provide for our intellectual and practical consistency without reducing it to mere regularity. Human beings are, we believe, distinctively free and rational beings; such beings must have reasons, not just causes, for their actions. To have a reason for an action is—

on this account—to perform that action in accordance with some rule or principle that one accepts, tacitly or explicitly, as properly governing one's behavior. Reasons are rules, then. To act rationally is to act in accordance with a rule that is (in some way) one's own.

Putting it that way reminds one immediately of Kant, of course, and there is no doubt that his fundamental notions of moral autonomy and self-legislation capitalize on the assumption I have noted. But the idea is not peculiarly Kantian, nor is its influence confined to the sphere of moral philosophy. It has become second nature to us now to think philosophically in these terms. To explain an action rationally, to say why one was doing what one was doing, is to invoke some rule or principle of which that action is a specific consequence. "What was your reason for doing that?" seems always to beg, sooner or later, a philosophical answer in the form of a rule: "I did it in accordance with my rule (or principle) that, in such-and-such a situation, given so-and-so, do this-that-and-the-other." To the extent that one cannot cite such a rule one is following, cannot exhibit a principle that one's action exemplifies, then to that extent the action looks less like an *action* at all. One is not really acting in such a case but merely behaving.

It may be that those who are engaged in a practice are not fully aware of the rules that the practice (ideally) exemplifies. They may also not be fully aware of the rules that they themselves as a matter of fact are following in doing what they are doing in this instance. In fact, both are likely to be the case with most of us most of the time. We are rarely aware of the precise rule (or rules) we are actually following when we decide, for example, that such-and-such piece of student work does not deserve an honor grade or when we decide not to let a baseless slur on an acquaintance pass unchallenged. Nor, although both may be practices we claim as our own, are we likely to be able, even on reflection, precisely to specify the (ideal) rules for fair grading of student work or the defense of an innocent acquaintance against slander. This is not necessarily to say that our actions in these cases are not what they should be. We do not usually demand absolute self-consciousness as a test of authority in practical matters.

Nevertheless, the standard philosophical assumption is that there *are* such rules that one is following in one's rational action, at least tacitly. And the further assumption is that by so doing, one is (at least tacitly) trying to conform one's actions to some rule that one (at least tacitly) understands to be one of the constitutive rules of the practice one is engaged in. If there is a practice of fair grading of student work, say, then that practice will be defined by particular rules to be followed in grading (however complicated such rules may be); and, insofar as one is trying to grade such student work fairly, one will be trying to follow those rules, whatever they are. One will be trying, that is, to match the regularities of one's actual behavior to the rules that govern and constitute the practice in terms of which one's behavior is to be characterized and evaluated.[9]

In some circumstances our usual rough-and-ready approach, our ordinary tolerance of murkiness, will not be acceptable. Perhaps the case is very complicated, or perhaps a very great deal rides on the outcome of our deliberations. In such matters one will want to make as explicit as possible both the (ideal) rules of the practice in question and the actual rules that, given one's ordinary dispositions and the traditions of one's community, one is inclined to act upon, so that one can do one's best to see that they—the ideal and the actual—will appropriately coincide. This, we think, is the natural home of philosophy. Philosophy should provide us with the tools of critical analysis sufficient to reveal both (1) the ideal rules constituting our epistemic or ethical practices and (2) the actual rules describing our own most likely behavior in such epistemic and ethical situations as those practices have to do with. The first task of philosophy, then, is the accurate *representation* of our practices, ideal and real.

Two familiar examples vividly illustrate philosophy conceived as this sort of representation. The first is the founding text of modern philosophical thought, Descartes's *Meditations on First Philosophy*. Descartes is concerned to establish the authority of certain epistemic practices (he wants to fix upon something "firm and lasting in the sciences," as he says in Meditation

9. In this discussion I am ignoring the vexed questions of how practices are to be distinguished from one another, who determines what practice is being participated in at a given time, and so forth.

One), and for that purpose he finds it necessary to submit to the test of doubt—his particular test of authority—the most fundamental epistemic practices he can identify. Notice how he goes about this. He does not attack the results of these practices, namely, the specific judgments in which they issue. Rather, he assumes that the epistemic practices themselves can be reduced to *principles*, to epistemic *rules* that are being followed by the thinker, whether tacitly or explicitly, and it is these rules that he subjects to his technique of doubt.

> And for [my purposes of epistemic critique] it will not be necessary for me to examine each [particular epistemic judgment], which would be an infinite labor; but since the destruction of the foundation necessarily involves the collapse of all the rest of the edifice, I shall first attack the principles upon which all my former opinions were founded. (Descartes, *Meditations*, pp. 75-76)

Notice: "I shall first attack the principles . . . ," and that is just what he does. Any adequate epistemology, he thinks, must be a set of epistemic rules to be followed once their acceptability has been established. Descartes now begins to determine whether our ordinary epistemic rules, once they are identified as such, are in fact rationally unobjectionable. If they are, then our epistemic practices do have the authority they claim.

He starts his examination with a very broadly conceived and naive epistemic principle (a principle of sensory evidence, in fact): "Everything which I have thus far accepted as entirely true and assured has been acquired from the senses or by means of the senses" (p. 76). That is, my ordinary epistemic principle has been: whatever the senses tell me, directly or indirectly, is true and assured. On reflection, of course, this is completely unacceptable as a general rule for acquiring true belief, since it quickly leads to inconsistent "truths": "But I have learned by experience that these senses sometimes mislead one, and it is prudent never to trust wholly those things which have once deceived us." Thus the principle must be modified. The rule of sensory evidence must be sharpened and clarified, first by identifying the external conditions (e.g., distance, light) and the internal conditions (e.g., inebriation, madness) that can affect the

veridicality of sense perception and then by formulating a re-
vised epistemic principle that takes them into account: "Whatever the senses tell me in circumstances when the external and
internal conditions of perception are known to be ideal, is true
and assured."[10]

It is frequently pointed out by philosophical historians that
the Cartesian revolution in philosophy turns upon Descartes's
thoroughgoing foundationalism, or his reliance on a particular
sort of doubt, or his establishment of the ego as metaphysical
subject. But what is often not sufficiently marked, I believe, is
another assumption alongside these very familiar ones, and
deeply connected to them: the assumption I want to call *rationality-as-representation*.[11] It is the assumption that having reasons for what one does is a matter of following tacit or explicit
rules for action, and thus that the various practices characteristic of the exercise of our rationality (in Descartes the focus is on
the epistemic practices necessary to the New Science) can be
fully described—*represented*, as I call it—as ideal structures of
such rules. Without that assumption, the Cartesian project of
doubt and self-correction couldn't get off the ground.

A second example will show that this Cartesian assumption
still lives and that it can be separated from the epistemological
critique, and the overt defense against skepticism, that one finds
in Descartes himself. I am thinking of John Rawls's enormously
influential *A Theory of Justice*. Rawls is not writing against the
moral skeptic in any very direct sense, since he assumes at the
outset an effective sense of justice in his reader. His book is an
attempt to *refine* that original sense of justice, to achieve (as far
as possible) a "reflective equilibrium" between our intuitions
about what is just, on the one hand, and the demands of self-
conscious moral theory, on the other. In doing so, he assumes
that any adequate theory of social justice will consist in what
he calls "principles of justice," that is, rules specifying (or at
least ruling out) certain courses of action for agents (and societies) who seek to be just. He assumes, that is, that our familiar

10. See Harry G. Frankfurt, *Demons, Dreamers, and Madmen: The Defense of
Reason in Descartes's "Meditations."*
11. I have used this phrase before, in *Ethics without Philosophy: Wittgenstein and the Moral Life*, but the emphasis there is not exactly the same.

moral practice of judging social arrangements in terms of their justice can be represented as our (tacit or explicit) comparison of the principles constituting those arrangements with certain principles of justice that we (tacitly or explicitly) accept as our own.

Philosophically considered, then, the social arrangement simply *is* a set of principles of action exemplified institutionally; so our moral critique of it must proceed in these terms as well. If reasons are rules, then moral reasons are the moral rules followed by moral agents; and thus our philosophical examination of the moral worth of a given practice (i.e., moral worth conceived as the quality and force of the moral reasons that support it) must first of all consist in our specification and critique of the moral rules it exemplifies. To have a sense of justice is, for Rawls, to have one's own principles of justice that can be brought to consciousness and thus made both the objects and the tools of critical scrutiny. Such consciousness raising, indeed, is a main task of moral philosophy, as conceived in *A Theory of Justice*. There can be no question that the book is a major achievement, but it is equally clear that its achievement rests solidly (and essentially uncritically) on the assumption that practices (including the practice of moral philosophy itself) can be represented as the exemplification of rules to be followed in action.

I have been trying to specify a sense in which philosophy is distinctively *vorstellendes Denken* ("representational thinking") and I have approached this by arguing that, since Descartes at least, philosophy has proceeded by *representing* human rationality and human action in a particular way. It has portrayed the distinctively human social practices as essentially rule-governed, as essentially constituted by principles accepted and followed (with some degree of awareness) by the agents participating in them. I have called the philosophical assumption behind this kind of description *rationality-as-representation*. At bottom, it is the assumption that being rational is a matter of having reasons for what one does, and that reasons are rules governing action. But it also incorporates the natural assumption that the more consciousness there is of these reasons, the more rationality there is present in both agents and practices. To be rational in a minimal sense is, on this account, to be acting in accordance with some rule or rules (rather than just exhibiting some regularity of behavior); to be *fully* rational is to be explicitly and self-critically *aware* of what rules one is following in one's actions. To be a minimally rational agent is to be capable of having one's behavior *represented*, that is, described in terms of rule following; to be fully rational is to be capable of *self*-representation, that is, capable of describing for oneself the rules that one's behavior (ideally and/or actually) exemplifies. This capacity for self-representation we might call *philosophical* rationality, and it is in this sense that philosophy is distinctively *"vorstellendes Denken* that gives reasons," to revert to Heidegger's phrase. Not only does it "set before" one the reasons that are there for one's behavior, it sets them before one in a distinctive way: as *rules* self-consciously to be followed in action, as *principles* deliberately to be exemplified in practice. Philosophy *represents* our lives as rule-governed social practices in the attempt to clarify and defend them; and the *fuller* that representation, the more complete and comprehensive and self-conscious it is, the better.

What is at stake in rationality-as-representation, then, is a particular way of describing rational human action, a mode of description that is peculiarly *modern* and *philosophical* in at least three of its central features. First, it emphasizes one's capacity and need for conscious and controlled self-reflection as a way to virtue. Such rigorous self-reflection on the epistemic and ethical rules one is following is assumed to be the only way to eliminate from one's thought and life both outright error and— what is apparently just as bad—the uncriticized traditional conceptions of the past. Second, it focuses attention upon one's capacity to distance oneself, at least in thought, from the routines actually constituting one's everyday life; thus it strengthens the distinctively modern picture of the self as finally independent of both nature and history. By representing one's ordinary practices as sets of rules to be followed (or not) by one, it makes the self seem an extensionless but powerful point, a disembodied spiritual entity that can float free above life, picking and choosing for itself the places and structures to inhabit. Third, all this lends weight to the Enlightenment (and ultimately existentialist) moral ideal of authentic self-responsibility, an ideal that throws back upon the individual the whole burden of achieving meaning and purpose in life. In this view, meaning comes only from within the self, that is, from the choices one does or doesn't make. By choosing, carefully and explicitly, the recipe for a particular life, one thereby makes for oneself the meaning that one hungers for. One is most fully oneself, most authentically self-responsible, when legislating for oneself the laws one will follow, the life that one will lead.[12]

This connection to authority returns us to the matter of skepticism, the more or less constant companion to modern philosophy. The philosophical skeptic insinuates that our actual lives are not what they seem to be, that our current practices do not, in some way or other, live up to their own billing. Thus our lives are claimed to be less than fully authentic. We can now see an important assumption common both to (modern) skepticism and to (modern) defenders of our epistemic and ethical practices. It is the assumption that these rational practices can be and should be fully *represented* in order to be attacked or defended. The philosophical opponent of skepticism has, by and large, accepted without demur the skeptic's initial reduction of our practices to sets of rules to be followed by action. Then the opponent's claim in response is either that the rules of the practice have been misidentified in the skeptic's attack on them and thus that the practice has unfairly been pronounced lacking (the straw-man defense), or that, while the correct principles have been identified, the skeptical attacks on them are in some way inconclusive or faulty. Perhaps the reason that (as Hume pointed out) such skeptical disputes seem to be both interminable and yet purely notional is that both sides accept the same purely notional presupposition of rationality-as-representation.

VII

I have followed a deliberately meandering path in this chapter, mainly because I have wanted to acknowledge that the threat of philosophical nihilism resists our standard philosophical ambi-

---

12. For further detail see Charles Taylor, "Overcoming Epistemology," pp. 464–88.

tion to formulate it as a clear and specific intellectual challenge. One can sometimes distinctly feel its cold breath upon one's neck, but even then one isn't quite sure that there's really anything there. My aim has been to get at the sense of nihilism gradually, by moving from particular to general and by using Heidegger's reflection on Nietzsche's use of the term as a bridge.

I began with a fantasy: the nihilist fantasy of a wholesale collapse of epistemic and ethical authority, a collapse brought on by philosophical reflection itself. Nihilism, so understood, is the specter of our rational capacities growing in power and sophistication until they finally grow powerful and sophisticated enough to undermine themselves, thus leaving us sunk in a fundamental despair. The pain we would feel in such a case would be particularly ugly and dangerous, because it would spring from so deep a dissociation in our sense of who we are. We would no longer be able to identify the most distinctive and honored part of ourselves, our rationality, with the lives we must actually live; the difference between our claims and our hopes for ourselves, on the one hand, and the reality we actually inhabit, on the other, would be crushing. The sense of life, of a distinctively human life, would therefore be in question. In the long run, human life would pass away, replaced either by something less than we are, or by something "more," like Nietzsche's Overman.

There is little question that such a fantasy has troubled some considerable philosophers. The important philosophical question for us now is: *should* it? Is there any basis for such a fear within the practice of philosophy itself? We have seen that Heidegger answers, emphatically, *yes*. For him, nihilism is more than just a constant *threat* to philosophical reflection: because philosophy is always at root *metaphysics*, and because metaphysics is "representational thinking that gives reasons," nihilism is the *necessary consequence* of philosophy, its hidden essence. The nihilist fantasy is a glimpse of things to come, he thinks.

The conclusion is certainly provocative, but the premises on which it rests are so idiosyncratic that few outside the circle of Heidegger partisans are likely to find it decisive. I have tried to argue something weaker than Heidegger's flat-out equation of metaphysics, philosophy, and nihilism. So far I have tried to show that there is a fruitful way to reinterpret his crucial claim that metaphysics is "*vorstellendes Denken* that gives reasons." My interpretation takes this to be a claim about (modern) philosophy's fundamental assumption that rational actions are to be described as instances of rule following and thus that the various social practices that constitute human life are best conceived as patterns of such rules for action. I have called this assumption *rationality-as-representation*. It is, I have claimed, a distinctive feature of philosophy (of *modern* philosophy, at least) that it has tried to represent our lives in this way.

All this has been a way to suggest, of course, that rationality-as-representation is the key to understanding the threat that nihilism poses to philosophical reflection. Unlike Heidegger, I am not claiming that nihilism is the essence of philosophy, whatever exactly that might mean. There is no need, and certainly no good reason, to maintain that the sort of nihilist collapse I hypothesized in section 1 of this chapter will ever actually take place, even if philosophy continues to advance forever in a perfectly straight line. We can even admit to skeptics of the transcendental standpoint that it may not be possible for us now to describe such a hypothetical collapse in a way free from all plausible philosophical objections. To admit these things is just properly to locate philosophical nihilism as a *threat*, not as an actuality; and, as I have already said, a threat need not finally be entirely rational in order to be a genuine threat. As every parent knows, the effective power of a childhood fear, and thus the need to take it seriously, does not depend upon a completely coherent conception of its object.

Our philosophical examination of nihilism has all along assumed that at this point we simply do not know how rational the threat of nihilism is, that is, that we do not know whether or not our fear of such a collapse has any coherent basis in the practice of philosophical reflection. But we are now in a position to find this out, I believe, because we can now see what at least part of that basis would need to be. It is the possibility that our lives can be *represented*, in my sense of the term; that our constitutive epistemic and ethical practices can be displayed as sets of rules to be followed by one in action. For once that set of structural assumptions about rational action is taken up into a

very natural *ideal* of practical rationality, namely, that the rules
one follows in one's actions ought to be rules that one could self-
consciously and wholeheartedly *accept* as rules governing action, then the possibility is there that the rules of one's practices
(whether actual or ideal) would *not* be acceptable to one on such
a reflection. Once one's life has been represented, then it can
become an object of either satisfaction or shame to one. Thus a
necessary condition of philosophical nihilism (I do not say *sufficient*, of course) is rationality-as-representation.

That claim is not an a priori one, based (à la Heidegger) on
some alleged insight into the essential nature of (modern) philosophy. It is simply an interpretation, a reading if you will, of the
philosophical tradition that shows itself decisively in Descartes,
reformulates itself in Kant's transcendental critique, and is still
found in philosophers as different as Husserl and Rawls. I am
suggesting that, all the way from Descartes to some forms of artificial intelligence research, one sees the steady persistence of
the notion that human life can be rationalized as a structure of
rules to be followed (tacitly or explicitly) by a potentially self-
conscious and potentially autonomous agent.

I am suggesting as well that the constant attention of modern
philosophy to the threat of skepticism (with philosophical nihilism as the most extreme result of such skepticism) is explicable in terms of the persistence of this notion. It is what gives
such skepticism the room to operate. I am not interested here in
trying to assign priority to either chicken or egg: it does not
matter for my purposes whether rationality-as-representation
first led to skepticism or whether skeptical threats produced the
self-conscious attempt to represent our lives in answer to them.
It is enough to see that the notions now take in one another's
washing. Modern skepticism consistently assumes such a possibility of representation; if there were no such possibility, there
would be no such skepticism, and thus no threat of nihilism.
(That is not to say, of course, that our inherent sense of frailty
would not find some *other* way to express itself.)

If the threat of philosophical nihilism has a rational basis,
then, it is because our lives can be represented in this distinctively philosophical way. So the philosophical question about
philosophical nihilism is, at first, the question about rationality-

as-representation: can our lives indeed be represented as a structure of rules to be followed in action? If they can, then the threat of nihilism does have a rational basis, since it makes sense to imagine that the rules that govern our lives might on reflection turn out to be unacceptable to us in some fashion, or at least that they might convincingly *seem* so.

If our lives cannot be so represented, however, then it is difficult to see how nihilism might be a genuinely *philosophical* threat. There would certainly remain the possibility of a deep disenchantment with one's present condition, an "arrest of life" (as Tolstoy called it in his own case), that would leave one permanently powerless and self-despising, or that would, like the Nietzschean Overman, free one for new forms of dominion and excitement; but it is hard to see how, without representation as a precondition, either of these outcomes could be brought about by pure *reflection*. Reflection that powerful seems to demand the sort of distance from its object that in the case of one's own life only some form of philosophical representation could supply. Only if one can see that life *impersonally*, as *a* form of life alongside others, can it become the object of a distinctively *philosophical* reflection capable of leading one to radical change. It is difficult to see how such impersonality could be achieved without the description of that life in terms of the rules for action that it (ideally and actually) exemplifies. Certainly, at any rate, that is how (modern) philosophy has tried to achieve it.

Can our lives be represented in accordance with the canons just described? This question, usually unformulated as such, underlies some of the most interesting and important philosophy written in this century; one could argue, in fact, that it is the (tacit) presence of this question—and thus the tacit presence of the question of philosophical nihilism—that gives our century's philosophy whatever unity it has. How can the question be answered? To many philosophers *language* has seemed to be the heart of the matter, since language seems necessarily to underlie, indeed to constitute, every epistemic and ethical practice we are tempted to claim as distinctively human. Language is not just an adjunct to our humanity, as if it were only a device we had developed for the purpose of sharing thoughts and feelings capable of existing independently of it; rather, the thoughts and feelings that make us human essentially depend upon language for their very possibility.[13] There could be no substantial, distinctively human epistemic and ethical practices apart from our ability to speak. The sorts of attentive discrimination, inner and outer, that those practices trade upon are conceivable only linguistically. Thus language is the essential and fundamental human practice; it is the human practice prior and common to all others.

Can language be represented, then? Can it be adequately described as a set of rules to be followed by speakers? If it can, there seems no reason not to expect that *all* our practices can be represented in a rule-referenced way, given world enough and time; and thus the threat—but still only the *threat*—of philosophical nihilism would be genuine. If language cannot be represented, then that threat is baseless, and our fears of unbridled philosophical reflection leading to nihilism can be appropriately treated as irrational. So the philosophical question of philosophical nihilism is, I believe, ultimately the question of the possibility of representing language as a structure of rules to be followed by speakers. In the next two chapters of this book I want to examine what seem to me to be the two deepest and most fruitful explorations of this question in the philosophy of this century, namely, the so-called later philosophies of Heidegger and Wittgenstein. By looking at their attempts to formulate this question adequately and to answer it decisively, we can not only reach a better understanding of what the threat of philosophical nihilism comes to, we can also travel some distance toward our second goal in this essay, that of appreciating the significance of this threat within a life both reflective and engaged.

13. See the essays in Charles Taylor, *Human Agency and Language*, for substantiation.

2

Heidegger and the
Speaking of Language

Heidegger's deliberate attention to the matter of language comes, for the most part, late in his long career of thinking. Early on there were some oblique approaches to the topic in lectures and classes, and there is, of course, the careful discussion of assertion and discourse in sections 33 and 34 of *Being and Time*, a discussion for which Heidegger himself apparently retained some measure of affection; but most of his explicit thinking about language belongs to the period well after his so-called turn in the mid-1930s and is of a piece with the rejection there of the "humanism" (as he calls it) that infects even his own earlier work.[1] In a 1944 lecture course on logic for the first time he directly exploits his conviction that only an altered philosophical relationship to language—Heidegger himself speaks of this as an altered *experience* of language—can free thinking from the exhausted categories of the Western metaphysical tradition. The point is then publicly made in the *Letter on Humanism* (1947), which contains his famous assertion "Language is the house of Being";[2] and the essays collected in *On the Way to Language* and *Poetry, Language, Thought* develop and consolidate his thinking about that new linguistic relationship or experience. These late essays will be the focus of my discussion in this chapter.

1. Martin Heidegger, *Being and Time*, pp. 195–210. See also Martin Heidegger, *On the Way to Language*, p. 92.
2. A translation by Frank A. Capuzzi and J. Glenn Gray of the *Brief über den Humanismus* appears in Martin Heidegger, *Basic Writings*, edited by David Farrell Krell.

I

The immediate philosophical background for Heidegger's thinking about language is set by two powerful and opposing accounts of linguistic meaning. The first we may call *language-as-representation*; the second, *language-as-expression*.[3] The first of these accounts came fully into its own in the seventeenth century, with the Lockean "Way of Ideas" and the Cartesian epistemological revolution. The second is in romantic revolt against the first and can be found initially in the linguistic speculations of Herder and Humboldt.[4] As is clear from the references in his essays, later Heidegger is most specifically concerned to oppose the second account, especially as it was developed by Humboldt; but this opposition to language-as-expression is in no way an attempt to rehabilitate language-as-representation. Both accounts are equally bad, he thinks, and for the same reason. Thus it will be useful to begin with a sketch of language-as-representation.

Although the representationalist account of language came to full bloom only with Locke and Descartes, its roots reach at least to Aristotle's *De Interpretatione*. Heidegger translates the crucial Aristotelian passage as follows:

> Now what (takes place) in the making of vocal sounds is a show of what there is in the soul in the way of passions, and what is written is a show of the vocal sounds. And just as writing is not the same among all (men), so also the vocal sounds are not the same. On the other hand, those things of which these (sounds and writings) are a show in the first place, are among all (men) the same passions of the soul, and the matters of which these (the passions) give likening representations are also the same. (Heidegger, *On the Way to Language*, p. 114)

3. I am indebted to Charles Taylor for these phrases. See his *Human Agency and Language: Philosophical Papers I*, pp. 215–92, 77–96. In this context I am of course not using 'representation' in the sense described at the end of chapter 1.

4. See Taylor, *Human Agency and Language*, pp. 254–57, for references and helpful discussion.

Whether directly in speech or indirectly in script, language is "a show," says Aristotle, of what is going on in the soul. The claim seems a truism: it is hard to deny that *one* function of language is to make public the hidden "passions." The philosophical questions about language become acute only when a more specific account of this "showing" is attempted. *How* does language reveal the soul's inner landscapes? What sort of connection exists between our words and our passions, such that the utterance of the former can "show" the latter? Aristotle seems to provide a decisive clue when he speaks here of sounds and writing as *signs* (*semeia*) of inner events and states. The representationalist account seizes upon this term: a language is nothing more than a *system of signs*. The sign relationship is taken to be the fundamental semantic tie of word to inner world.

And what is a sign? A sign is, in this account, a *conventional designation*, an agreed-upon mark standing for something that exists independently of it. Here is the thing; there is its sign. Here is a particular "passion:" *fear*, for instance; there is the word 'fear'. Fear and 'fear' are not at all the same, of course: the first is a passion common (Aristotle believes) to all human beings; the second is a word of a particular language, namely, English. Everyone knows what fear is, but not everyone knows what 'fear' means. Indeed, one could just as well use another sign altogether to designate that same passion. Calling it 'fear' is neither better nor worse than calling it '*Angst*'. The sign is doing its work so long as it is understood by its audience. Aristotle himself in the passage quoted from *De Interpretatione* specifically mentions the word differences found among the natural languages.

In this way, the linguistic sign becomes interpreted as a pure *name*, as a sort of *proper* name, a written or spoken mark with which the passion is (conventionally) associated and that can be used, in virtue of that association, to refer to it. The sign thus becomes a *representative*, a deputy, a handy substitute for the thing itself. The word becomes, in Hobbes's famous image, a *counter*. Language then can be understood, it seems, as an ordered system of such representatives. When these individual representatives are combined in particular, conventionally specified (i.e., grammatical) ways, the result is a true or false *representa-*

tion of a relationship among the passions that those representatives represent.

The Lockean/Cartesian "Way of Ideas" accepts and extends this attractively simple account of language-as-representation. Like Aristotle, both Locke and Descartes take language to be the outer (public, "physical") expression of the inner (private, "mental") landscapes of the soul. The advance they mark over Aristotle is the relatively plausible and well-developed philosophy of mind they share as the basis for this conception of language, a philosophy of mind admirably suited to the powerful new sciences beginning to come on line in the seventeenth century. It is a philosophy of mind that builds in *representation* (understood to take place by means of the mechanism of *natural resemblance*) at the most fundamental level of mental operation.[5]

Both Locke and Descartes erect their philosophies upon a simple but apparently very fruitful metaphor, or family of metaphors, for the basic cognitive power of human beings: mind is (in Locke's phrase) *the mirror of nature*; it is a passive medium that naturally reflects, well or ill, the reality that stands before it.[6] These natural reflections of reality Locke and Descartes call *ideas*; and they assume that, like the images appearing in an actual mirror, our ideas are the more or less accurate copies of the things that originally cause them to appear to us. At bottom, then, mind is quasi-mechanical reflection. As a result of their "natural" resemblance-relations to reality, our ideas are, on this account, *representatives*: the inner "mental" image becomes the deputy, the substitute, for the "physical" thing itself. All thought, all cognition, occurs in the medium of the idea thus defined. All our beliefs about ourselves or the world are, on this account, simple or complex constellations of these "natural" representatives. Out of our ideas we form (for ourselves and others) *pictures of facts*, representations of reality as we take it to be. Thus we think, truly or falsely, *about* the world; but that intentional connection of thought to reality is possible only because

5. See Richard Rorty, *Philosophy and the Mirror of Nature.*
6. Even this philosophy of mind is not completely original with them, of course. Its seed can be found in Aristotle's account of the passions as "likening representations" of matters outside the soul. See the passage from *De Interpretatione* quoted in the text.

the universal medium of thought, the idea, has an immediate "natural" connection of resemblance to the reality that caused it to appear.

Language, the medium in which our thinking is made public, is for Locke or Descartes simply an artificial iteration of the essentially representational structure of mind itself. Words are the names of ideas. As ideas represent (i.e., resemble) reality, so do spoken words represent (i.e., name, designate) ideas. Spoken language is thus the *representation of a representation*, the (artificial) sign of a (natural) sign; written language is merely another step up the same ladder, the sign of a sign of a sign. While Descartes and Locke do not agree on how all our ideas actually come to be present to consciousness (whether some are "innate," as Descartes believes, or whether all come through "experience," as Locke has it), and while Locke stresses much more than does Descartes the *conventionality* of our words, the ways they come to be connected to our ideas through our own decisions and associations, both agree that language, written or spoken, is a system of designative representation founded on the "natural" resemblance of idea to object.

Thus both for Aristotle and for the "Way of Ideas," the representationalist account of language rests upon a philosophy of mind that builds in a form of "natural" representation, of "natural" intentionality, as the basic structure of human consciousness. In *De Interpretatione* Aristotle calls this *homoiosis*; in the *Essay* Locke calls it *resemblance*. It is the "natural identity" of idea and object that is supposed to underwrite our original linguistic designations of reality, connecting word to world—common sign to particular thing—through the necessary medium of the resembling idea. These immediate designations make possible all subsequent linguistic representations. When this notion of "natural" mental representation began to collapse, as it did in the eighteenth and nineteenth centuries, some new account of language was therefore demanded. Its criteria of adequacy were set by the criticisms that demolished the philosophical foundations of the earlier account. A quick review of those criticisms is thus in order.

The immediate weakness of representationalist philosophy of mind and language is its account of human consciousness, and thus of linguistic representation, as essentially passive and receptive. Locke's favored image for the mind's receptivity is, as we have already noted, *reflection in a glass*. In a more Aristotelian vein Descartes sometimes speaks of mental *impression*, such as a seal makes in soft wax. In both tropes, human consciousness is taken to be essentially plastic. It yields itself up to reality, passively conforming to it and thus becoming its proper representative. But this rhetoric is profoundly misleading, as Kant realized. It obscures the presence—indeed, the necessity—of *will* at the center of any genuinely *thinking* consciousness. To think is to order and to judge. The human mind cannot be merely a passive receptor of impressions and images, therefore. We must first *construct* our representations of reality from the representative ideas we are (*ex hypothesi*) given. And even if (*per impossibile*) our representations were to come to us full-blown, we must still in our judgments either *assent to or dissent from* the representations thus given, and such assent or dissent is an act of will.

The entire Cartesian project of systematic doubt, for example, gets its sense only from the presupposition that some of our representations are more acceptable than others, that some more than others accurately reflect the structure of reality *sub specie aeternitatis*. Not all our representations, however powerfully impressed upon us, are of equal value. Thus the Cartesian ego, whose salvation depends upon accurate and comprehensive knowledge (something "firm and lasting in the sciences," as he puts it in Meditation One), must *pick and choose* among the various representations that beset it. Adequate knowledge (as distinct from the grounding certainty of the ego's immediate self-presentation) is an *achievement*. Thus the mind that achieves this knowledge could not be pure receptivity; on the contrary, it must also be *will*, the will to truth.

Pressed on the point, then, even Descartes would have to yield. In spite of the official rhetoric, mind is not *just* the mirror of nature or yielding wax. But that admission alone seems to pose no real problem for the die-hard representationalist: so long as nothing compromises the basic idea of mental representation itself, then the structure of Cartesian or Lockean epistemology can easily be altered to accommodate a knowing consciousness that is will as well as receptivity. For even if the representationalist must now admit that hidden in the kernel of *res cogitans* is the will to truth, he can still insist that the truth it wills is the accurate and comprehensive representation of the real. The image of the mirror has been supplemented but apparently not compromised.

But *can* the representationalist continue to make that last claim? Apparently not. The immediate indications of trouble are the familiar epistemological difficulties one encounters here. Given the representationalist account of consciousness as immediate awareness of ideas, there is no way for the mind to verify the accuracy (i.e., the actual resemblance to reality) of its most fundamental representations. How could I know, for example, that I have constructed my representations in the appropriate way, that I have put the ideas together correctly? I couldn't. Worse yet, there is even no way for me to be sure that the basic connection of idea to reality is such that my constructions out of the former could *ever* appropriately resemble the actual structures of the latter. Resemblance *itself*, the "natural identity" of idea and object, is in question. Let us see why.

In the representationalist account, consciousness is *directly* aware only of its own ideas. Conceived as the mirror of nature, mind "contains" only the images of things, not the actual things themselves. One's knowledge of any reality thus can come only through one's representations of it; and however coherent and convincing a given set of representations may be, there is always the possibility of its falsity. The essential nature of a representation is that it is always distinguishable from, and therefore possibly different from, what it represents. *No* representation carries its warrant of truth on its face, not even the second-order, philosophical representation that our ideas resemble the objects that cause them. What then could be the source of one's assurance that (at least sometimes) the things-in-themselves match up appropriately with the things-as-they-seem? What could be our guarantee of the "natural resemblance" of idea to object asserted to be at the heart of all representation? *None*, it seems, barring some Cartesian deus ex machina. Such assurance would require that the mind be able to escape from its own representations so as to check directly their fundamental resemblance to the reality they purport to represent. Mind in that case would have to be much more than just a mirror.

The immediate upshot of this recognition is a virulent epistemological skepticism, verging on the rigorous solipsism entertained (in his philosophical moments) by Hume. The notion of knowledge itself is in danger of collapse under the weight of the image of representation. Kant tried to meet this skeptical challenge with a sort of holding action: he argued that human experience is constituted by the ego, thus admitting that representation is not a mechanical isomorphism like the production of a mirror image; but he insisted as well on an ineffable thing-in-itself outside consciousness as the necessary anchor of the representations thus constituted. Representation must, at least in its ideal, answer to something beyond itself.

But to paraphrase Wittgenstein, a wheel that when turned turns nothing else is not a part of the mechanism; and so it is with the Kantian *Ding-an-sich*: one could eliminate it with no discernible epistemological loss. Thus in the representationalist account, objective reality (i.e., the *Ding-an-sich*) has become completely inaccessible to thought; one is left only with the representations themselves. But this breaks the back of the philosophical metaphor of *representation* altogether. If there are *nothing but* representations available to me for inspection, then there are *no* representations. The sense of the metaphor itself depends upon the possibility of comparing representations to what is represented. When that possibility is void, as it now is, the image has ceased to function. Epistemological skepticism of the Humean sort only points out how empty the representationalist philosophy of mind was to begin with. The wheel of "mental representation" has been found not to be connected to any working mechanism.[7]

II

So a representationalist philosophy of mind turns out to be a dead letter. With this, the charm of a representationalist philos-

7. See Friedrich Nietzsche, "How the True World Became a Fable," pp. 485–86.

ophy of language disappears as well. For all its simplicity and attractiveness, language-as-representation required some trope of quasi-mechanical isomorphism to make it go. Because such tropes so decisively failed to live up to their promises, a new philosophy of mind was required; and with its advent, a new account of language began to emerge in the late eighteenth century. Following Heidegger's lead, we will call this new account *language-as-expression*. Heidegger finds it most clearly developed in the work of the linguist Wilhelm von Humboldt, especially in his "On the Diversity of the Structure of Human Language and Its Influence on the Intellectual Development of Mankind," but there are other, even more powerful, versions in play.[8] As the name suggests, one may summarize this account as the view that language is the *fundamental activity of human self-expression.*

Of course, simply to say that language is human self-expression is just as harmless, and just as uninformative, as to say that language represents reality. The interest of either claim resides in the philosophy of mind that supports it. In contrast to its predecessor, however, it is not so easy to sketch in a few words the conception of mind that underlies Humboldt's view of language. For us *expression* is a much less distinct and familiar philosophical image than is *representation*. Nevertheless, the essentials of the expressionist conception can be grasped by starting with its emphasis on human *activity*.

The emphasis on activity is largely absent from representationalist accounts of mind and language. The official rhetoric of such accounts stresses the essential passivity and receptivity of human consciousness. These accounts put forth a picture of the person as essentially a *thoughtful spectator*, whose thinking about reality is essentially detached from any particular context of purposeful action or social relationship. A mirror is not an agent, after all, and neither is a piece of soft wax.

In this respect, as in so many others, Descartes is a paradigm of the representationalist; and his description of the actual circumstances of his philosophical thinking vividly reveals some of his most basic assumptions about the self. At the beginning

8. Heidegger, *On the Way to Language*, p. 116. See also Taylor, *Human Agency and Language*, p. 254.

of Meditation One he presents himself as one who is luckily freed of all worldly cares and disturbed by no unruly passions. He is fortunate (he thinks) to be able to do his thinking in a serene retreat of peaceful solitude. Later in the same meditation he describes himself as clothed in a dressing gown and seated by a fire, presumably therefore in a comfortable private room, another image of isolation and detachment. Descartes's situation of placid withdrawal thus becomes a trope for Cartesian mind itself. Mind too exists in a room of its own, in a space freed from the bustle of the street outside the window. It too is independent of any particular immersion in action or society; thinking is essentially separate from (and, ideally, prior to) any doing. The Cartesian thinking self, the *res cogitans*, is both epistemologically and metaphysically prior to the "bodily" self involved in the world's schemes and arrangements; and the secure knowledge at which Cartesian thinking aims is the representation of a world that lies at an inescapable epistemological and metaphysical distance from the transcendental subject that surveys it.

As we have already noted, however, this detached and spectatorial image of mind cannot be fully sustained even by Descartes himself. Even he must admit (in Meditation Two) that thinking is inseparable from some forms of willing: the *res cogitans* revealed by his systematic doubt is a being that affirms, denies, rejects—that *wills*. The expressionist conception of mind tries to make this recognition of will *central* rather than a grudging or peripheral admission. Human life is *essentially* purposeful activity in a social context, the expressionist maintains, and all forms of human consciousness, even the most abstract, must be understood as forms of that activity. Mind is not a preexistent, independent spectator of one's life of activity and social relationship; rather, mind is the *expression* of that active and communal life itself.

Of course it is difficult to say, exactly and economically, what 'expression' means here, and for our purposes it will not be necessary to trace this notion all the way through the daunting complexities it generates in Hegel, who was its great champion. Nevertheless, the fundamental idea is clear: mind shows itself *as* certain complex and complicated forms of human activity.

The presence of mind is constituted by particular sorts of social practices and "products," not (as in Descartes or Locke) by some metaphysically distinct substance; and the relationship of mind to these constitutive "products"—i.e., to sentences, buildings, works of art, theological systems, political institutions, etc.—is not like the relationship of an approaching storm to a falling barometer but more like the relationship of anger to the scowl that shows it.[9]

Both the barometer and the scowl can be understood as *signs*, of course; as such, either can thus be the basis for an inference. From Smith's scowl I can predict a storm in the Smith household, just as from Smith's barometer I can judge the likelihood of a change in the fair weather. But the sign relationship that underlies the inferences is very different in the two cases. Charles Taylor puts it clearly:

> The barometer 'reveals' rain indirectly. This contrasts with our perceiving rain directly. But when I make plain my anger or my joy, in verbal or facial expression, there is no such contrast. This is not a second best, the dropping of clues which enable you to infer. This is what manifesting anger or joy *is*. They are made evident not by or through the expression but in it. (*Human Agency and Language*, p. 91)

Expression, then, is *embodiment*. It is the appearance, the immediate and inseparable presence, of mind in some medium. As Taylor points out, the embodiment of anger in a scowl is neither "accidental" nor "indirect." The scowl and the passion are not two genuinely independent things, which just happen to have become associated with each other, like a red traffic light and the necessity to stop one's car. Nor is the connection between the facial expression and the feeling a factual link that might not have been discovered by us, like the connection between a lowering barometer and the approach of rain. Does it make sense to imagine that we might *not* have known of the connection between scowls and anger? ("How lucky our ancestors were to realize that. Life must have been chancy before

9. Here I am gratefully indebted to Charles Taylor.

they did.") No, the scowl *is* the anger, anger embodied; while the falling glass is only an indication of a storm, not the storm itself. Fundamentally there is only one thing in the first case: the anger. It is only with practice and instruction that one learns how artificially to separate the "reality" of anger from its "sign," as in cases of pretense.

Ceteris paribus, then, mind is present only as embodied or expressed in some medium. Mind is not an independent, incorporeal substance that just happens to attach itself to some physical gesture or construction; mind is human activity of a certain level of complexity necessarily embodying itself in some medium of expression. It is not the mirror of nature; it *is* nature: natural activity grown complicated enough to have become *self-reflective*, activity so complex and sophisticated that it can (and needs to) cast off exterior expressions (embodiments) of itself. Thinking, then, is nature's self-expression, not its representation from someplace "outside."

This expressionist philosophy of mind leads, naturally enough, to a corresponding philosophy of language. Language, in this account, is the fundamental medium of self-expressive mind. It is the basic "material," the fundamental social practice, in terms of which human beings embody their intelligence. Notice that I say 'embody' rather than 'encode' or 'represent'. Language is conceived here not as a fixed and orderly set of conventional designations (a "code," a "system of signs") used to construct representations of an antecedent and independent world; rather, it is the activity itself of world-*creation* through human self-expression: "Language must be regarded not as a dead product of the past but as a living creation. It must be abstracted from all that it effects as a designation of comprehended ideas" (Heidegger, *On the Way to Language*, p. 117). As Humboldt says at another place:

> In itself language is not work (*ergon*) but an activity (*energeia*). Its true definition may therefore only be genetic. It is after all the continual intellectual effort to make the articulated sound capable of expressing thought.[10]

10. Quoted in Heidegger, *On the Way to Language*, p. 117.

Energeia not *ergon*. As the fundamental medium of human self-expression, language grows and changes as does the human world. Indeed world and language are not, as in the representationalist account, two separable items; they are not *fact* and its *picture*. They are *one*. World first of all shows itself—expresses itself, embodies itself—in the language that human beings use in their relations to one another. Without language there is no human world at all. In this way language becomes an essential feature of human spiritual development. It is the medium in which human beings create a habitable world to live in together. "When we understand the nature of language in terms of expression, we give it a more comprehensive definition by incorporating expression, as one among many activities, into the total economy of those achievements by which man makes himself" (Heidegger, *Poetry, Language, Thought*, p. 192).

As my quotations illustrate, Heidegger's explicit references in his attacks on language-as-expression are mostly to Humboldt, but I suspect that another thinker is his true opponent in this matter: Nietzsche. Coming to terms with Nietzsche's work (lectured on again and again by Heidegger after the mid-1930s) was a large factor in his decisive turn away from humanism, a turn of which his mature reflections on language are part and parcel. The account of language (sketchy as it is) in *The Will to Power* certainly develops even further the sort of expressionist views to be found in Humboldt. So it is not unlikely that Heidegger had Nietzsche in mind. At any rate, it will be useful to introduce Nietzsche as an object of comparison here, not only because he shows us an even starker version of language-as-expression, but also because by reference to his account we can see even more clearly the sort of relationship to language—and to life in general—that later Heidegger is struggling to avoid.

III

Nietzsche accepts with neither reservation nor regret the failure of representationalism as a philosophy of mind and language. For him, the human being is a center of creative will to power, not a tape recorder of what there is. There is no serene, Cartesian "knowing subject" to gaze placidly upon reality like a transparent eyeball (in Emerson's phrase). The basic activity of consciousness is not representation but *interpretation*, where interpretation is an act of force, the introjection of meaning into some plastic material. Interpretation is embodiment, in other words. Even rationality, that idol of philosophers, is not—as the tradition has it—a style of representation according to the final order of things; it is only a final failure of the imagination and of its power to create new interpretations.

> *Rational thought is interpretation according to a scheme that we cannot throw off.*
>
> . . .
>
> "Interpretation," the introduction of meaning—not "explanation." . . . There are no facts, everything is in flux, incomprehensible, elusive; what is relatively most enduring is—our opinions. (Nietzsche, *Will to Power*, sec. 522, 604)

Our virtue, our defining excellence as human beings, is not some alleged capacity for grasping secure metaphysical truth, as Plato and Descartes both believed. Rather, it is our creative power to push through, again and again, our own ends of self-mastery and control. It is our capacity to be active, self-defining, self-interpreting individuals, not thoughtless and reactionary members of a herd.

> The individual is something quite new which creates new things, something absolute; all his acts are entirely his own.
>
> Ultimately, the individual derives the values of his acts from himself; because he has to interpret in a quite individual way even the words he has inherited. His interpretation of a formula at least is personal, even if he does not create a formula: as an interpreter he is still creative. (*Will to Power*, sec. 767)

Naturally enough, Nietzsche's account of language reflects this radically nontraditional epistemological and metaphysical perspective. A single highly compressed section from *The Will to Power* shows the essential elements of his view:

We cannot change our means of expression at will: it is possible to understand the extent to which they are mere signs. The demand for an adequate mode of expression is senseless: it is of the essence of a language, a means of expression, to express a mere relationship—
The concept "truth" is nonsensical. The entire domain of "true-false" applies only to relations, not to an "in-itself"—There is no "essence-in-itself" (it is only relations that constitute an essence—), just as there can be no "knowledge-in-itself." (Sec. 625)

Language is, as he puts it here, "a means of expression." A language is not an impersonal and objective photographic medium; on the contrary, its vocabulary and idiom are always the expression of a particular and quite specific way of seeing—i.e., interpreting—what is there. As such a means of expression, moreover, it always embodies a "relationship," not a "fact," not an "essence-in-itself," as he says. Let us try to unpack these claims a bit.

As noted, the representationalist account of language construes the proposition, the basic unit of language, as a kind of *picture*, as a "true" or a "false" reflection of some independently existing state of affairs. There are the things-in-themselves, says the representationalist; here is their recapitulation in words, like flies trapped in amber for all eternity. But for Nietzsche the proposition is a "means of expression"; it is a "sign"—we might better say a *symptom*—of a particular state of the will to power in relation to what confronts it. Language *expresses*, says Nietzsche; it does not *represent* reality, external or internal, any more than the symptom "represents" the disease. The symptom *presents* the disease; one might even say, it *is* the disease showing itself. The symptom is a particular embodiment (perhaps incipient and therefore incomplete) of the pathological syndrome itself. The rash does not "recapitulate" or "represent" the antecedent and independent "fact" of measles. The rash is part of the illness itself, just as the boiling clouds we see on the horizon are part of the approaching storm.

Just so, for Nietzsche, the proposition/judgment symptomatically expresses a relation of the will to power to its world. It shows, not what that world is like (or even *thought* to be like) in some static and "objective" way but what a particular constellation of the will to power has made and is making it to be. True, the proposition does "reveal the world," but not as the published photograph reveals the contents of a pharaoh's tomb. It reveals *symptomatically*; it *expresses*. In the uttered proposition the world is *present*, not pictured. Life—i.e., will to power—is embodied there in an attempt to preserve and enhance itself in relation to other life. The proposition is both expression and intervention, therefore. It presents—expresses, embodies—the quality of the speaker's will to power in relation to the other forces that confront him, and it functions in that embodiment as an instrument of that will to power in its attempt at self-overcoming and self-enhancement. The words of the judgment are simultaneously both symptoms and tools of the will to power's self-overcoming.

Life at a given moment is always a "relationship," as Nietzsche says in section 625; that is, it is always a particular disposition of the will's forces in relation to other centers of power. The world is not a stage set of lifeless props for the free standing ego to represent and then to manipulate. The world is, in his word, *Becoming*, an endless play of forces against other forces. "Our" world, the world as we actually encounter it, is Becoming itself: *living powers* confronting other living powers, not dead "objects" displayed before a mysteriously vital "subject." There is no "essence-in-itself," he says, only "relations" (sec. 625). A particular language in use, then, is the timely, historical expression (symptom, "sign," embodiment) of a particular life being lived. It reveals not the world's "essence" (understood traditionally, that is, Platonically) but its "relations." A particular idiom, grammar, and vocabulary—that is, a particular set of possible judgments to be made or questions to be asked—shows (but does not represent) the whole disposition of life-forces operating there at a given moment. In particular, it shows these forces as they embody themselves in a specific (and ultimately temporary) center of will—what Nietzsche calls "a complex form of relative life-duration within the flux of becoming" (sec. 715)—namely, the "speaker" from whom the utterance of this language issues.

But an account of language must look two ways: toward language as understood as well as toward language as uttered. If for Nietzsche the utterance of a proposition is the natural, symptomatic expression and effort of a particular center of will to power in its relation to other such centers, then what is it to *understand* such a proposition? Nietzsche does not directly answer this question in *The Will to Power*, but it seems clear that, like utterance, understanding must also be an act of interpretation. It too must be a symptomatic, embodied expression of will to power in its attempt at self-overcoming, in this case the "hearer's" will to power rather than the "speaker's." Understanding the propositions one hears is not, for Nietzsche, a matter of grasping someone else's "pictures" of the world. Understanding is not intrinsically "mental." Rather, to understand a proposition is just to *respond* to its utterance in some "appropriate" way. It is to share with the speaker a form of life, a publicly recognizable congruence of speaker's action and hearer's response. Understanding a proposition is, to put it flatly, seeing the symptom and "appropriately" responding to it, as the mother comforts the crying child or the physician springs to help the convulsive patient.

There are, of course, various degrees of understanding between speakers and hearers, depending upon the degree of shared identity in their forms of life. The ideal understanding is between those Nietzsche calls *nobles*, those whose will to power is openly active, self-conscious, and growing. They fully "understand" one another: they act congruently in response to the disposition of forces then in evidence, moving to manipulate the rabble and to strengthen the power of their own kind. "Linguistic" understanding, the understanding of a proposition, is for Nietzsche just a specific case of this congruence of action and response, a congruence founded upon an (almost) identical disposition of the will to power within a shared set of practices. There are, of course, substantial (perhaps insoluble) philosophical problems that attach to this sort of behavioralist account of language; but what is crucial for us to see here is that understanding a proposition is not, for Nietzsche, some private "mental" act of grasping another's "representation" of reality but just a public, active agreement in action and response. To understand one another is to go on together "in the same way."

Thus the traditional notion of truth—truth as accurate representation of the real—has no place in Nietzsche's account: it is, as section 625 has it, "nonsensical." There is no static essence of things to be ahistorically represented by an ahistorical "knowing subject." There is only a dynamic, historical relation of force to forces, a relation to be expressed and embodied in speech. The proposition is a sign, all right, but only in the way that a rash is a sign of measles or a scowl is the sign of anger. The proposition is a presentation, not a representation.

If one is to speak of propositional *truth* at all, therefore, it must be the truth of the force-relation symptomatically expressed in the proposition. "The entire domain of 'true-false' applies only to relations, not to an 'in-itself' " (sec. 625). To characterize a proposition, a judgment, as true or false can only be to characterize the truth or falsity of the life, the relation of forces, from which the judgment issues and which it therefore embodies. "Truth," applied critically to a given judgment, is an honorific of *quality*; it characterizes the quality of the life of the one who made the judgment. Judgments are genuinely true if and only if they naturally arise from *true lives*: from lives, that is, that are "truly alive," lives in which the will to power is active, self-conscious, expanding, instinctual, and so on.

For Nietzsche, then, truth is always and only a *value*, not a metaphysical matching of words and the world. Life is the will to power's struggle for mastery of the forces that confront it, and the "products" of human consciousness are no more than interpretations of those antagonistic forces, interpretations intended to facilitate their comprehensive mastery by human will. A people's language in use is therefore an expression of a certain quality (i.e., power) of consciousness; in its range of judgments and questions are posited and expressed those structures of interpretation, those values, by means of which a particular constellation of will to power is seeking (perhaps fruitlessly, of course) to push itself through to control and self-command. Truth is such a value; indeed, it is apparently a "higher" value, a meta-value, since with its help one judges (i.e., interprets) the value of other value expressions, other interpretations.

If I say, "N.N. is neurotic," I am expressing (*not* representing) in that judgment some relationship of "my" will to power to N.N. (and to everything else, ultimately). If I subsequently reflect on my initial judgment and say, "The judgment 'N.N. is neurotic' is true," I am (apparently) making a metajudgment, a judgment about the first judgment about N.N. But I cannot be, as one might at first think, judging that initial judgment in its relation to "the facts." (Such a "metaphysical" notion of truth is *nonsensical*, according to Nietzsche.) I am, rather, characterizing (positively) the quality of the life from which the initial judgment issued. I am judging the *speaker* (in this case, myself) by reference to the value or values exhibited in what was spoken, just as one might judge the health of a child by reference to the complexity and the difficulty of the games she wants to play.

Some such metajudgments are essential to any moderately sophisticated form of human life. Insofar as we organize our lives by reference to our own and others' judgments (and we *do*), we apparently must avail ourselves of some way of characterizing the value of the lives those judgments embody. But what can "characterizing" mean in that last sentence? It certainly cannot mean *representing accurately*, or even *inaccurately*, those values, nor can it mean specifying their relationship to what "makes" them truly valuable. The idea of language (or metalanguage) as representation is dead and gone for Nietzsche, as is the Platonism that refers a value to a "true world" beyond itself. A "characterization" of someone else's values can only be *another primary expression of one's own will to power*, another expression of the disposition of various active and reactive forces at a given moment in the flux of Becoming, as Nietzsche might put it. A truth judgment about a proposition is thus just another judgment, not one in any way philosophically privileged. There is no hope of traveling up the ladder of metalanguages to a place where judgments can be tied down to "things-in-themselves."

In this way the philosophical inquiry into the truth of one's judgments leads one inevitably, according to Nietzsche, to an analysis of the notion of truth as itself nothing more (nor less) than a value posited by the will to power, an analysis that undermines truth's habitual place as the "highest" of our values.

That is a considerable shock to the system. In line with our culture's underlying Platonism, the value of our values has always been thought to depend upon their truth. Only those claims, especially those claims about value, determined to be *true* are supposed to be worthy of our acceptance. The basic intellectual and moral structures of our civilization have thus traditionally depended upon truth as a second-order predicate, that is, as a judgment made on other judgments per se, as a judgment made within a metalanguage. In a Nietzschean account of language-as-expression, however, the very idea of such a metalanguage has become empty. A symptom is a symptom is a symptom: there are no *meta*symptoms. So a judgment is a judgment is a judgment; an expression is an expression is an expression; and thus a value is a value is a value. My assertion that my propositions, or the values of my form of life, are *true* is just another instance of my self-expression as will to power, completely on a par with the will to power embodied in the initial utterance of the propositions and the initial affirmations of the values of the form of life. All these expressions are simply iterated forms of "I will." There are no "higher" values, no metajudgments. Life is just the wash of judgment against other judgments, just the push of interpretation (i.e., force) against other interpretations. Thus the highest values devaluate themselves, which is, of course Nietzsche's own definition of 'nihilism' (*Will to Power*, sec. 2).

At this point one seems in a cruel bind. As we have seen, the traditional representationalist account of mind and language is bankrupt. Mind is not the mirror of nature, so the proposition cannot be the publicly exhibited photograph of the image caught in one's inner glass. But the only apparent alternative to this account of language has grave problems of its own. If language is not representation, then must it not be some immediate "means of expression"? If so, then the slope from Humboldt to Nietzsche seems a slippery one. One seems inevitably led into some form of linguistic behaviorism, into some form of transcendental Skinnerianism. To speak and to understand a language is, on this sort of account, just to be a part of a very complicated form of life. It is to be adept at an extraordinarily complex set of linguistic actions and reactions, which are interwoven with other complicated forms of behavior and are shared by (some) other human beings. To be able to speak and understand a language is, in other words, to be able to play a sophisticated verbal/behavioral game.

Internal and external difficulties abound, however. The internal philosophical difficulties incurred by the behavioralist account of language are immense and well known, and this is not the place to try to take their measure.[11] The external ones are equally troublesome. If language is understood as a "means of expression," doesn't the notion of truth become nugatory? Will it not become, as it does in Nietzsche, only a value, and not even the highest value at that? And will that not lead, again as Nietzsche expected, to a devaluation of those lives, like ours, that have been thought to rest on something "truer" than just themselves?

IV

The later Heidegger's essays on language should be read as responses to this Hobson's choice between language-as-representation and language-as-expression. Curiously enough, he does not challenge the *correctness* of these traditional views.

> No one would dare to declare incorrect, let alone reject as useless, the identification of language as audible utterance of inner emotions, as human activity, as a representation by image and by concept. The view of language thus put forth is correct, for it conforms to what an investigation of linguistic phenomena can make out in them at any time. (Heidegger, *Poetry, Language, Thought*, p. 193)

So Heidegger admits that all the empirical and conceptual data available to us from linguistic study favor some form of representationalism or expressionism. Nevertheless, he says, these perfectly correct accounts of language are somehow still seriously inadequate to our needs as thinkers: "Thus, despite their antiquity and despite their comprehensibility, they never

11. See Noam Chomsky, "A Review of B. F. Skinner's *Verbal Behavior.*"

bring us to language as language" (*Poetry, Language, Thought,* p. 193). Their very correctness, so charming in its promises of work to be done and progress to be made, obscures the primordial *truth* of language on which all such conceptual correctness *about* language is parasitic.[12] Heidegger wants more of his linguistic reflections than just another philosophical or scientific *theory* of language, however "accurate" and powerful it might be.

> We do not wish to assault language in order to force it into the grip of ideas already fixed beforehand. We do not wish to reduce the nature of language to a concept, so that this concept may provide a generally useful view of language that will lay to rest all further notions about it. (*Poetry, Language, Thought,* p. 190)

He wants to go behind such "accounts" of language to discover what makes them possible. He wants to experience language preconceptually, so to speak; to get behind all our current (and very useful) theories about it. That his essays are so strange —almost incomprehensible—to us is due (at least partly) to our conviction that the representationalist and the expressionist accounts must completely exhaust the alternatives in philosophy of language. After all, if a proposition is not some sort of picture of antecedent reality, what else could it be but a complicated verbal self-expression, a gesture set within a language-game? What "truth" about language could possibly lie behind the "correctness" of that choice? These are, I believe, the guiding questions of the work collected in *On the Way to Language* and *Poetry, Language, Thought.*

When philosophers meet an impasse of this sort, they typically begin to look for a determining assumption shared by both the untenable positions; Heidegger is no exception to the rule. He too begins to cast about for what is *un*thought here that forces our thoughts about language so inexorably into this bind. His answer: for all their differences, both language-as-representation and language-as-expression agree in the assumption that

12. See Martin Heidegger, "On the Essence of Truth," especially secs. 1, 2, and 3. A good translation (by John Sallis) of this essay can be found in Heidegger, *Basic Writings,* pp. 117–41.

language is essentially a human instrument adapted to human purposes. *We speak* [a] *language*. Language is our creation, a human invention, and it is used by us to further our own purposes: communication, first of all; then whatever other purposes—science, art, grocery shopping—communication itself serves.

From the representationalist perspective, this assumption certainly seems correct. If the essence of language is an orderly system of conventional designations by means of which our ideas (and thus, presumably, "the facts") can be represented, then what is language but an instrument for human communication? One can see this "humanist" assumption very clearly at work in the seventeenth-century attempts to "improve" language by increasing its precision and carrying power. Some philosophers (Leibniz, for instance) went so far as to anticipate the deliberate development of a perfect language, the *characteristica universalis*, which would make possible the fully adequate representation of all our ideas. Language is here clearly understood to be a human instrument, and one that, like any tool, can be self-consciously refined and adapted.

The expressionist perspective is much the same, of course. We are creatures who want to flourish, it says, and we congregate to serve that end. Thus there naturally arise among us various cooperative practices, various systems of coordinated human behavior, that help us to defend ourselves against dangers and to further our goal of life-in-abundance. On this account, language is just another system of cooperative human behavior; it is another form, that is, of human self-expression aiming at human good. Like farming, or chess, or the democratic state, a language is a set of normative practices whereby the will to power embodies itself in order to push itself through. The expressionist will admit, of course, that a language is an especially complicated and powerful form of self-expression, since the extraordinary degree of cooperation and coordination it affords makes possible the improvement of all the other cooperative practices that constitute human culture. Indeed, a language even makes possible its *own* development: the invention of new and more powerful languages adapted to specific ends has now become an honored human practice all its own. In all of this one clearly sees language understood as a tool in service to the end of human flourishing. To paraphrase Wittgenstein, language is a form of (human) life.

Heidegger wants to get behind the linguistic "humanism" he finds common both to language-as-representation and to language-as-expression, just as he wants to get behind all other philosophical expressions of the centrality of the human.[13] Certainly we human beings naturally and urgently speak, and certainly that speaking is often directly or indirectly in aid of our various purposes. But is our speaking in that way a *primordial* or *essential* speaking? Heidegger says, startlingly, *no.*

> Language *speaks.* This means at the same time and before all else: *language* speaks. (*Poetry, Language, Thought*, p. 198)

Die Sprache spricht. To understand Heidegger's alternative to representationalism and expressionism as philosophical accounts of language we will need to unpack that compact but cryptic claim.

Language speaks, he says. But how can that be, when the sounds and the gestures are so clearly our own? But are they? Mostly as we speak, we do not really *speak* at all, but only thoughtlessly mouth the words and phrases we have already heard from others. Most of our time is passed in fruitless curiosity, in tireless gossip about what others have said or done (whether low-level gossip, of the sort retailed by *People* magazine, or gossip of a more rarefied variety, as found in this book), and in other kinds of addictive but idle chatter (*Gerede*).[14] In all these everyday activities we are "speaking" only in the most deracinated sense of the term; one might just as well say that the mechanical Gypsy in the carnival booth is "speaking" as the tape replays its prerecorded prophecy. We cannot look to everyday speech, to the speech of "the Anyone" (*das Man*), if we are truly to experience language.

If we must, therefore, seek the speaking of language in what is spoken we shall do well to find something that is

13. See the "Letter on Humanism," pp. 193–242.
14. The ideas here are from Heidegger, *Being and Time*, sec. 35. In this respect Heidegger's ideas seem much the same both before and after the "turn."

spoken purely rather than to pick just any material at
random. What is spoken purely is that in which the
completion of the speaking that is proper to what is
spoken is, in its turn, an original. What is spoken purely
is the poem. (*Poetry, Language, Thought*, p. 194)

In his seminal essay "Language" (delivered in 1950) Heidegger
chose a short poem by Georg Trakl, "A Winter Evening," as an
example of that pure speaking of language to which the philosopher must learn to listen.[15] He summarizes what he learns
from it in these dense, resonant sentences:

Speaking occurs in what is spoken in the poem. It is
the speaking of language. Language speaks. It speaks
by bidding the bidden, thing-world and world-thing, to
come to the between of the dif-ference. What is so bidden
is commanded to arrive from out of the dif-ference into
the dif-ference. . . . The dif-ference lets the thinging of
the thing rest in the worlding of the world. The dif-
ference expropriates the thing into the repose of the
fourfold. Such expropriation does not diminish the
thing. Only so is the thing exalted into its own, so that it
stays world. To keep in repose is to still. The dif-ference
stills the thing, as thing, into the world. (*Poetry, Language, Thought*, p. 206)

Here in short compass are the essential elements in Heidegger's
experience of language, artfully placed; but one needs a thread
to follow through the labyrinth his claims make. I propose to
give the most attention, as does Heidegger himself, to the puzzling notion of the dif-ference (*der Unter-schied*, in his deliberately fractured German) between thing and world. It is in that
"dimension," as he calls it, that a primordial experience of language is to be found. We will approach *der Unter-schied* through
Heidegger's own reading of the poem.

Trakl's poem is first of all a matter of *naming*, says Heidegger
(p. 198). It names the snow falling silently on the windowsill; it

15. A translation of this poem can be found in *Poetry, Language, Thought*,
pp. 194–95.

names the winter eventide marked by the vesper bell tolling its call to prayer; it names the table laid with provisions for supper. Here we seem on familiar (if not entirely safe) philosophical ground in our attempt to understand the speaking of language in the poem. It can seem initially quite plausible to us, just as it seemed plausible to Plato and St. Augustine, that, like the poem, *all* language begins with naming, that words and the world first hook up with one another through (individual or communal) acts of object-baptism: "This is (to be called) a *chair*, and this is (to be called) a *table*, and this is . . . ."[16] Perhaps language can be understood as an orderly system of names; perhaps naming is the fundamental semantic tie. (One hears, of course, the distinct intimations of language-as-representation.)

As Heidegger himself might put it, however, such an account of linguistic meaning would not be positively *incorrect*; but it nevertheless fails to do justice to language as such. That is because it makes *naming* seem much more philosophically innocent and straightforward an activity than it really is. To name is not, *pace* Plato or Augustine, merely to attach preexisting labels to objects already present-to-hand, as I might right now "name" my pen 'Sam'. That sort of "naming," since it depends both upon a prior ability to recognize my pen as a distinct and reidentifiable "object" and upon a stock of already available name-words recognizable as such, is obviously parasitic upon a great deal of what Wittgenstein called *stage-setting*, and what Heidegger would call a *more primordial* kind of naming. It is that "more primordial" kind of naming, the naming that first reveals what there is to *be* named, that gets covered over in the Plato/Augustine accounts of language. To understand the poem —and thus language itself—as an original act of naming, as Heidegger claims it is, we need a deeper understanding of what it is to name something at all.

Primordial naming, says Heidegger, is *calling*. We say in English, when explaining the name of something, "That is called a . . . ." Or we say, "The team calls him *Flash*, mainly because he's so slow." So naming is calling. But what is it to call? It is *to bid something to come into nearness*.

16. For a discussion of Augustine's views, see Ludwig Wittgenstein, *Philosophical Investigations*, sec. 1.

> This naming does not hand out titles, it does not apply
> terms, but it calls into the word. The naming calls. . . .
> Thus it brings the presence of what was previously un-
> called into a nearness. (Heidegger, *Poetry, Language,
> Thought*, p. 198)

Notice that to call something to come close implies that, before
the calling, the thing called was *not* close. It was not already
there, as the pen called 'Sam' in my example was already there
as an object represented to my consciousness. To "call into the
word," as true naming does, is always an act of *revelation*,
then. It first *shows* the thing to us by naming it. The same point
is made in "The Way to Language" (1959):

> *The essential being of language is Saying as Showing.*
> Its showing character is not based on [antecedently ex-
> isting] signs of any kind; rather, all signs arise from a
> showing within whose realm and for whose purposes
> they can be signs. (Heidegger, *On the Way to Language*,
> p. 123; my bracketed addition)

Primordial naming cannot rely upon a stock of names already
in place, as ordinary naming does. That stock is called into being only through the call of primordial naming itself. Language
does not preexist this call; rather, it is in this first naming that
language as we know it comes originally to be. More, to call in
this way is always to call "into the distance," Heidegger says,
and what is named in the poem is called only into *nearness*, not
to full presence-at-hand like the pen. What is truly called into
the word as present remains also at the same time absent (*Poetry, Language, Thought*, p. 199).

What naming calls from absence into nearness is a *thing*.

> What does the first stanza call? It calls things, bids
> them to come. . . . It invites things in, so that they may
> bear upon men as things. (*Poetry, Language, Thought*,
> p. 199)

The word 'thing' is, for most of us, rather a colorless one. It usually just means "that which exists in some way or other," an
"entity." A hat is a "thing," and so is an idea, a color, a politi-

cal system, and so on. Insofar as the term has a technical meaning within philosophy, it means either something like *res extensa*, a lump of inert stuff, or a conceptual representation of a *res cogitans*, the "object" of an idea present to the ego-subject. In either case—thing as brute stuff or thing as represented object—a thing is understood as an entity that "stands over against" the human being and other entities. A thing is something that exists (or could exist) on its own, something essentially "separable" from other things. But Heidegger means something very different by the word:

> However, the thingly character of the thing does not consist in its being a represented object, nor can it be defined in any way in terms of the objectness, the over-againstness of the object. (P. 167)

A thing is not independent of ("over against") other things; on the contrary, without its correlative *world* the thing cannot be what it is. For Heidegger it is always "thing-world" and "world-thing." As he puts it, a thing *gathers a world*.

> The things that were named, thus called, gather to themselves sky and earth, divinities and mortals. . . . This gathering, assembling, letting-stay is the thinging of things. The unitary fourfold of sky and earth, mortals and divinities, which is stayed in the thinging of things, we call—the world. In the naming the things named are called into their thinging. Thinging, they unfold world, in which things abide and so are the abiding ones. By thinging, things carry out world. (Pp. 199–200)

If this intimate correlation of things and world seems mysterious, and it is likely to at first blush, think instead of *words* rather than of things and of *a language* rather than of a world. Imagine that one has been living outside one's native land—living in Switzerland, say—and one day as one is walking in the woods, far away from any tourist areas, lost in the landscape and in one's thoughts, one suddenly hears, behind one, another—unexpected—walker say something about *fried chicken*. Those words, 'fried chicken', immediately gather to one the language of their utterance. Suddenly one is in English, and one waits for the other words in the same family ('white gravy', 'sweet potato pie') to make their appearance. One listens for the familiar rhythms and inflections; in a flash one hears and feels about one the whole of one's native language. The words 'fried chicken' are not mere sounds (mere heard "objects" or "representations" to one's consciousness), of course; they are *words* (compare: things), and thus always and already the words of a certain *language* (compare: world). As words they immediately gather the language that, simultaneously, makes them intelligible *as* the words they are: words-of-that-language; language-of-those-words. Without the language they gather, they would not be words at all. But to gather the language is to gather the *world* of those words too. 'Fried chicken' heard unexpectedly on a Swiss *Wanderweg* brings one not just English, but *home*: parents, sister, the Sunday table, love and pain.

So it is that the things named in a poem like Trakl's—snow, the vesper bell, the well-laid table—gather a world. By "thinging," by appearing there as the things they are, these things "carry out world." They bring near the referential totality within which they are what they are. And the world borne by things is not the traditional philosophical one: it is not a collection of mental or physical "objects" or "experiences."

> The word 'world' is now no longer used in the metaphysical sense. It designates neither the universe of nature and history in its secular representation nor the theologically conceived creation (*mundus*), nor does it mean the whole of entities present (*kosmos*). (*Poetry, Language, Thought*, p. 201)

Heidegger's "world" is a holistic system of back-and-forth references among the things that constitute it; it is a structured totality (like a language) within which each part is just the part it is only because of its relationships to all the other parts.

Ultimately, the world revealed in the poem is the realm of things appropriated in the unity of what Heidegger calls the "fourfold" (*das Geviert*). To be aware of the world of the thing named there in the poem is to hear and respond to its necessary *resonances*, resonances that move imaginatively in four different directions (sky, earth, divinity, mortality) arranged on two perpendicular axes (earth/sky, mortals/divinities). At the point these axes of resonance cross, says Heidegger, lies the thing that gathers its world. But that way of putting it may be dangerously misleading, for it can make it sound as if these "resonances" of a thing are mere psychological "associations" it has accidentally acquired. (Perhaps one's farewell meal at home was fried chicken, so that one has come to associate it with fond leave-taking: that is why hearing someone in Switzerland talk about fried chicken makes one sad.) This is not at all what Heidegger means. "World" is no more a matter of individual psychological associations than is language.

Let us look more closely at this mysterious gathering of the fourfold in the thing. First, how can a thing—what we typically want to call a "physical object"—gather a world in the way that a word "gathers" its language? What could be the "language" of a thing? Doesn't the linguistic analogy break down too soon to be useful? Let us see. In "Building Dwelling Thinking" (1951) Heidegger takes as his example of a thing a bridge over a stream. The bridge, a human artifact, was not always standing there, connecting the banks and allowing the traffic to pass unimpeded. When the bridge was built, certainly the "physical" and the economic, and perhaps even the "aesthetic" and the "social," circumstances of the neighborhood changed: there is now a new "physical object" at location L; it is now easier and cheaper than it used to be to get one's crops to market; people now have something to admire and be proud of; and so on. So the bridge makes a difference. But why call any of this "gathering a world"? Isn't that, at best, rather a highfalutin way of stating some quite ordinary facts? And aren't these facts, like all facts, essentially independent of one another? They do not in any interesting sense form a "language," do they?

As a first pass, here is a comparison that may help. Think of someone at work on a painting. She thinks she has finished with it; she has done what she originally planned to do in her sketches and her notes. But as she finally surveys the piece, she is dissatisfied. It doesn't work; it just sits there, competent but moribund. So she steps up to the canvas and adds a few broad strokes of chrome green to the lower-left quadrant. Suddenly everything is different. That added patch of color gathers the rest of the design into a clear, powerful, and resonant structure; it *focuses* the painting's shape and color into a *work*. The green lets one see the internal and external relationships that (now) give the painting its reality and force. It makes visible what was not visible before it was there. The new strokes add to the work not just another quantity of paint; they give it an altogether new quality: it is now fully itself. The painting has, we may say, *come together*, letting us see it (and, if it is a great work, many other things besides) in a new way, in *its* way. The chrome green gathers the painting to itself, just as the painting itself may gather—focus, reveal—its world.

The bridge may do the same for its circumstances. What the building of the bridge allows us to see is not (just) another single thing, namely, the bridge itself; rather, it allows us to (begin to) see the *relationships* among all the things that are there: relationships that *make* these things what they are, but relationships we are inclined to forget or to ignore. A given relationship thus shown is a part of what Heidegger means by the *world* of a thing. As a language is a set of synergistic relationships among words, relationships that create the words *qua* words that then in their turn create the relationships themselves, so world is a set of such relationships among things. The bridge *gathers a world*. It *makes a neighborhood*, one might say. It becomes the point from which distances are computed, thus making one newly aware of one's location and of its locality. It becomes a treasure to be defended against natural and human enemies, thus showing one those enemies and reminding one of one's own capacities for care, neglect, and violence. It becomes a way to the other bank, thus reminding one of the benefits and the burdens of commerce with those on the "other side." And so on. Like the green paint, the bridge focuses attention on a radiant whole; it reveals relationships—strikes resonances, one might say—that show one one's place within that whole. In that deep sense, it *gathers* to itself, and to us, a *world*.

And these relationships that the bridge reveals are not merely "accidental" or "psychological" ones. They are not just "associations" we human beings "happen" to have made. I suppose it can be called a "fact" about human beings that they have enemies, or that they live in intimate contact and commerce with other human beings, or that they identify themselves and their fortunes with particular localities, and so on; but these are "facts" of a very peculiar kind. We could say that "facts" of this sort constitute human life as such; if they were to change, human life itself would disappear, to be replaced with something more heavenly (or more hellish). (Some facts *are* "accidental" to human life, of course, such as the fact that most of us get thirty-two teeth, rather than thirty or thirty-four.) The bridge gathers those "constitutive" facts of human life; it is what it is—viz., a bridge—only because of them. It simultaneously reveals and depends upon them. The human landscape is (*essentially* is, one wants to say) a place of locality, commerce, aggression and defense, trust and mistrust, "here" and "over there," and so on; and the bridge "speaks" all these things. It "makes sense" to build bridges only because these things are true.

The bridge is no more an "accidental" addition to the human landscape than the strokes of chrome green are an "accidental" addition to the work of the painting. Once completed, the painting is seen to be a radiant whole, and the green strokes put on at the last are a constitutive part of that. They cannot be removed and leave the work undestroyed. The painting exists as a "world" of relationships, internal and external, and each part of the painting speaks in terms of all the others. So it is with the bridge. It is not so much that it *reminds* us of these relationships (though true enough to say, that is almost too psychological an idiom in which to say it); rather, it *shows* them, and through them, it *shows* itself. It is what it is only in their light. It is a "word" within the "language" of the human world. It too is a part of a radiant whole.

Heidegger goes even further. With his claims about "the fourfold" he wants to describe the "grammar," so to speak, of the world-language gathered by things like the bridge. The four poles of the fourfold are *sky, earth, divinities, and mortals*; and just like the parts of a natural language's grammar, they cannot fully be separated from one another. The world of the fourfold is a holistic system. The things named in a poem thus reveal the "unitary" nature of the fourfold shown there: no one aspect of this unity makes sense apart from its internal reference to all the others.

In "Building Dwelling Thinking" one gets perhaps Heidegger's clearest account of a life that is lived in tune with this fourfold "grammar" of existence. He calls it there a "dwelling" life, where —as the lack of commas in the essay's title makes clear—dwelling means at the same time *building* (making *things: poiēsis*) and *thinking*. The poet, the thinker, the builder are for Heidegger one and the same. In such a life, mortals dwell (1) in that they "save the earth," (2) in that they "receive the sky as sky," (3) in that they "await the divinities as divinities," and (4) in that they "initiate mortals" into the nature of death (*Poetry, Language, Thought*, pp. 150–51).

To save the earth is "to set [it] free into its own presencing" (p. 150). Such a life does not try to master nature, to subjugate it wholly to human will and purpose. Nor does it refuse to act, resisting all forms of cultivation and change. Rather, to live a "saving" life is to enter into a cooperative venture *with* the earth. It is to see oneself as a natural process of transformation, assisting the earth as it grows tomatoes, or children, or democratic states. It is, therefore, to remember oneself *as* the earth, as genuinely earthly, as a part of *its* will and life; not to think of oneself as the ghostly, immaterial, godlike Cartesian ego resting at the center of reality.

To receive the sky as sky is "to leave to the sun and moon their journey, to the stars their courses, to the seasons their blessing and their inclemency" (p. 150). It is to pay attention to, and thus to recognize one's own submission to, these celestial cycles within which all human life is set, and upon which it ultimately reckons. It is to acknowledge, without regret or anger, that the inhuman is prior to the human, that human purposes do not originally constitute what there is. Receiving the sky as sky is, then, the death of all "humanism." It acknowledges the contingency, not just of every specific human practice, but of human being itself. The human world shelters beneath and within that which is not human. The sky, not *Dasein*, is the open region in which things appear and truth occurs.

To await the divinities is "in hope [to] hold up to the divinities what is unhoped for" (p. 150). Heidegger's point here is not essentially theological. A divinity is a presence from another world, a messenger (of whatever kind) from a realm of haleness and wholeness, qualities manifestly lacking in our world. Thus a poem, or a piece of philosophy, might partake in divinity: it might be that sort of messenger. To await the divinities is to remain open to—to hope for—that hale and wholesome future we cannot even yet foresee. It is to refuse cynicism and despair; it is to stay on the track of eschatological transformation but without seeking to reproduce it at will. It is to remain a poet, or a philosopher, in spite of one's own barrenness and the darkness of one's time.

Finally, to initiate mortals into their mortality is to make them "capable of death as death . . . so that there may be a good death" (p. 151). This means more than just reminding oneself of one's own approaching death and thus warring against one's constant liability to self-deception about it. It means also to live so as to *rejoice* in our finitude as well as to fear it. It means to see and to appreciate that "pain and death and love belong together" (p. 97). Without the recognition of suffering and death, our capacity to love anything at all would be lost. One cannot love what is invulnerable. Rather, we can only love what we can pity, truly pity, for its fragility and its inevitable dissolution. If I could not see death in my father's face, it would not be so precious to me; it is the preciousness of this man, at this moment, neither of which will endure. To initiate mortals into their mortality is thus to make them capable of loving the things they are given, and given only for a time.

The dwelling life whose "grammar" is constituted by the unity of the fourfold is revealed by the things named, for example, in a poem like "A Winter Evening." In the first stanza of that poem there is named a house. A house, so spoken, is not just (as we might think "scientifically" or "philosophically") a particular concatenation of physical objects, nor is it just (to quote Le Corbusier) "a machine for living in."

> Let us think for a moment of a farmhouse in the Black Forest, which was built some two hundred years ago by the dwelling of peasants. Here the self-sufficiency of the power to let earth and heaven, divinities and mortals, enter in *simple oneness* into things, ordered the house. It placed the farm on the wind-sheltered mountain slope

looking south, among the meadows close to the spring. It gave it the wide overhanging shingle roof whose proper slope bears up under the burden of the snow, and which, reaching deep down, shields the chambers against the storms of the long winter nights. It did not forget the altar corner behind the community table; it made room in its chamber for the hallowed places of childbed and the "tree of the dead"—for that is what they call a coffin there: the *Totembaum*—and in this way it designed for the different generations under one roof the character of their journey through time. (*Poetry, Language, Thought*, p. 160)

Such a house is, in the fullest sense, a *thing*. By naming it, one gathers the whole world, the whole set of relationships, in which it dwells. All the poles of the fourfold are present, the axes of resonance crossing in the unity of the Black Forest farmhouse. *As the thing that it is*, the house cannot be present apart from its world, that is, apart from its relationships to other things, relationships traced and articulated in the "grammar" of the fourfold. To think of it as a buzz of elementary particles, or as a sensible tax shelter, or as a quaint piece of folk art, is to lose it *as a house*. These are not, for Heidegger, merely alternative ways of describing "the same thing"; only in a world of other things, a world that shows the unity of the fourfold, is the house a *thing* at all.

This now means: things, each in its time, literally visit mortals with a world. (*Poetry, Language, Thought*, p. 200)

V

So, in the pure speech of the poem there is the primordial *naming* of *things*: things that, as the things that they are, necessarily bear a *world* of other things, a world whose basic "grammar" is revealed in the holistic unity of the fourfold. A complete account of Heidegger's thinking would now need to say a great deal more about each of the poles of the fourfold; in particular, it would need to explain how these resonances of the thing escape becoming rigid philosophical categories, and how they fail to be tarred with the brush of Platonic metaphysical dualism. It would also need to uncover why, and to what extent, Heidegger believes his fourfold grammar of existence to be universal and immutable. All this is beyond the scope of the present essay.

Instead, and in order to pursue directly the question of how *die Sprache spricht,* I will try to get clearer about the peculiar relation between thing and world in his account. (Heidegger himself explicitly denies, of course, that the thing/world relation is truly a "relation" at all. He calls it a "dimension," actually, "*the* dimension" [*Poetry, Language, Thought,* p. 203]. His reasons for insisting on this terminology will become clearer as I proceed.) He calls this relation *the dif-ference (der Unterschied),* and he says some very obscure things about it:

> · In the midst of the two, in the between of world and things, in their *inter (Unter),* division prevails; a *difference (Unter-schied).*
>
> · · ·
>
> It exists only as the single difference. It is unique. Of itself, it holds apart the middle in and through which things and world are with one another.
>
> · · ·
>
> The dif-ference carries out world in its worlding, carries out things in their thinging. Thus carrying them out, it carries them toward one another.
>
> · · ·
>
> The dif-ference is *the* dimension, insofar as it measures out, apportions, world and thing, each to its own. Its allotment of them first opens up the separateness and towardness of world and thing. (Pp. 202–3)

In spite of the apparent darkness of these remarks, there is quite a real philosophical problem that Heidegger is gnawing on. The issue can most easily be seen by returning for a moment to the linguistic comparison I used earlier: thing is to world as word is to language. With this ratio in mind, one can begin to see why Heidegger says:

> For world and things do not subsist alongside one another. They penetrate each other. Thus the two traverse a middle. In it, they are one. Thus at one they are intimate. (P. 202)

There cannot be a word that is not the word of a specific language. 'Water' is a word at all only because it is a word *of English*. Its reality as a word, as a sign, is completely dependent upon its relation to—i.e., its differences from—all the other words of English. (This is Saussure's point, of course: *la langue* is nothing but a holistic system of significant differences.) Thus the sense of 'water' is "granted" by the English language, by 'water' being a word, a particular word, of that language. At the same time, the English language itself exists only as the collection of its various words and operations. There is no English apart from words like 'water' and 'father' and 'patter' and so on. In this way, the words and the language "do not subsist alongside one another" (p. 202), as if they were separable, independently existing entities. The word 'water' *is* a word only because it is *not* finally separable from (although it must of course be *distinguishable* from: so much for Hume's famous dictum to the contrary) all the other words of English. The word and the language—*la langue*: the system of significant differences—thus "penetrate each other," as Heidegger puts it; they are "intimate."

So it is with thing and world. The Black Forest farmhouse, for example, is the particular thing that it is only because, like the word, it exists within a set of relationships—one might better say, a set of social *practices*—that grant it the rich significance it has. The altar corner of that house—to take a concrete instance—means what it means, that is, *is* what it *is*, only because outside that house and family there are the various practices of worship and prayer to which it is directly related. Those practices are the "language," so to speak, within which this particular altar and its use by the family are "utterances." Without those practices, the cross on the wall would be nothing (nothing) at all, or at most an idiosyncratic affectation, like a family habit of clearing one's throat before every sentence. So too for every genuine thing within that farmhouse: it is what it is only because it is set within practices—within a world—through which it is determinately related to an indefinite number of other things.

> The world grants to things their presence. Things bear
> world. World grants things. (*Poetry, Language,
> Thought*, p. 202)

Thing and world "penetrate each other," just as do word and language. A world or a language is, as we have been taught to say, a holistic system.

But to fall back upon such philosophical terms of art as 'holism' should not blind us to the puzzle that remains. What exactly is the relation between the "part" (the word or the thing) and its sense-giving "whole" (language or world)? There cannot be words without a language; we have seen that there cannot be signs at all without some system of differences to grant them their significance as such. Yet there cannot be a language without words either; there cannot be a system of differences unless those differences are somehow *marked* (carried, "borne," says Heidegger) *as* differences. How is that possible?

Ordinarily we think of a difference as a distinction established between entities within some system of representation, as when we say that in English there is a clear verbal and definitional difference between 'sleet' and 'snow' (and thus for us a clear practical difference between sleet and snow.) We can easily imagine other, rather finer, differences in frozen precipitation being noted by a given representational system, as they are reputed to be in the language of the indigenous Alaskan people, for instance. Call this *difference-as-established-distinction.* But how do such differences arise? Does a given difference-as-distinction arise from the refinement of a *prior* one, as when we take the basic difference-as-distinction between sweet and dry wines and spin it out into a whole system of subtle discriminations? Well, certainly *some* differences can come to be distinguished in that way; but how do the *initial* differences-as-distinction get established? How do we first get the difference between sweet and dry, or between wine and water, and so on? By learning

English, one may (truly) say. But that merely pushes the question back one more step, for how do the constitutive differences of English—that system of significant differences—come to be? How is difference possible *primordially*, one might ask in a Heideggerian vein?

Here is an uncomfortable dilemma. On the one hand, there can be no differences—i.e., no sense in a claim about differences—unless there is some public system of description (i.e., a language) within which those differences can be established and employed. *Real* differences are *established* differences, i.e., *linguistic* differences. (That now familiar equation is, of course, the force of Wittgenstein's so-called private language argument in the *Philosophical Investigations*.) On the other hand, there can be no language in the first place without the recognition of linguistic *norms*, that is, without the recognition of differences acknowledged *as* differences. In a genuine language there must be the possibility of making a linguistic mistake *and recognizing it as such*. That too is a point emphasized by Wittgenstein.[17] (It is also a point implicit in the structuralist accounts of language that derive from Saussure.) So it seems—and here is the bind—that there can be difference only if there is *already* difference; there can be language only if there is *already* language. (To put it in the material mode: there can be things only if there is a world to "grant" them, but there can be a world only because there are the things that "bear" it.) How then is language (or world) possible at all?

This question poses a deep problem for the advocates of language-as-expression, thinkers such as Humboldt and Nietzsche. Their accounts of language are, in Heidegger's term, essentially "humanistic." That is, they are committed to the view that language is just a "product"—an "expression," they call it—of a particularly complex form of "life," namely, *human* life. They must, therefore, somehow argue that the established differences (i.e., the norms) originally necessary to language are, either consciously or unconsciously, human "products" too.

But they could be conscious human "products" only if one can ignore the first horn of the dilemma just set out. To get lan-

17. See *Philosophical Investigations*, sec. 270, for example.

guage going, on the "conscious human product" account of linguistic norms, one would need to be able to note and remark a difference before one had any public system of description (i.e., a language) available within which the difference could be noted or remarked. All language would therefore need to originate as "private language." Increasingly, of course, this has come to be seen by philosophers as a hopeless position: after Wittgenstein's work, a difference existing altogether outside a system of representation looks like a senseless notion.

What, then, about the alternative claim, that these linguistic norms just arise *unconsciously* out of complex forms of human interaction? But that is to say no more than: "They arise." One has in no way explained their occurrence by waving about the words 'unconsciously' or 'human'; their nature and their genesis are just as mysterious as ever. From this viewpoint, the origin of language looks like a bit of magic. So much for "humanism": the appeal to the "human" factor in such magical explanations does no work at all. It is void of all substantial content, then, to think (as Humboldt and Nietzsche do) of language as a form of *"human"* expression. And once "human" goes, it is not clear that the metaphor of *expression* does any real work either.

The same problem arises for the language-as-representation account. If language is conceived as a holistic system of signs used by us to represent facts to others, how did that system of signs originate? How did the original normative designations of *this* thing by *that* name get established so as to make representation possible? Any account of their origin that refers them to human beings will find itself faced with the unhappy choice we have just seen. If "consciously" established, such norms commit one to the possibility of "private language." If established "unconsciously," the account of their origin is void of explanatory power altogether; it is a piece of conjuring. Thus the representationalist account falls to the ground too, independent of its familiar epistemological problems.

The recognition that the things primordially named in the poem are holistically related to one another in a world that "grants" them, gives Heidegger a crucial insight into language, therefore. It lets him see that the holistic "relation" of words to one another to form a language poses an apparently insuper-

able difficulty for any form of linguistic "humanism." I do not
want to claim that Heidegger was fully aware of the extent to
which this difficulty depends upon something like Wittgenstein's
animadversions on "private language"; certainly there is no
clear reason to believe that he was aware of Wittgenstein's work
on this issue. But subliminally, at least, he must have seen that
linguistic holism makes the part/whole relation exceedingly
mysterious; and that mystery is only turned into philosophically
unacceptable magic by appeals to "private" or to "unconscious"
norm establishment. That is why the part/whole (i.e., word/lan-
guage or thing/world) "relation" becomes instead the "dimension" of *dif-ference.*

> The dif-ference is neither distinction nor relation. The
> dif-ference is, at most, dimension for world and thing.
> (*Poetry, Language, Thought,* p. 203)

As the necessary condition for language *überhaupt,* dif-ference
is prior to any system of description (it is not a "distinction");
and the holism of language and world cannot be construed in
ordinary part/whole terms (dif-ference is not a "relation"). Thus
the "dimension" of dif-ference is *sui generis*: "It exists only as
this single difference. It is unique" (p. 202).

> The dif-ference is *the* dimension, insofar as it mea-
> sures out, apportions, world and thing, each to its own.
> Its allotment of them first opens up the separateness
> and towardness of world and thing. (P. 203)

That is to say, there must be some primordial "activity" of
"differing" by means of which things and world, word and language, become possible both in their interpenetration ("intimacy") and in their division ("separation"). There must be some
primordial articulation of things into a world, of words into a
language. A language is not just a "collection" of words, a static
sum of them, like apples in a bin. It is an ordered system of differences, and it exists only as the dynamic tension of these differences. A language *is* tension; it is the play of differences, the
attunement of simultaneous "separateness and towardness," as
Heidegger puts it. Those differences must be opened up and
maintained *as* differences in order that language be at all. And

that opening up of difference and keeping it open cannot originally be done by human beings: that is the point of the foregoing argument. This primordial "activity" of "differing" is what he calls *dif-ference (der Unter-schied)*.[18]

Of course, nothing can be said directly about it. It cannot become its own (or our) object of scrutiny, since any such scrutiny would have to be linguistic (the "private language argument" once again) and thus must presuppose and employ the very dif-ference it is trying to capture and explain. One remains, therefore, in the possession of exactly that which one wants to distance and possess. Human being *is* language, *is* being-in-the-word/world. Therefore it *is* dif-ference; it cannot rise above it or dive below it.

And thus the speaking of language—not what it speaks *of*, of course, but its ability to speak of anything at all—must remain mysterious, ungrounded, encompassing. The worlding of the world and the thinging of the thing are equally impervious to philosophical explication or understanding. There remains to philosophical thinking only one essential but unanswerable question: Why is there something (some *things*) rather than pure Being's nothingness? Why is there difference at all? The only proper response to such queries is: *dif-ference*; but that is an "answer" to them only in a highly attenuated sense.

Die Sprache spricht, then. In the masterful poem it speaks directly by naming, by bidding the things of the world to come close to us, to disclose themselves as the things they are in the unity of the fourfold. Heidegger calls this, curiously, the *stilling* of the dif-ference: the thing released into its world, the world simultaneously borne by the things thus granted (*Poetry, Language, Thought*, pp. 206-7). Both thing and world are brought thereby into their essential truth, *stilled* there in their reciprocity. But the stillness of dif-ference is not motionlessness: "As the stilling of stillness, rest, conceived strictly, is always more in motion than all motion and always more restlessly active than any agitation" (pp. 206-7). Stillness means here not *stasis*, but something more like *perseverance*, as when we say, "Even after his retirement from teaching, Heidegger still held regular

18. 'Activity' is a loaded word, of course; one that Heidegger would certainly avoid. I use it *faute de mieux*.

philosophical discussions." Dif-ference is *still* (i.e., *always*) in motion, so to speak. Language continues to speak of new things in new ways. The worlding of the world is never over and done with, once and for all. In a poem a new thing, a new world, is not of course *represented*, but in the poem such newness may be coming to be, nevertheless. Language may still be speaking in those images; the hidden world of the divinities may be showing us a new face.

> The poet makes poetry only when he takes the measure, by saying the sights of heaven in such a way that he submits to its appearances as to the alien element to which the unknown god has "yielded." Our current name for the sight and appearance of something is "image." The nature of the image is to let something be seen. By contrast, copies and imitations are already mere variations on the genuine image which, as a sight or spectacle, lets the invisible be seen in something alien to it. . . . That is why poetic images are imaginings in a distinctive sense: not mere fancies and illusions but imaginings that are visible inclusions of the alien in the sight of the familiar. The poetic saying of images gathers the brightness and sound of the heavenly appearances into one with the darkness and silence of what is alien. By such sights the god surprises us. (*Poetry, Language, Thought*, pp. 225–26)

Thus the god surprises us. Thus in the resonant things named in the poem the new world of the divinities may break in upon the one with which we are familiar. This brings us to a second, and deeper, way in which language speaks in the poem. It speaks dif-ference itself. In naming things, and thus in the reciprocity of dif-ference calling near as well the world the things bear, dif-ference itself is (silently) acknowledged. It is not named per se: to try to name the primordial possibility of all naming is to chase one's tail. But dif-ference is nevertheless there in the poem, in the possibility of its speaking and our hearing. Whether we fully know it or not, as we listen to the language of the poem we are attending to dif-ference. In what seems to me rather a forced reading, Heidegger claims to find dif-ference specifically imaged as *pain* in Trakl's third stanza. "Pain is the dif-ference itself," Heidegger says. At issue here is the puzzling line: "Pain has turned the threshold to stone." Heidegger's reading of it is frankly philosophical. The threshold "bears the between" of inside and outside, and pain "joins the rift," bringing them together as firmly as stone.

> The verse calls the dif-ference, but neither thinks it specifically nor does it call its nature by this name. The verse calls the separation of the between, the gathering middle, in whose intimacy the bearing of things and the granting of world pervade one another. (P. 204)

Even if one finds this sort of exegesis a bit too much, as I do, the fact remains that Trakl's poem is beautifully sensitive to the surprising resonance of "ordinary" things; it speaks to us of the transubstantiations that (can) occur daily and unexpectedly, as when the winter supper table becomes for the wanderer the altar of the Lord, when generously shared bread and wine become the flesh of the god eaten in communion. And we do not *will* these alterations, although we must be appropriately willing for them to occur (pp. 140–41). In that sense, then, this is certainly a poem that speaks dif-ference. It surprises us into recalling the unforeseen and uncontrolled pregnancy of things, the way they can come to "bear" a world either unknown to us or long ago forgotten. And in so doing, it recalls to us the way in which the "meanings" (to use a crude word) of things like tables and bread depend upon the worlds they bear. And that in its turn reminds us of something essentially true about *us*, for it is not mere things we live on, but the meanings of things. Ours are lives lived in the "dimension" of endlessly dif-fering world and thing. We live in the dif-ference.

So, in the pure speaking of the poem, dif-ference is acknowledged and hallowed as such. Thereby all the standard philosophical contrasts, all the divisive differences given in a language and its concepts, are silently referred to an originary dif-ference prior to them all. Dif-ference is simultaneously *both* (and, in a certain way, therefore *neither*) One and Many, Word and Language, Thing and World, Matter and Spirit, and so on. This recognition of the insuperable priority of dif-ference over all particular differences means, of course, that the familiar rag-bag of philosophical arguments and "problems" is emptied at the start. Such differences, along with their associated meta-physical quandaries, can now be seen as mere vicissitudes of dif-ference, rather than as fundamental antinomies of thought per se. Their depth is shown to be *grammatical*—one might also say *historical*—rather than truly metaphysical; thus they lose their obsessive hold on our attention. The fly is out of the fly-bottle, as Wittgenstein put it.

Within the precincts of dif-ference, within the speaking of the poem, there can be no (hopeless) call for an ontotheological ground for thought and life; there can be no deified "highest values" to become devaluated; there can be no philosophical casting about after transhistorical certainty. To live in "the di-mension," to "dwell poetically on the earth," is to have been freed of the illusions that give sense to the ambition to escape by philosophical thought from things into the Absolute. In the poem and its life there are "only" things, one might say. Thus philos-ophy—i.e., metaphysics: the rational search for *super*-things—has (or should have) come to an end. The poets—not, of course, the particular human beings like Hölderlin and Trakl who write the verses (to honor them as exceptional individuals would be to fall headlong into the "humanism" Heidegger so despises) but the anonymous, impersonal poetic voices that are indistinguish-able from the speaking of language itself—are our only resource against the nihilism that (according to Heidegger) such meta-physics cultivates.

To summarize, I have been arguing that Heidegger's mature reflections on language should be understood as an attempt to steer a course that avoids both linguistic representationalism (Descartes and Locke) and linguistic expressionism (Humboldt and Nietzsche). Both these accounts, as we have seen, construe language as an instrument of human will: either as the conven-tional depiction of the inner display of ideas to consciousness or as the natural, behavioral expression of our communal needs, desires, and purposes. For all their differences, therefore, both these accounts of language are profound instances of "human-ism"; both locate the origin and nature of language within hu-man life. And because of this essential "humanism," both accounts must fail, according to Heidegger, since neither can make intelligible that original recognition of difference *as* difference that is apparently both *dependent upon* language and simultaneously *necessary to* it.

His guiding dictum—*die Sprache spricht*—is at once both an acknowledgment of this antinomy within our philosophical thinking about language and an attempt to gesture at a way through it. To say that language speaks is ultimately to gesture at the mystery of *dif-ference*, that unifying differentiation (or differentiating unification) that makes human life and thought possible. *Our* speech is thus not originary but responsive.

> The way in which mortals, called out of the dif-ference into the dif-ference, speak on their own part, is: by responding. Mortals must first of all have listened to the command, in the form of which the stillness of the dif-ference calls world and things into the rift of its onefold simplicity. Every word of mortal speech speaks out of such a listening and as such a listening. (*Poetry, Language, Thought*, p. 209)

We speak only because we were first spoken to, only because we listened to language primordially speaking in the words of some poem.

VI

This expository foray into Heidegger's thinking about language has been motivated by my assumption of its relevance to the issue of philosophical nihilism described in chapter 1. That relevance is partly due to a general interpretive assumption I make about the later Heidegger, namely, that he is in virtually constant argument with Nietzsche and with the elements in his own earlier thinking that he came to see as unwholesomely Nietzschean. His so-called turn away from "humanism," a turn most easily seen in the essays on language, is really a turn away from *will*, or at least from that notion of self-mastering, self-determining will that comes to glory in his description of the "completed nihilism" of Nietzsche's Overman.[19]

After the middle 1930s Heidegger was growing increasingly frightened, I think, by the prospect of those "more comprehensive forms of domination, whose like has never yet existed," that Nietzsche had prophesied as the consequence of his ideas; and he was even more frightened that important elements of his own "existentialist" phenomenology in *Being and Time* gave aid and comfort to such horrors.[20] The reflections on language are, in part, an attempt to back away from that abyss. They are examples of a philosopher trying to think outside the Platonic metaphysical categories that must, sooner or later, be "inverted" to form something like Nietzsche's equally metaphysical anti-Platonism: "In its essence metaphysics is nihilism."[21] Thus, the essays on language can be seen as a fundamental part of Heidegger's attempt to sidestep metaphysical nihilism altogether, a nihilism he in practical terms identified as the final accession of human will to the status of philosophical *hypokeimenon*.

As we have seen, Heidegger's attempt to dethrone human activity and will shows itself most vividly in his efforts to undercut the expressionist account of language found in a theorist like Humboldt. Language, Heidegger argues, cannot be understood as a "product" of human "activity"; it cannot be simply (to quote Nietzsche himself) a "means of expression." Thus, since human life is always and everywhere a life of language, the failure of expressionism shows that human activity, human will, cannot be at the center and origin of even *human* life, much less at the center and origin of the rest of what there is; it cannot be the philosophical *subject*. Language, not man, originally speaks. Human life must therefore answer to something beyond itself. I will return to these claims against Nietzsche in the next section.

But even if I am incorrect in my interpretation of later Heidegger as in continual *Auseinandersetzung* with Nietzsche, the essays on language can still fruitfully be read as a response to philosophical nihilism. In chapter 1, I argued that such nihil-

19. See chapter 1 above, pp. 27–32.
20. The quotation is from sec. 960 of Nietzsche's *The Will to Power*.
21. Martin Heidegger, "The Word of Nietzsche: 'God is Dead'," p. 110.

ism cannot simply be identified as a doctrine internal to a particular philosophical conception like Nietzsche's or Heidegger's. I tried there to suggest that philosophical nihilism—understood as a wholesale collapse in the authority of our most fundamental epistemic and ethical practices, a collapse somehow brought on by philosophical reflection itself—is a threat internal to philosophy per se, at least in its modern style and self-conception; and I tried to articulate the apparent basis of this threat, an assumption I called *rationality-as-representation*.

That basis is, as the name indicates, first of all a philosophical assumption about what human rationality is. It is the assumption, as we have seen, that being rational is a matter of having and following *rules for action*; to be a rational agent is, on this account, to act on general *principles, laws*, that give form to one's behavior, that shape the chaos of one's multitudinous "movements" into a coherent fabric of "action." Some of these rules, or principles, or laws (one can use the terms more or less interchangeably in this context) match means to given ends. Others specify the ends themselves. In any event, the question "What is she doing?" asked about a rational agent must always (according to this assumption) be appropriately answered by citing some set of instrumental and/or teleological rules (laws, principles) that she is, tacitly or explicitly, following in her behavior. To be rational is to act on reasons, and to act on reasons is to follow a rule. Reasons are rules, therefore.

These interconnected assumptions about what human rationality is lead quite naturally to some strong claims about the final representability of the forms of human life. If to act rationally is to follow, either tacitly or explicitly, certain rules governing action, then the basic structures of such rational action, what we might call the constitutive social practices of a particular form of human life, can be conceived as patterned sets of such rules. When reasons become rules, practices become programs. A given epistemic or ethical practice, say, can thus be presented as a kind of formal structure. It can be set out as something like a set of instructions to be followed by the agent in pursuit of some goal. It can be *represented*, in a rather special sense of that term. And what can be done for one social practice ought to be able to be done for all. The ultimate end of such a philosophical account would be the representation of a whole form of human life: setting it out as a complex and interlocking structure of the rules, principles, and laws that constitute the rational practices of the human beings who live it.

Leaning a bit on Heidegger, I have called this perspective on human life *vorstellendes Denken*, or *"representational"* thinking that gives *reasons* in the form of *rules*. I have suggested that it is the apparent success of such *vorstellendes Denken* in modern philosophy that makes the threat of philosophical nihilism increasingly effective. The possibility of such representation of one's life means the possibility of disillusionment with it, perhaps even the possibility of corrosive shame at it.

If the basic springs of our rational action can be set out so formally and explicitly, if they can be represented as rules for us to follow, then it may be possible, even *necessary*, that we refuse in good conscience to follow them. Our lives, represented as such structures of rules, may fail to engage our own effective sympathies. In the worst case, we may be deeply ashamed, either of the content of some of our ruling reasons or of their lack of deep and smooth connection to one another. Our lives might, it seems, turn out to be less noble, less coherent, and—perhaps worst—less interesting than we thought. That disappointment, produced by a certain style of philosophical reflection and critique, might be crushing.

I do not say that it *will*, of course. *Vorstellendes Denken* and philosophical nihilism remain (for the most part) threats, not realities.[22] But some threats are idle, and one is foolish to waste one's time on them. Is the threat of philosophical nihilism one of these? If I am correct in my analysis, that question can only be answered by looking at the basis of such nihilism's threat to us, namely, at *vorstellendes Denken* itself. Can human life be represented in that distinctively philosophical way? Are there any fundamental human practices that cannot be construed as programs, as sets of rules to be followed in action?

For Heidegger, of course, the issue of whether human rationality can be construed in terms of rationality-as-representation

---

22. For some stimulating reflections on the relation of philosophical theory to moral practices, see Annette Baier, *Postures of the Mind*, especially essays 11 and 12.

must be a question about language, since both our notions of "reason" (hence *rationality*) and "word" (hence *language*) hark back to the original Greek experience of the *logos*: that which is law, logic, reason, word, and meaning all in one.[23] To be rational at all is to be a creature of the *logos*; human beings are, in George Steiner's neat gloss on Aristotle, "word-animals."

> It is held that man, in distinction from plant and
> animal, is the living being capable of speech. This
> statement does not mean only that, along with other fac-
> ulties, man also possesses the faculty of speech. It
> means to say that only speech enables man to be the liv-
> ing being he is as man. It is as one who speaks that man
> is—man. (*Poetry, Language, Thought*, p. 189)

Can language, then, be represented as a structure of rules to be followed by speakers?

Nowhere in all his reflections on language does Heidegger address this question directly. Perhaps his least indirect approach is found in a few paragraphs toward the end of "The Way to Language," where he briefly addresses the relation of "formal" languages to "natural" ones (*On the Way to Language*, pp. 132–33). There he is concerned with the attempts of information theory to create a linguistic vehicle that, as he puts it, " 'informs' man uniformly" (p. 132). Presumably, the ultimate goal of such formalization is to remove from language all occasions for misunderstanding, so that it becomes a perfect tool for the communication of information from one human being (or one machine) to another. Although Heidegger does not make the point explicitly, it seems plain that an essential part of a complete linguistic formalization of this sort would be the representation of language as a system of explicit, recursive rules to be followed by speakers; so his expressed distrust here of formalization would seem to be a distrust of the possibility of such representation as well.

It is curious, then, that Heidegger never flatly claims that the formalization of language is impossible. He seems content to remark at first that even the most optimistic information theo-

23. Martin Heidegger, *Early Greek Thinking*, p. 60

rists currently must "admit that formalized language must in
the end always refer back to 'natural language' " (p. 132). For
them, of course, that necessity is just a "preliminary stage in
the current self-interpretation of information theory." Formalization remains "the goal and the norm." For Heidegger, the
matter is very different:

> But even if a long way could lead to the insight that
> the nature of language can never be dissolved in formal-
> ism to become a part of its calculations, so that we ac-
> cordingly must say that "natural language" is language
> which *cannot be* formalized—even then "natural lan-
> guage" is still being defined only negatively, that is, set
> off against the possibility or impossibility of formaliza-
> tion. (P. 132)

Any transcendental philosophical argument against the possibility of representing language as a formal structure of rules
will, he seems to be saying, give away far too much to the for-
malizers: it will still define natural language "only negatively."
The impossibility of formalization will still be understood as a
lack of *human* power rather than as an acknowledgment of the
original power of language itself. Human power thus remains
the benchmark: "The 'natural' aspect of language, which the
will to formalization still seems forced to concede for the time
being, is not experienced and understood in light of the originary nature of language" (p. 132). And what is *that*? That nature is *physis*, which in its turn is based on "the appropriation
which Saying arises to move" (p. 132).

But what is *physis*? Here is Heidegger from "The Question
concerning Technology":

> *Physis* also, the arising of something from out of itself,
> is a bringing-forth, *poiēsis*. *Physis* is indeed *poiēsis* in
> the highest sense. For what presences by means of *phy-
> sis* has the bursting open belonging to bringing-forth,
> e.g., the bursting of a blossom into bloom, in itself (*en
> heutōi*). In contrast, what is brought forth by the arti-
> san or the artist, e.g., the silver chalice, has the bursting

open belonging to bringing-forth not in itself, but in another (*en allōi*), in the craftsman or artist. (Pp. 10–11)

The account in sections one through five of this chapter shows what Heidegger has in mind with the comparison. To experience the "originary nature" of language as *physis*, bringing-forth in itself, is to experience it as dif-ference; it is to experience that *poiēsis* of the masterful poem that, by naming the different things that there are, first calls near the world they bear. It is to acknowledge the primordial agency of language itself: before all else, *die Sprache spricht.*

And once language has been experienced in that way, the idea of representing it as a human practice constituted as a set of rules will seem silly. The power of language itself lies behind, and therefore beyond, any human power to construe its effects in an orderly way. Any representation one might give of it, even the most abstract and formal, even the most empirically "correct," will itself be necessarily linguistic and therefore given to one by the language one hopes to capture with it. It will itself be an instance of *physis*, a bringing-forth of dif-ference, as he would put it. And as such, it must always be *historical, destined, sent,* like a letter.

> There is no such thing as a natural language that would be the language of a human nature occurring of itself, without a destiny. All language is historical, even where man does not know history in the modern European sense. Even language as information is not language *per se*, but historical in the sense and the limits of the present era, an era that begins nothing new but only carries the old, already outlined aspects of the modern era to their extreme. (*On the Way to Language*, p. 133)[24]

No representation of language, however attractive and powerful, is the thing itself, any more than a single letter, however rich or lengthy, could reveal to one the whole truth of one's

24. The word translated 'destiny' here is '*Geschick*'. It derives from 'Schicken', which means to *send* or *dispatch*, as when one sends a letter. Destiny is something that is sent.

correspondent. Any particular form of speech, any thought, therefore—any representation—is only a sending.

In particular, the representation of language as a practice defined by a system of recursive rules is such a sending; it cannot be taken as the thing itself. This is not to claim that *vorstellendes Denken* applied to language will necessarily produce an account of it that is "incorrect." On the contrary, such an approach may lead directly to a "technology" of language that will better and better suit it to human purposes, a technology that will confirm and reconfirm itself in its various results. But— and this is Heidegger's point—such "correctness" and its technological payoffs will come only at the price of forgetting what originally makes them possible: language's "truth," so to speak. And that truth is the originary dif-ference behind and beyond *any* conceptual representation of language, including this one. To *appreciate* that truth, to acknowledge it in thought and in practice, is to live in a way that puts *vorstellendes Denken*, and thus the threat of philosophical nihilism, in its place. Such appreciation involves a kind of humility—perhaps one ought even to call it a kind of *submissiveness*—that is unfamiliar and uncongenial to us.

One can illustrate the unfamiliarity by asking a single, currently unprofessional, yet deeply philosophical, question: Where do our thoughts come from? Most of the time that is easily answered, of course. They come from other people. Their ideas are variously mangled and modified to suit our own purposes, scaled down to fit our own capacities for understanding and use, sometimes, perhaps, extended or connected in surprising ways. Such intellectual modulations pose no great difficulties for explanation. But what of those very rare thoughts that seem genuinely original, that mark a sharp break with past ways of thinking? What about those thoughts that constitute revolutions within a culture, or, even more rare, found new cultures altogether? Where do *they* come from? Or, to put it somewhat more philosophically, how are such remarkably original thoughts possible?

We cannot now return to recollection of the Forms, or to divine revelation, or to inspiration by the *Zeitgeist* in order to account for them: the myths and the metaphysics that gave support to such explanations are now moribund. So what do we do? If we consider the matter at all, which is rare, we usually revert, unthinkingly, to some sort of quasi-Nietzschean naturalism. We "invert" our outmoded forms of Platonism, putting the "true world" here below. Thoughts are natural human expressions, we say. Like all human products, they are fully explicable in terms of human beings and their attempts to survive and to flourish. We think in order to live. Of course we will quickly admit that we cannot yet give the fine-grained explanations that will account for a Plato, a Newton, or a Shakespeare; we cannot yet do the utopian neurophysiology or sociology (or whatever) that can explain how the will to power can constellate itself in such patterns of unexpected brilliance. But some such explanations are on the way, we are sure.

Heidegger believes that his reflections on language put the lie to this sort of vulgar naturalism. The acknowledgment of dif-ference requires us to acknowledge the primordial power of language in a way inconsistent with any such naturalistic account of thought. Naturalistic representations of thinking (and hence of language) are first of all *representations*. (There is no place for us to dwell, to think, outside the house of language.) And as representations they are "sendings"; they have a historical provenance and destiny. To make some range of them absolute, as vulgar naturalism does, is senseless. It is to forget what makes representation itself possible, namely, the primordial work of dif-ference.

More important, this acknowledgment of dif-ference, an acknowledgment brought about by the considerations recounted in section five of this chapter, undercuts the *motivation* of vulgar naturalism. For this naturalism is, Heidegger believes, deeply infected with "humanism." It is not disinterested in looking to account for thinking as a form of human expression and will. It does so because it wants our thoughts, especially the best ones, to be fully accountable as *ours*. Vulgar naturalism is *itself* part of an attempt at human self-mastery and self-command. But dif-ference, as the necessary condition of thought and language, cannot be a human product or expression; the basic differences marked in our thinking cannot be originally spun out of reality by the will of human beings. There must be, according to Hei-

degger, the primordial "activity" of dif-fering prior to all specific languages, i.e., prior to all thinking human beings at all.
Language must speak before human beings can speak their natural languages in creative response. In this sense, at least, human beings and human life must answer to something beyond
themselves. The vulgar "naturalist" metaphysics of will to power, the basis (according to Heidegger) of Nietzsche's nihilism,
cannot, however "correct," be *true*.

But this disavowal of vulgar naturalism is not a return to a
metaphysical *super*naturalism, to be sure. To answer to dif-ference is not to answer to a traditional god or to any other kind of
supernatural entity. The full recognition of dif-ference is, or
ought to be, the end of the Platonism that divides what there is
into two camps, the "natural" and the "supernatural." The acknowledgment of dif-ference is the realization that this ancient
metaphysical division is itself only a "destiny" and that none of
the categories "sent" by dif-ference can be sensibly applied to
dif-ference itself. Heidegger believes he has thus escaped (how
successfully, we shall have reason to question) from metaphysics altogether. Dif-ference is a notion outside all philosophical
characterization, including the most sophisticated.

Thus our thoughts, sent as they are by dif-ference, are not
finally our own; they possess us, not we them. They are not, in
any interesting sense, *human expressions* at all. And that means
that the same must be said of our *lives*: we no more own them
than we own the unexpected thoughts that call them forth. Our
lives are "sent" too; they are just as much our "destiny" as are
our forms of speech. We can no more finally control one than
the other, since neither has its source in us.

While this insistence on the uncharacterizable yet all-encompassing dif-ference at the source of all does seem to sail dangerously close to the *via negativa* stressed in some forms of Christian theology, Heidegger claims to be remembering another
tradition, that of the pre-Socratic Greek thinkers like Heraclitus.

Once, however, in the beginning of Western thinking,
the essence of language flashed in the light of Being—
once, when Heraclitus thought the *Logos* as his guiding
word, so as to think in this word the Being of beings.

But the lightning abruptly vanished. No one held onto
its streak of light and the nearness of what it illumi-
nated. (*Early Greek Thinking*, p. 78)

Heidegger is trying to return to a "naturalism" older than the
Platonic metaphysical distinction, a "naturalism" of nature as
physis: "the arising of something from out of itself" (*The Question concerning Technology*, p. 10). Language/thought/world
is, in *that* sense, perfectly *physical*, perfectly *natural*, where nature is not conceived as a realm of "matter" entirely lacking in
"spirit" or "life." Language—thought, the human world—arises
"from out of itself." In the dimension between thing and world
there is ever-active dif-ference, appropriating each to its own.

This dif-ference is, according to Heidegger, very close to what
Heraclitus called the *Logos*, to whom all are directed to listen
(Fragment B 50) (*Early Greek Thinking*, pp. 59-78). It both does
and does not want to be called "Zeus" (B 32). That is, it both
tempts one to identify it with something "supernatural" (the
Platonic error) or with something non-"supernatural" (the Nietzschean error) and then it rebukes one for doing either (pp. 72-73).
It is continually removing itself from the philosophical/theolog-
ical gaze. In the fragments of Heraclitus and the other pre-
Socratics, Heidegger finds indications of a form of life that is
free of both vulgar "naturalism" and vulgar "supernaturalism,"
that is, free of metaphysics *überhaupt*. It is a life that answers
to something beyond itself but without any prideful or fearful
attempt to lay hands on that and to make it one's own. The key
to that nonmetaphysical life was a certain experience of language, one now lost to most of us, but an experience remembered in Heideggerian dif-ference.

VII

It is clear, then, that Heidegger's experience of language as the
dif-fering, appropriating *Logos* sets him free of the threat of nihilism. In the first place, it sets him free of what *he* understands
to be the philosophical root of Nietzsche's own original nihilism,
namely, the metaphysics of the will to power and its underlying

"humanistic" anthropomorphism. For all his attacks on the Western philosophical tradition, Nietzsche's concept of the will to power is—according to Heidegger—itself stoutly metaphysical; it merely inverts the Platonism he affects to despise, thereby elevating "this world" to the status formerly held by the Forms.[25] The upshot of that inversion is a valorization of the human.

Here is the practical force of the Nietzschean metaphysics, as interpreted by Heidegger:

> But, because "God is dead," only man himself can grant man his measure and center, the "*type*", the "model" of a certain kind of man who has assigned the task of a revaluation of all values to the individual power of his will to power and who is prepared to embark on the absolute domination of the globe. (Heidegger, *Nietzsche*, 4:9)

Notice: "only man himself can grant man his measure and center." Such a self-measurer and self-granter Nietzsche calls the *Overman*. Overman and self-conscious will to power are one and the same. If, therefore, the "complete nihilist" is the Nietzschean Overman, as Heidegger insists, and if the Overman is defined as the self-measurer and self-granter, as one who recognizes without fear or regret that his life—indeed, life itself—answers to nothing beyond its own needs for self-command and self-overcoming, then no one who has experienced language as dif-ference could be such an Overman. To respond to dif-ference is to recognize that one *does* answer to something beyond oneself and one's aims, to something beyond the "human" altogether. It is to recognize that behind all self-consciousness there is language, and that behind language there is that which cannot be brought to light as such *in* language. This unrepresentable region "sends" all forms of self-consciousness, including that of the Nietzschean Overman.[26] Nietzsche's metaphysics of the will to power, like any metaphysics, cannot therefore be taken

25. Again I want to make it clear that I am not endorsing Heidegger's "metaphysical" reading of Nietzsche.

26. The notion of the "region" (*Gegnet*) that "sends" is explored in Martin Heidegger, *Discourse on Thinking*.

as the final truth about what there is. It forgets its own "destiny" as language. If that metaphysics is, as Heidegger believes, the philosophical basis of Nietzschean nihilism, then the experience of language as dif-fering, appropriating *Logos*, as the poetic word that measures out to one one's dwelling on the earth, removes one from such nihilism's grasp.[27]

Second, and more important in the long run, the experience of language Heidegger names as dif-ference appears to remove the threat of a philosophical nihilism that is wider than the one he locates in Nietzsche's (alleged) metaphysics of the will to power. That is because Heidegger's account seems to undercut rationality-as-representation and its corollary, the *vorstellendes Denken* that holds our lives up to the philosophical possibilities of wholesale disappointment and shame. In the last section I have already indicated part of the reason why: once the essence of language is experienced as that dif-ference necessarily prior to all the differences (concepts, distinctions) marked within it, then there is an obvious argument to the claim that that essence cannot be captured in language itself. All conceptual differences, and therefore all conceptual representations, including the representation of linguistic practices as constituted by rules, are "destined," "sent," by originary dif-ference itself; thus none can *be* that dif-ference *tout court*. Language, so understood, cannot say what Saying is. And therefore human life, a life utterly inseparable from language, cannot be represented either; its truth cannot become the object of *vorstellendes Denken*.

As I noted in my discussion, however, Heidegger seems hesitant to avail himself of such direct claims and arguments. Nowhere in his discussion of the question of linguistic formalization, for example, does he forthrightly deny the possibility of such formalization; much less does he argue the point. Why not? I doubt it is because he is unaware of the transcendental arguments available to him. Nor is it due, in my opinion, to a professional love of obscurity per se, or to an unwillingness to risk a stand. I suspect that his reticence, or indirection, has its root in his recognition that the hold of what I have been calling

27. For poetry as the measure, see *Poetry, Language, Thought*, pp. 213–29.

rationality-as-representation goes deeper than any purely transcendental/philosophical argument could reach; indeed, that such argument ends up reinforcing what it wants to remove.

To appreciate the point, it will be useful to return to a distinction made in section six of chapter 1. In my discussion there of rationality-as-representation, I distinguished between *simple rationality* and *philosophical rationality*. Under the general philosophical conception of rationality-as-representation, to be *rational*, pure and simple, is to be acting on the basis of (tacit or explicit) *reasons*, where reasons are understood to be *rules* governing one's actions. To be a rational agent is thus to be capable of having one's behavior *represented*, that is, described in terms of rule following, rather than in terms of randomness or mere regularity of movement. *Philosophical* rationality, then, is the capability of *self-representation*, that is, the capability of describing for oneself the rules that one is following in one's actions.

To these two conceptions, let me add a third, equally a part of our modern philosophical consciousness, a conception I will call *moral rationality*. It is the assumption that the rules one is following (or seeking to follow) in one's actions ought to be rules that are *self-reflectively acceptable to one as such*. Following Kant, one could, of course, call this the moral ideal of *autonomy*; and it is important to see that, as such an ideal, it goes beyond purely philosophical rationality. That is so because it is perfectly possible for one to represent to oneself one's actual behavior in a certain case, that is, to describe for oneself the rules that one is actually following there, and yet *not* find those rules acceptable to one as such. This is often so in certain forms of weakness of will, and also in some other cases of moral conflict, as when one, as an institutional representative, say, must act in a way that goes against one's own principles or temperament. In such cases one knows exactly what one is doing, and even why one is doing it, yet one despises oneself for doing it nevertheless. *Ceteris paribus*, one would not "freely choose" to follow the rule one is in fact following. Yet one is not truly "out of control" or "unconscious" in such cases; that is what makes them so awful. Autonomy goes beyond mere philosophical rationality, therefore. It is properly an ethical ideal; thus I call it *moral rationality*.

Let us think about the threat of philosophical nihilism in relation to these three conceptions. I have argued that this threat ultimately depends upon rationality-as-representation, since only if one could explicitly set out one's form of life as a set of social practices constituted by rules for action—only if one's life could be thus *represented*, as I call it—only then could it be found radically wanting by some process of general philosophical reflection. Philosophical self-criticism (of the modern sort, at least) depends upon a certain distance from its object, and only through some sort of *vorstellendes Denken*—"philosophical rationality"— can one's life become the abstract, formal object of one's own philosophical scrutiny, and thus perhaps of one's shame and disgust. If this is so, then a sure way to block the threat of philosophical nihilism would be to show that a human life *cannot* be represented in this wholesale way, to show that not every practice of human rationality can be construed as a patterned set of rules. We have just been looking at Heidegger's reflections on language in this light, of course; and we have seen that his experience of originary dif-ference means that language, the definitively human practice, indeed cannot be represented in this way. So it might seem that Heidegger's work should be seen as an attack on what in the preceding paragraph I called *simple rationality* and *philosophical rationality*. He is attacking the notion that when we are speaking or thinking, what we are doing can be represented (or self-represented) as a set of rules we are following in doing so.

While such an interpretation certainly reveals a great deal of what is at work in later Heidegger's reflections, it does not cut deep enough to do them full justice. Something rather more profound, and rather more disconcerting, is present in his insistence that *die Sprache spricht*. Part of that is indicated by his own refusal to deal in explicitly transcendental arguments against the representation of language, thus refusing to cast his work in a clearly philosophical form, especially one that belongs to the Kantian tradition. The reasons for that refusal should now be clearer. The first two conceptions of rationality-as-representation ("simple rationality" and "philosophical rationality") have their point only given the assumption that the character of our lives is our own to choose: a rule—the basic explanatory device of those conceptions—is something one can choose to follow or choose not to. The philosophical idea that a form of life can be described as a pattern of rules does not stand alone, therefore; it is not independent of a particular moral ideal, namely, the Kantian (perhaps ultimately Cartesian) ideal of the autonomous individual, the self-legislator, who chooses for himself or herself a form of life. Only to such a self, one might say, could it ever have seemed that rationality-as-representation was true; only such a self would have ever needed such a conception. Without the ideal of the self-legislating self behind it, rationality-as-representation would never have gotten off the ground as a philosophical program.

So, if rationality-as-representation is the historical condition of philosophical nihilism, as I have argued, and if the ideal of moral rationality is the true spring of rationality-as-representation, as I am suggesting now, then it is *that* ideal that must be the target of any thinker who wants to dispose of such nihilism. And that ideal cannot be successfully attacked with arguments that, qua arguments, presuppose the standpoint of the ideal itself, as transcendental/philosophical arguments do. Such arguments, presupposing as they do the power of mind to specify its own constitutive conditions, properly belong to the Kantian self they were originally designed to establish and refine. It is no wonder that Heidegger declines to use them. That is why he speaks of a certain "experience" of language as the foundation of his reflections (*On the Way to Language*, p. 119). One is not originally brought to those reflections, or sustained in them, by philosophical argument per se.

The ultimate destination of Heidegger's reflections shows itself in these two paragraphs from "The Way to Language":

> Appropriation grants to mortals their abode within
> their nature, so that they may be capable of being those
> who speak. If we understand "law" as the gathering
> that lays down that which causes all things to be pres-
> ent in their own, in what is appropriate for them, then
> Appropriation is the plainest and most gentle of all

laws, even more gentle than what Adalbert Stifter saw as the "gentle law." Appropriation, though, is not a law in the sense of a norm which hangs over our heads somewhere, it is not an ordinance which orders and regulates a course of events.

Appropriation is *the* law because it gathers mortals into the appropriateness of their nature and there holds them. (*On the Way to Language*, pp. 128–29)

If one were to focus only on the last sentence of the first quoted paragraph, one would likely see here just another Heideggerian insistence that language cannot be represented as a practice constituted by "norms" or "ordinances," that is, rules. Language is not, *pace* naturalists like Nietzsche, a "course of events" to be explained in terms of what "orders and regulates" it.

But that is to miss the real force of the paragraphs, which is, I believe, the image of Appropriation as "*the* law" that "gathers" and "holds" mortals. To speak of Appropriation is, of course, to speak of the persistent dif-ference of thing and world, of word and language. Appropriation is "what brings all present and absent beings each into their own, from where they show themselves in what they are and where they abide according to their kind"; it "yields the opening of the clearing in which present beings can persist and from which absent beings can depart while keeping their persistence in the withdrawal" (p. 127). To insist, as Heidegger does here, that Appropriation is "*the* law" is to say more than that it is general, regular, or coherent; it is to insist that it must be *obeyed.* The point of the comparison is not to stress the *formal* features of Appropriation (actually, of course, such claims would be senseless); rather, the point is to remind us of its ultimate authority over all that is human.

And that authority does not, *could* not, derive from some autonomous act of prior consent (tacit or explicit) on our part. "*The* law" of appropriating dif-ference "gathers" and "holds" us as mortals. It *creates* us as the mortals we are; we do not give *it* power with our nods of rational agreement. We must recognize, says Heidegger, that we speak (think, indeed *exist*) *only by answering* to language already speaking; and to respond in that way is, however "gentle" the word of address, always a form of obedience.

I am suggesting, therefore, that the later Heidegger's essays on language most truly ought to be interpreted as an attack on the Enlightenment ideal of *moral rationality*. To experience language as the Heraclitean *Logos* is to acknowledge that all authority—intellectual, practical, political—lies outside the human pale. At the bottom of all is obedience to what is spoken by language itself. The Kantian notion that we give authority to our intellectual and practical canons by our acts of rational consent to them is, for Heidegger, ultimately incoherent. "Our" consent is not our own to give. We are "gathered" and "held" by the *Logos* in all we say and do—in all that we *are*. We obey it, first and last. And that is not a condition to be remedied with deeper philosophical penetration into the nature of things; it is not "false consciousness" to be overcome in some Hegelian, or Marxist, or Freudian fashion. Dif-ference cannot be got behind and rationalized; it is "*the* law."

The Kantian myth that refers all authority to human autonomy cannot survive this insight. Kantian "rationality," understood as self-conscious self-direction in terms of self-consciously acceptable principles of action, has *itself* no intrinsic authority, once it is recognized that such self-consciousness is created and governed by that which *cannot* become conscious: "*the* law." Whether one knows it or not, such "rationality" is *already* obedience, and blind obedience at that. The Enlightenment ideal of autonomy, of moral rationality, flattering to us as it no doubt is, fails to acknowledge the truth that *language*, not woman or man, first speaks; and thus it fails to see that our lives are ultimately lives of obedient response to that speaking, not lives of self-conscious and principled self-direction. Human will is finally and always the will to obedience, not (*pace* Nietzsche) the will to self-command.

So Heidegger's deepest attack on philosophical nihilism, and on the intellectual and political culture that makes it possible, is not just the claim that philosophical rationality is, as a matter of fact or logic, impossible ("language cannot be formalized as a system of rules"). That would be, from his point of view, only a "correct" philosophical/scientific result, not the "truth" we so desperately need. His is also, and much more interestingly, the claim that the *hope* that lies behind such attempts at rationalization is perverse. He is not trying to block rationality-as-representation as a philosophical program; rather, he is trying as well to engage and to undercut the moral ideal that has given the program its deep appeal to us all along. To acknowledge that *die Sprache spricht* is not just to realize that one's life cannot finally be reduced to sets of rules to be followed in speaking and acting. It is also to realize that therefore one is not finally responsible for the shape of that life, whatever it is; that one is neither required nor able to "approve" of its constitutive elements; that one is not and never has been the potentially autonomous, self-legislating, self-owning being of Kantian myth.

And once that is clear to one, then philosophical nihilism is absolutely no threat. One didn't (and couldn't) invent the game one is playing, or even ask to join the party at the table, so now one must play the hand that one has been dealt. There is no cause for shame in that. Of course, one must try to play it as well as one possibly can. One can certainly be disappointed in, perhaps even ashamed of, one's own particular infelicities of bid and response. But that does not mean that the game itself is no good, or that one might be responsible for reforming or revolutionizing it.

It is, I suspect, this deep current of anti-Enlightenment animus that gives to Heidegger's later work its power both to compel and to chill. It answers to our sense, nourished by the bloody rain of recent history, that the Kantian rational self is a weak reed on which to rest all hopes of intellectual and practical authority. Once one's form of life begins to seem detached from one, to seem an abstract set of rules and procedures that must be clarified and endorsed in acts of quasi-divine individual or collective self-consciousness, then the threat is quite real that such endorsement will not, for one reason or another, be forthcoming, and thus that one's form of life, perhaps even life itself, will lose one's allegiance. Apathy and barbarism are the two sides of this coin. The loss of (what seemed) one's true authority demands, on pain of death, its immediate reinvention, often through the suppression of both intellect and fellow-feeling.

Jumped-up gods quickly appear; the trains will be made to run on time again. Confronted with these frightful realities of alternative despair and enthusiasm, as we are, and believing them to be the bitter fruits of the Enlightenment, as we sometimes do, it is no wonder that Heidegger's call to *Andenken*, to remembrance of an earlier experience of authority centered in the *Logos*, not in the Kantian rational self, has the power to hold our attention.

But this is, as Derrida and others have pointed out, "logocentrism" with a vengeance. In the beginning was the word—*die Sprache spricht*—and this primordially speaking word is the father god, the *Logos*. It is the single, central source of all meaning, all authority, and thus all truth. From it comes *"the* law" that must be followed in all our intelligible speaking and acting.

What is crucial here is to see that this is not just a "philosophical doctrine" of Heidegger's, not just a "philosophical account of language." What one sees here are the elements of a kind of ethical vision (to use an admittedly unsatisfactory phrase), a kind of basic stance or attitude that shapes all of later Heidegger's more explicitly "philosophical" thinking. It is a stance that looks to authority from somewhere "above"; it is a stance that assumes a primal, patriarchal source for *"the* law" that creates and governs us. I call it an ethical vision because it shapes the very way the sense of life comes to us. That sense is first of all something *given*, not made, and given by something described as *numinous, powerful,* and *sovereign*: "Language speaks." Therefore for Heidegger—and against his explicit wishes and claims—the source of life's meaning remains something *supernatural*—not in the sense that it is a particular or traditional divine entity but in the sense that it is "above nature," that it "sends" (the German verb is *'schicken'*) from outside history the history that thus becomes our "destiny" (*'Geschick'*).

So the *Logos* casts a strong shadow. Philosophical nihilism and cultural "pluralism" (read, for Heidegger: cultural *collapse*) may be genuine threats, but the loss of the Kantian ideals of rational authority and individual autonomy is at least equally frightening. The crucial question one faces here can be simply put: What sort of politics would Heidegger's pre-Socratic experience of language require? This is not yet the place to try to answer it; suffice it to say that it is unlikely to be the democratic liberalism most of us cherish. It is hard to see how the politics of individualism, of human rights, and of personal and national self-determination could flourish apart from the Enlightenment notions of rational authority that gave them birth and succor. To surrender to the authority of the unrepresentable, all-encompassing—hence uncriticizable—*Logos* is, in practical terms, to put oneself at the mercy of history, which Heidegger calls *destiny*, and to do so in a way that goes far beyond the Nietzschean and pragmatist recognition that there is no appeal outside its vicissitudes to a "true world"; there is no way to defend oneself against the "sendings" of the *Logos* when *that* is what both the ravings of madmen and the lines of strong poets must be called.

Granted, the pragmatist lesson to be learned from Nietzsche and others is that our history is all that we have, is all that we *are*, all the way down; but that is not so much a counsel to disavow that Kantian rational individual as the locus of authority as it is to insist that we recognize the fragility, the historicity, of that ideal, and of our use and affection for it. Nothing "in the nature of things" ensures that such an ideal will endure and flourish: only time will tell. All that is true enough, and sufficiently worrisome, but it provides no reason to begin to worship history itself under the name of 'dif-ference' or 'Appropriation', to begin to think of it as *destiny*.

To recognize our fallibility, our partiality, and our lack of final power over our lives—that is, to recognize our inevitable historicity—does not require the Heraclitean and Heideggerian rhetoric of religious submission, nor does it require a mystical name (*Logos*, Appropriation, dif-ference) for the forces of history and language that define us. To trade in such images, and to proffer such names, is dangerous; and not, I believe, an accident on Heidegger's part. He is not just a pragmatist that dare not speak the name. His attempt at a postphilosophical rhetoric, with its impressionistic wordplay, its portentous indirection, and its scriptural cadences and repetitions, strongly suggests that he retains a hankering for the Absolute. Better than most, and much to his credit, he sees the danger of making human will the locus of that Absolute. I suspect, however, that he only raises another, more mysterious—and therefore more dangerous—god in place of the noumenal self. There is something in Heidegger, one sometimes feels, that cries out to be ravished, or at least radically transformed. And that is frightening, since history—not destiny now, but just the natural lottery of time and chance—throws up so many who are eager to undertake the job. A politics that, like Heidegger's later thinking, tries to go beyond all "humanism" runs the risk of becoming manifestly inhuman. Heidegger's horrifying personal involvement with National Socialism may have been, in relation to his philosophical thinking of that period, just an accident, just the expression of a residual racism, or xenophobia, or greed, untouched by all his erudition. But it is no accident, I believe, that one should suspect the peculiar religious tenor of his later work to be a threat to Western political democracy. And that is why, for some of us, his work's undeniable illumination strikes so cold.

Since my purpose here has been to trace the internal conceptual contours of Heidegger's later philosophical thought, rather than to detail the sad (and often frightfully ugly) events of his life as a German citizen, I have omitted from the argument of this chapter any discussion of the historical material that has surfaced (or resurfaced) in connection with the publication of Victor Farias's book *Heidegger et le Nazisme* and Hugo Ott's book *Martin Heidegger: Unterwegs zu seiner Biographie.*[28] Suffice it to say that there is now on record abundant evidence to show that Heidegger's temptation to various forms of fascism, linguistic and otherwise, was neither superficial nor short-lived. The ideological burden of his philosophical work did not disappear after the fiasco of the Rectorship in 1933–34 nor did his gradual (*very* gradual) disillusionment with National Socialism propel him toward more liberal-democratic views. What Jürgen

28. An English translation of Farias's book was published by Temple University Press in 1989. A very useful review article on the German reaction to the book is Thomas Sheehan's "Heidegger and the Nazis," *The New York Review of Books*, 16 June 1988, pp. 38–47. There is also a fine symposium on Heidegger and Nazism in *Critical Inquiry* 15:2 (Winter 1989), pp. 407–88; it contains a long introduction by Arnold I. Davidson and essays by Hans-Georg Gadamer, Jürgen Habermas, Jacques Derrida, Maurice Blanchot, Philippe Lacoue-Labarthe, and Emmanuel Levinas.

Habermas calls Heidegger's "critique of reason"—closely connected with the demolition of the Enlightenment self I have just rehearsed—was a feature of his thinking until the very end of his life, and that critique was the engine that moved him toward the peculiar and unsettling quasi-religious transformation of language into the primordially-speaking *Logos*. My claims in this chapter about the presence (and the ethical and political dangers) of that transformation should be able to stand on their own, independent of what we know about Heidegger's actual political sympathies and activities. But such knowledge as we also have of those facts may strengthen my claims to find objectionable ideological elements in the philosophical texts themselves.

VIII

Having come this far in our exploration, one is tempted by precedent to a summing-up. Is Heidegger *right* in his claims about language? In spite of the weight of philosophical tradition on its side, I doubt that it is the appropriate question to ask, at least at this point. Not only is it presumptuous, it also persists in assuming a point of view "outside" the matter at issue, a "point of view" that Heidegger's work is constantly concerned to question. Thus it seems unfair, as well as foolish, to press it. Better, especially in an essay like this, simply to let the exposition stand, along with all the questions, tacit and explicit, that it raises.

One can, however, say this: there is every reason to believe that later Heidegger's experience of language as the dif-fering, Appropriating *Logos* is a genuine one. By that I mean more than just his *own* relationship to language—and thus to thing, world, and history—was actually of the sort I have recounted. We do not know that it was, as a matter of fact; and in any event I am not merely commending his sincerity, faint praise in the best of circumstances. I mean that we can recognize that the form of life congruent with that relationship is a real possibility *for us*; it is not so idiosyncratic as to be either incomprehensible or negligible. Indeed, in very profound ways it recalls forms of life that gave birth to our civilization and that still sing, like drowned ghosts, in many of the texts and practices we most revere. We cannot help but find it resonant. Moreover, it is a form of life that is not threatened, as ours seems to be, by philosophical nihilism. So long as we hear language speak, and so long as we speak only in knowing response, there is no real danger that the sense of life can disappear. Since there is no conceivable authority outside the speaking *Logos*, there is no fear (or hope) of judging what it says to be inadequate.

But if the specter of philosophical nihilism has been driven off, the shadow of philosophical totalitarianism remains. To locate authority absolutely in the *Logos*, as Heidegger does, is to risk the rule of the Absolute. By undercutting the metaphysical "humanism" that can lead to intellectual and political anarchy, he has removed the most effective, perhaps the *only* effective, barrier against the various despotisms of "destiny." Thus the question remains: Is there an experience of language that, like Heidegger's, exorcises the threat of philosophical nihilism but that does so without opening one to threats from the side of authoritarianism that are just as fearful? With this question in mind, we will turn in the next chapter to the work of the other great philosopher of our century, Ludwig Wittgenstein. Then we will be better able to return to the ethical and political questions about Heidegger's work raised in the last section.

3

Wittgenstein and the
Scene of the Language Game

In comparison to Heidegger's, Wittgenstein's philosophical reflections on language are likely to strike us—initially, at least—
as clear and straightforward. Gone are the carefully cultivated
jargon and the sometimes muddy prose. The controversial ety-
mologies, the stirring poems, and the dark Greek aphorisms
have been replaced by homely reminders and by the "quiet
weighing of linguistic facts."[1] There is even a lengthy and explicit examination of what has come to be the philosophical focus of this book, namely, the question of whether our language
can be represented as a social practice defined by rules to be followed by speakers. No wonder we at first feel less at sea.

Nevertheless, Wittgenstein's work is not without its difficulties. It is a grave error, I believe, to assume that the apparent
plainness of its presentation should be matched by the reader's
assumption that it means exactly no more than it says. In the
Tractatus, of course, the distinction between what can be *said*
and what must be *shown* appears as an explicit theme of the
work, thus inciting the reader to look beyond the achievements
of the text itself. Something of the same insistence recurs in the
Philosophical Investigations:

> I make [this book] public with doubtful feelings. It is
> not impossible that it should fall to the lot of this work,
> in its poverty and in the darkness of this time, to bring
> light into one brain or another—but, of course, it is not
> likely. (P. x)

Such a remark is not just a confession or a complaint; it is a
warning to the reader that things are not always, or not just,

1. Ludwig Wittgenstein, *Zettel*, sec. 447.

what they seem. As we saw in our discussion of Heidegger, the point of raising the question of whether language is a social practice constituted by rules is not just to get a simple yes or no answer to it; such a result might be "correct," yet trivial. The point is what gets uncovered in the attempt to answer this question as Heidegger might: in particular, the point is what we learn thereby about the relation of the self to language, to authority, and thus to life itself. The same holds for our attempt to understand Wittgenstein's reflections. I do not want just to piece together here a reasonably coherent account of what he says about rules and language in the *Philosophical Investigations* (that has already been done);[2] I want, to put it crudely, to discover the philosophical *moral* behind his discussions of rule following, training, obedience, agreement, and the like. Such attempts to expand or to penetrate the thoughts of another are risky, of course, but only thus does one engage Wittgenstein's philosophical work in a way that does justice to the intention that guides it:

> I should not like my writing to spare other people the trouble of thinking. But, if possible, to stimulate someone to thoughts of his own. (*Philosophical Investigations*, p. x)

I

The proper philosophical backdrop for these reflections we have on Wittgenstein's own authority:

> Four years ago I had occasion to re-read my first book (the *Tractatus Logico-Philosophicus*) and to explain its ideas to someone. It suddenly seemed to me that I should publish these old thoughts and the new ones together: that the latter could be seen in the right light only by contrast with and against the background of my old way of thinking. (*Philosophical Investigations*, p. x)

2. See the essay by Gordon Baker in Steven H. Holtzman and Christopher M. Leich, eds., *Wittgenstein: To Follow a Rule*.

The *Tractatus*, published in German in 1921 and in an English translation in 1922, is a deep and complicated piece of work, and there is naturally no hope of specifying all the ways that the equally complex *Philosophical Investigations*—published a full thirty years later, in 1953, two years after Wittgenstein's death—responds to the earlier book. The books face one another in a peculiar tension, a tension difficult to characterize as a familiar sort of philosophical opposition. Although in the preface to the *Investigations* he flatly asserts "grave errors" in the *Tractatus*, he nevertheless is slow to dismiss its conclusions outright, so as to clear a space for a presumably better account of its matters. The first book's failure to hit the mark, clear enough to him already by 1928, had left its author wary of *all* philosophical theorizing, thus provoking a self-criticism whose peculiar rhetoric, while often noted, has not yet been fully appreciated. It is not, to his mind, a simple matter of: *Tractatus*—wrong; *Philosophical Investigations*—right. Although it is very hard to tell a story (especially when it is one's *own*) without a well-defined hero and a decisive triumph, such seductive models for the construction of our intellectual history, familiar as they are, fail to meet our real needs as philosophical thinkers; or so Wittgenstein believes. He is trying for a less romantic relation to his past. This is not the place to attempt a general hermeneutic for Wittgenstein's later work, but at least a few reminders of its radically nontraditional character can be entered in the hope of forestalling some tempting and familiar misunderstandings of what is going on there. I will limit myself to three points, each of which I have developed at greater length elsewhere.[3]

First, it is crucial to keep in mind that Wittgenstein's fundamental term of criticism in the *Philosophical Investigations* is *nonsense*, not falsity.[4] The philosophical positions he attacks there—primarily his own, of course—are not faulted for being untrue or ill-argued, as one might fault a scientific or historical claim, but for being nonsensical.

> 119. The results of [my] philosophy are the uncovering
> of one or another piece of plain nonsense and of bumps

3. James C. Edwards, *Ethics without Philosophy: Wittgenstein and the Moral Life.*
4. Here I am indebted to the work of Stanley Cavell.

the understanding has got by running its head up against the limits of language. These bumps make us see the value of the discovery.

Again:

464. My aim is: to teach you to pass from a piece of disguised nonsense to something that is patent nonsense.

At first glance, of course, this may not seem the least bit untraditional. Did not the *Tractatus* itself make the same claim about earlier philosophy?

4.003   Most of the propositions and questions to be found in philosophical works are not false but nonsensical. Consequently we cannot give any answer to questions of this kind, but can only point out that they are nonsensical. Most of the propositions and questions of philosophers arise from our failure to understand the logic of our language. (They belong to the same class as the question whether the good is more or less identical than the beautiful.)
And it is not surprising that the deepest problems are in fact *not* problems at all.

The difference, however, is profound. In the *Tractatus*, the charge of nonsense rests upon a particular, and distinctively philosophical, account of the limits of sense and nonsense per se, the so-called picture theory of the proposition. To claim that a certain proposition or question is nonsense is to claim that it fails to meet the canons of sense inherent in the essential possibility of language itself, canons Wittgenstein claims to have traced and set forth in his book. In the *Investigations*, by contrast, it is just that sort of canonical account of language that is *pronounced* nonsense: it is the ultimate nonsense, he has come to see, to try to split off sense from nonsense in an abstract and philosophical sort of way. The "limits of language," a notion that crucially occurs in both books, are in the *Tractatus* defined by a *theory* and in the *Investigations* are defined by a *practice*, or by what he calls a *form of life*. They are defined there by the form of life that shows itself specifically *in* the *Philosophical Investigations*, in that book and in what it took to be able to write it.

The point is crucial to understanding the force and discretion of Wittgenstein's self-criticism. He believes that his early work is a kind of philosophical nonsense. By that he does not mean, of course, that it is literally unintelligible, a melange of words that lack any clear meaning. Nor does he believe it to be just radically incomplete or inaccurate: he does not believe that he has omitted certain important facts from his survey or that he has constructed his theoretical account of the facts in the wrong way. Of course he may have done these things (he *has*, in fact), but that is not what finally makes the *Tractatus* unacceptable to the sound human understanding. To claim that it is nonsense is to claim that it has *no real point*, no real use or value for sound human beings. Whatever it does, it does nothing worth doing in the healthy human life. That sort of criticism, unusual in philosophy, locates fault not so much in the theory produced as in the character of the one who needs to produce it. It is, one might say, essentially *moral* criticism; it is criticism of a practice—a practice both intellectual and social—from the perspective and sensibility characteristic of another practice. It is the criticism of a particular sort of *life*, therefore, not just a set of intellectual constructions.

In particular it is criticism of the life that Wittgenstein calls *philosophy*.

> The philosopher is the man who must cure himself of many sicknesses of the understanding before he can arrive at the notion of the sound human understanding.
>
> If in the midst of life we are in death, so in sanity we are surrounded by madness.

Again:

> The sickness of a time is cured by an alteration in the mode of life of human beings, and it was possible for the sickness of philosophical problems to get cured only through a changed mode of thought and of life, not through a medicine invented by an individual.

And most bluntly:

> Philosophizing is an illness and we are trying to describe minutely its symptoms. Clinical appearance.[5]

The life of philosophy anathematized here, what one might also call the diseased philosophical *character* he opposes to true human soundness, is neither single nor simple; but for Wittgenstein its central feature is plain. Philosophy is first of all the intellectual attempt to view the world *sub specie aeternitatis*, to "see the world aright," as he puts it at *Tractatus* 6.54. In Wittgenstein's view, the sort of comprehensive understanding aimed at by philosophy takes a particular form and has a particular (usually hidden) motivation. Its form is *theoretical representation*. For the philosopher, to understand is to be able to depict metaphysically. It is to be able to fix the "object" of one's understanding in some medium of abstract and impersonal representation. It is to be able to *say* what that "object" truly *is*; and the less one's vocabulary for such representation is local and idiosyncratic, the less its comprehension depends on particular experiences or on specific initiations into practice, the better. The philosophical ideal of theoretical understanding anticipates a vocabulary of precise and universal application, a method of metaphysical representation whereby in its use one becomes Emerson's "transparent eyeball," viewing the world without distraction, partiality or error, becoming (as in the *Tractatus*) the "godhead of the independent I" that can see *sub specie aeternitatis* (Wittgenstein, *Notebooks 1914-1916*, p. 74).

Such theorizing disguises its own character. It appears—at least in its own self-descriptions—as pure and disinterested, as an attempt to reveal the truth for the truth's own sake; but in fact it belongs to an attempt to control reality through one's comprehensive knowledge of it. Put in Nietzschean terms, the will to metaphysical "truth" is for Wittgenstein always at bottom the will to power. In the grip of philosophical theorizing, infected by what Wittgenstein calls "the sickness of philosophical problems," one's relationship to life is radically diseased: curiosity replaces wonder; the world as miracle becomes the world

5. This remark occurs in a notebook written in 1934 or 1935. It is found in volume 50 of the Cornell edition of the *Nachlass*.

as riddle; the *Pathos* of nature degenerates into superstition; action becomes technology. In such a life, progress becomes a fetish (think of the motto for the *Philosophical Investigations*); and progress always means, one way or the other, one's own advance.[6] Life appears as a set of problems to be mounted, challenges to be met, threats to be avoided, attacks to be repelled, and so forth; and the key to all of this is the achievement of a comprehensive theoretical representation—i.e., a metaphysics—of the field of play. Philosophy is a means to "preserve and enhance" (Nietzsche) one's life through its rational representation; one's practices of self-maintenance and self-strengthening are given a firm foundation in "truth." Theory supports practice.

Such an attitude corrupts (*inter alia*) one's relationship to one's language. Obsessed by the desire to control and to conquer one's life, to make "progress" with it, and recognizing the importance of theoretical representation to that ambition, the grammar of one's language gets pressed into service as a metaphysics. The grammatical images of one's speech are transformed into metaphysical pictures of reality, and one's thinking is thus (unconsciously) constrained by the historical conventions of a natural language.

> 104. We predicate of the thing what lies in the method of representing it. Impressed by the possibility of a comparison, we think we are perceiving a state of affairs of the highest generality.
>
> . . .
>
> 115. A *picture* held us captive. And we could not get outside it, for it lay in our language and language seemed to repeat it to us inexorably.

That is why Wittgenstein can say, at section 109 of the *Investigations*, "Philosophy is a battle against the bewitchment of our intelligence by means of language." Our intelligence is be-

6. The motto of the *Investigations* is from Nestroy: "Überhaupt hat der Fortschritt das an sich, daß er viel größer ausschaut, als er wirklich ist." Andrew W. Baker translates it as, "The thing about progress is that it appears much greater than it actually is." For a helpful discussion of the motto, showing that it reflects Wittgenstein's animadversions on the idea of progress itself, see Baker's essay, "Nestroy and Wittgenstein: Some Thoughts on the Motto to the *Philosophical Investigations*."

witched not because language is somehow inherently an evil enchanter; the true source of our captivity to our grammar lies, rather, in the philosophical ambitions we bring to it. It is the metaphysical intellect that binds our intelligence with loops of words and grammatical images. And thus it is that intellect, and ultimately the form of life that it epitomizes ("the vast stream of European and American culture in which all of us stand"), that is the true target of Wittgenstein's self-criticism (*Philosophical Remarks*, p. 7). That form of social life with its intellectual manifestations is finally pronounced *nonsense*.

So the nature of Wittgenstein's criticism of his own earlier philosophy is not just philosophically untraditional; it is manifestly antiphilosophical. It opposes the kind of human character, the form of human thought and life, that he thinks of as typically philosophical: the character apotheosized in the metaphysical self—the godlike transcendental subject—of the *Tractatus*. That self, floating free of the world that it finally sees aright, is a perfect image of philosophy's founding hope. It is an image of power, of freedom from mere circumstance, a power vouchsafed by philosophical self-knowledge. The world is now a "happy" one, made happy by the "will" (i.e., attitude) of its metaphysically enlightened subject. This hope, the hope of salvational power granted by comprehensive theoretical representation, is what he is most concerned to oppose in the later work. It is the heart of the disease he (often) calls 'philosophy'.

This brings me to my second hermeneutical reminder: because the aim of Wittgenstein's later work is the destruction (or salvation *through* destruction: one can tell the story either way) of philosophy itself, the form of his own work cannot be a philosophically traditional one. We cannot present that work as a reasoned and comprehensive theoretical account of the matters with which it has to do; we cannot look to it for arguments, or pieces of arguments, designed to meet our representational and foundational expectations of philosophical discourse. Or, rather, we *can* do that (and most *have*), but only at the cost of underwriting Wittgenstein's own pessimism about the value of his influence. He was very explicit about the peculiar form of his contributions, which here (in a salvational frame of mind for the moment) he allows himself to call 'philosophy':

124. Philosophy may in no way interfere with the actual use of language; it can in the end only describe it. For it cannot give it any foundation either. It simply leaves everything as it is. . . .

. . .

126. Philosophy simply puts everything before us, and neither explains nor deduces anything.—Since everything lies open to view there is nothing to explain. For what is hidden, for example, is of no interest to us.

One might give the name "philosophy" to what is possible *before* all new discoveries and inventions.

127. The work of the philosopher consists in assembling reminders for a particular purpose.

128. If one tried to advance *theses* in philosophy, it would never be possible to debate them, because everyone would agree to them.

These are puzzling claims, and his summary account of his antiphilosophical philosophical form is not a model of clarity either:

122. A main source of our failure to understand is that we do not *command a clear view* [*übersehen*] of the use of our words.—Our grammer is lacking in this sort of perspicuity [*Übersichtlichkeit*]. A perspicuous presentation [*übersichtliche Darstellung*] produces just that understanding which consists in 'seeing connections'. Hence the importance of finding and inventing *intermediate cases.*

The concept of a perspicuous presentation is of fundamental significance to us. It earmarks the form of account we give, the way we look at things. (Is this a 'Weltanschauung'?)[7]

What is a "perspicuous presentation" and why is it so important? We can defer positive answers to these questions until we have actually examined Wittgenstein's discussion of rule following. Here it is only necessary to emphasize what it is *not*, so

_____

7. Note the slight change from Miss Anscombe's translation.

as to try to prevent some typical misreadings of that discussion. A "perspicuous presentation" is not a metaphysical representation. It is not an attempt to lay out, and then to support by rational considerations, a comprehensive account of (some) reality, an account capable of serving as an objective ground for (some of) our practices of self-preservation and self-enhancement. It is not even an attempt comprehensively to represent those practices themselves. Rather, it intends, as Wittgenstein says, to help us to "oversee" the uses of the words that we are likely to use in such representations, to see that these uses are more complex and more flexible than we are likely to realize off the bat. "The theorizing mind," says William James, "tends always to the oversimplification of its materials." Nowhere is this tendency more apparent than in the philosophical attempt to read off "the nature of reality" from the grammar of some natural language. The point of a perspicuous presentation is to block such metaphysical oversimplification by reminding one (sec. 127) of overlooked connections and/or differences in our uses of words. For that purpose, as he says in section 122, invented cases may be equally as effective as discovered ones: by pointing out that we might just as well have said so-and-so rather than such-and-such, that a particular idiom or construction is not sacrosanct, the paralyzing cramp of a particular grammatical picture may be released, allowing one's view to pass freely over the whole range of such images. One begins to "see connections" that one had missed.

The end in view here is not a "total picture" of one's grammar, one that could then be mined for a metaphysics to explain and to underwrite our linguistic practices. The invented and discovered uses of words are not data for the development of theory.

> 130. Our clear and simple language-games are not
> preparatory studies for a future regularization of
> language—as it were first approximations, ignoring fric-
> tion and air-resistance. The language-games are rather
> set up as *objects of comparison* which are meant to
> throw light on the facts of our language by way not only
> of similarities, but also of dissimilarities.

The irreconcilable differences among our usages, the fragments that cannot be knitted into a coherent fabric, are just as important to the philosopher as those that allow a smooth combination—perhaps more so. The point is not to regularize language by means of its objective representation but to be able to *oversee* it: to allow the mind's eye to pass unimpeded across and through its complicated landscapes, to be at home there without maps.

"Is this a 'Weltanschauung'?" The question is complex. In one sense the answer is clearly *no*. I have just been pointing out that the aim of a Wittgensteinian *übersichtliche Darstellung* of our grammar is clearly *not* the production of a metaphysical representation of what there is; Wittgenstein does not anticipate—in fact he *despises*—the achievement of a "worldview" through such philosophical theorizing. "Philosophizing is an illness. . . ." On the other hand, that very rejection, given its characteristic form and intensity, comes from *somewhere*. It is not *trivial* for Wittgenstein to insist that the philosopher must give up explanatory theories for *übersichtliche Darstellungen*; indeed, it is profoundly subversive. Such claims against the traditional ideals of intellectual endeavor indicate the presence of another form of life in opposition, one from which such criticism proceeds. Should *that* be called a 'Weltanschauung'? The word itself is harmless and may even be useful so long as one remembers that this other form of life cannot fairly be represented as itself a set of basic theoretical representations: that is just its own point against traditional metaphysical philosophy. Such representation would be unfair not only because it assumes that theory logically must precede practice; it would also ignore the *ethical* point at issue in Wittgenstein's self-criticism, namely, the question of whether life is *fit* to be made the object of that sort of scrutiny, the question of whether, for example, the world is a miracle to be hallowed rather than a riddle to be solved. Suppose one finds, as on his own last admission Wittgenstein did, one's life to be "wonderful"—i.e., full of wonders, full of wondering.[8] Is that a Weltanschauung? It is certainly not a *theory*.

The recognition that the *übersichtliche Darstellung* "earmarks

---

8. Norman Malcolm, *Ludwig Wittgenstein: A Memoir*, p. 100.

the form of account we give, the way we look at things" (*Philosophical Investigations*, sec. 122), leads to a third and final hermeneutical reminder. If the point of Wittgenstein's philosophical reflections is not to produce a general theoretical representation (and hence justification) of our grammar and our lives, then the individual philosophical remarks that constitute those reflections cannot be treated simply as representations, either. If, as I have claimed, these remarks proceed from a form of life radically at odds with "the vast stream of European and American civilization in which all of us stand," they cannot simply be intended to mark truths that "everyone would agree to" (sec. 128). They *do* that, of course, if they are successfully drawn. When Wittgenstein says, "To use a word without a justification does not mean to use it without right" (sec. 289), or, "Justification by experience comes to an end. If it did not it would not be justification" (sec. 485), he wants us to reply, "Of course!" He wants our acknowledgment that what he says is undoubtedly true. But that is only part of the story, since just that acknowledgment may also leave obscure the point of eliciting it. (As any teacher soon learns, securing the sincere and even enthusiastic agreement of one's pupils to what one has said is no guarantee that one has taught them what one wanted, or what they need.)

Wittgenstein's philosophical remarks must finally be understood as *initiatory* rather than purely descriptive; or, to put it more exactly, they are initiatory *through* their being true descriptions. The truths they mark are not intended to add up to one big truth, any more than his "sketches of landscapes" (p. ix) are supposed to be incorporated by later draftsmen into a single representation of the countryside. An album (p. ix) like the *Philosophical Investigations* is not the first draft of a treatise, as its author discovered for himself when he tried to turn it into one: "After several unsuccessful attempts to weld my results together into such a whole, I realized that I should never succeed" (p. ix). Nevertheless, the remarks do point beyond themselves, and thus they demand a particular sort of attention and response from us. The recalcitrant style of the *Investigations*, its refusal either to collapse into a jumble or to form itself into linear argument, aims to initiate the reader into the nonphilosophical sensibility that is its ultimate source and object. In reading its sections, therefore, we must remain alert for such translations. It will not be enough either to agree or to disagree with what he is saying (though that is essential); it is also necessary to understand why he feels it *worth* saying. And that means more than simply furnishing an intellectual context for his remarks. It means opening oneself to the spirit that informs them.

II

Even if not wholly sufficient for understanding the work of a philosopher like Wittgenstein, describing its immediate intellectual context is nevertheless often necessary. Without much oversimplification one can begin to plot the course of Wittgenstein's self-criticism by attending to the fate of two of the central themes of the *Tractatus*: first, the claim that the essence of language is its capacity to represent, truly or falsely, a world of hard facts existing independently of it; and second, the atomistic ontology and theory of inference that make the elementary propositions of language truth-functionally independent of one another. Neither claim was surrendered without a struggle (though the second went more easily than the first), and the discussion in the *Investigations* of rule following can be seen as the final campaign in that long war. Let us see how.

The representationalist account of language is formulated in the *Tractatus* as the famous "picture theory of the proposition," and the essentials of this account are by now well documented.[9] As the name indicates, its crucial insight is the comparison of the individual proposition to a picture. How is a picture possible in the first place? How does it manage to represent, whether truly or falsely, some concrete state of affairs? According to Wittgenstein, the representational capacity of a given picture is a function of its internal structural complexity in relation to the internal structural complexity of the fact being pictured by it. First, in any picture P of a fact F, there must be at least as many discrete picture elements in P as there are discrete objects in F. If, to take a simple case, in F there are three discrete objects in relation to one another (say, an apple, an orange, and a

9. See, for example, Anthony Kenny, *Wittgenstein*, chapter 4.

wooden table), then in any picture of F there must be at least three discrete picture elements (shapes, colors, sounds, or whatever) that can go proxy for the objects in F (see *Tractatus*, 2.13, 2.131). Second, if P is to be a picture of F, there must be some distinguishable relationship among the discrete picture elements of P that is capable of being mapped onto the relationship of the objects in F. If in F the apple and the orange are lying upon the wooden table, there must be some relationship among the elements of P that can be mapped onto the spatial relationship: x and y rest upon z. For example, if P is a true, iconic representation of F, the relationship of the picture-apple and the picture-orange to the picture-table will be visibly *the same as* the relationship of the real apple and the real orange to the real table, namely, the two former will visibly *rest upon* the latter. In that case, the mapping of the one relationship onto the other, so that P can be a picture of F, will be trivial. In non-iconic picturing, for example, a phonograph record of a piece of music, the mapping is more complicated, but the principles involved are precisely the same. (See *Tractatus*, 2.14, 2.15, 2.151, 2.17, 2.18.)

Language can represent reality because elementary propositions, the fundamental units of language, are themselves literally pictures in the sense just defined. In the elementary proposition there are discrete elements—names—that go proxy for the objects in states of affairs (*Tractatus*, 3.2, 3.202, 3.22, 4.22), and these elements are concatenated in such a way that their relationships to one another can be mapped onto the relationship of the objects named by them (3.21, 3.22, 4.032, 4.04). Thus elementary propositions are *logical pictures of facts*. True or false they share logical form (the possibility of the mapped relationship) with the states of affairs they (intend to) depict.

It is clear that Wittgenstein's picture theory of the proposition belongs to the representationalist tradition we have already seen stretching from Aristotle through the "Way of Ideas" and on past Kant. In the *Tractatus*, as with these others, language mirrors, or attempts to mirror, a reality that objectively stands over against the words brought to bear on it; the truth or falsity of a given proposition depends upon whether that objective reality is accurately set forth in those words, upon whether there is a proper "correspondence" between the fact and its conventional linguistic representation. But it is also clear that Wittgenstein's account is very different from the earlier forms of representationalism we have discussed. Its basis is logical rather than psychological; it proceeds by means of an analysis of the nature of representation *überhaupt*, rather than through a particular understanding of how the human mind words. In fact, its most immediate strength seems to be exactly this independence of any specific (and therefore controversial) philosophy of mind; it seems completely free of such mysteries as Aristotelian *homoiosis* or Lockean *resemblance*. In the long run, of course, no account of language can be entirely unencumbered by the sorts of implications one might call a "philosophy of mind," and a major weakness of the *Tractatus* in fact turns out to be the largely incoherent conception of mind and action it surreptitiously requires; but at first blush it seems that Wittgenstein has set the rigorously representationalist account of language on a sturdy logical foundation. In a rigorously Kantian spirit he has identified the necessary and sufficient conditions for the possibility of representation *überhaupt*, and thus of linguistic representation in particular; and he has done this—apparently—without any "psychologistic" appeal beyond the resources of philosophical analysis itself. Language-as-representation, recently given up for dead, seems to have been resuscitated.

A second Tractarian theme, closely connected to the picture theory of language, is the logical atomism of the individual elementary propositions. This atomism has both an ontological and an inferential dimension: just as each state of affairs in the world can exist or cease to exist without in any way affecting the existence or nonexistence of any other state of affairs, so too the truth or falsity of a given elementary proposition is inferentially unconnected to the truth or falsity of any other elementary proposition (*Tractatus*, 5.134, 2.061, 2.062). Exactly why Wittgenstein felt constrained to affirm such an atomism is a question that can be ignored here, but it is important to my account of his development to note the way he began to back away from it. On his return to Cambridge and to philosophical work in 1929, he undertook a fresh examination of his earlier convictions; a long typescript known as the *Philosophical Remarks* was one of its first fruits.[10] Most of its ideas are still of a piece with those in the *Tractatus*, but there is also the recognition that the fabric of the earlier book must be altered in some major respects if its fundamental ideas are to survive. In particular, if the Tractarian idea of propositions as logical pictures is to remain viable, it has to be cut loose from the doctrine of the inferential atomism of the elementary propositions.

It is easy to see that this atomism is untenable. Consider an ordinary color attribution: one points to a red object, call it '*O*', and says, "*O* is red." It is hard to imagine a proposition less likely to be a truth-functional construction from other propositions than such a color attribution; so if the Tractarian idea of an elementary proposition cuts any ice at all, then a color attribution of this sort is a prime candidate for being one.[11] Yet such a proposition is not, in spite of its apparently ground-level representation of reality, inferentially discrete, for if it is true (at t_1) that O is red, then it is false (at t_1) that O is blue. Color words form a system; if a particular color is (truly) predicated of an object at a given time, then it can be inferred that none of the other colors can be predicated of that object at that time. From "At t_1 O is red" it can be inferred that "At t_1 O is not blue"; "At t_1 O is not green"; "At t_1 O is not yellow"; and so forth. Such apparently necessary relationships make the author of the *Tractatus* uncomfortable. His edifice is built upon the notion of the elementary proposition, the concatenation of absolutely simple signs immediately depicting the concatenation of absolutely simple objects; without the elementary proposition there is, apparently, no direct and unambiguous hook of language to world and thus no philosophical content to the trope of linguistic representation. And the elementary proposition requires the "simple sign."

> 3.23 The requirement that simple signs be possible is the requirement that sense be determinate.

But if something like 'red' is not such a "simple sign," that is, the linguistically simple name of an ontologically simple object,

---

10. See the editor's note in Wittgenstein, *Philosophical Remarks*, for details.
11. This was Bertrand Russell's view.

then what *could* be? Yet 'red' is clearly *not* simple, at least in the sense that inferential atomism requires, for it is inextricably involved in the whole system of color words. 'Red' does not stand alone, so to speak; it is not a pure sign, a pure name, matched up independently with a given object. Are there then no truly elementary—i.e., inferentially discrete—propositions at all, and thus no "determinate sense" in language? Is representationalism, even of the Tractarian variety, really as dead as it had heretofore seemed?

Confronted by such difficulties, Wittgenstein tries in the *Philosophical Remarks* to save the picture theory by detaching it from the individual proposition. Language hooks up to reality, not single proposition to single fact, but by means of *systems* of propositions.

> I once wrote: 'A proposition is laid like a yardstick against reality. Only the outermost tips of the graduation marks touch the object to be measured.' I should now prefer to say: a *system of propositions* is laid like a yardstick against reality. What I mean by this is: when I lay a yardstick against a spatial object, I apply *all the graduation marks simultaneously*. It's not the individual graduation marks that are applied, it's the whole scale. If I know that the object reaches up to the tenth graduation mark, I also know immediately that it doesn't reach the eleventh, twelfth, etc. The assertions telling me the length of an object form a system, a system of propositions. It's the whole system that is compared with reality, not a single proposition. If, for instance, I say that such and such a point in the visual field is *blue*, I not only know that, I also know that the point isn't green, isn't red, isn't yellow, etc. I have simultaneously applied the whole color scale. (P. 317)

In this way, "the concept of an 'elementary proposition' now loses all its earlier significance" (p. 111). The Tractarian idea of language as a picture remains in place, but it is now self-contained systems of propositions that are the "elementary" representations compared to reality. The individual proposition in its representational relationship to the facts is only, so to speak, a particular application of a large, self-contained, and internally articulated range of possible judgments about them.

This emphasis on self-contained systems of propositions hooking up to reality, an emphasis that was Wittgenstein's stab at preserving some force to the idea of language-as-representation, leads fairly directly to the discussion in the *Philosophical Investigations* of rules and rule following. Given the image of such pictorial systems of possible judgments to be made, it is natural to wonder how the connection, or "application," to reality is actually made in the particular case. There are two questions here. First of all, granted that color words, say, "form a system" (*Philosophical Remarks*, p. 317), how is that system constituted as such—what makes it genuinely "systematic"? And, second, what makes it possible for that "system" to be applied in such a way that determinate *sense*, and therefore possibly *truth*, is made by means of it?

Wittgenstein offers the same answer to both questions: *rules*. A system *is* a system because it is defined by, governed by, clear and definite rules. If, therefore, a series of possible judgments "forms a system," then those judgments must be internally related to one another in a way that can be represented as a set of rules to be followed in making them. An example of such an internal rule of a system of judgments would be something like: "No single surface of an object can be characterized as being two different colors at the same time." Moreover, rules are supposed to account for one's ability to apply the system of judgments in a concrete instance. There is, as it were, a rule to be learned by means of which a given "yardstick" is used to measure in the first place. So, to learn the system of color words is not just to learn the "internal" rules governing their relationships to one another; it is also to learn "external" rules for their application to reality. So, to know what 'red' means is to have learned a rule that governs the application of that term (and related others) to a range of objects: the meaning of 'red' is the rule for its application.

In this way, the idea of a *rule* apparently becomes fundamental to a philosophical understanding of language, since rules constitute systems of linguistic representation both "internally" and "externally." And in fact, says Wittgenstein, these two dimensions are the same:

> The system of rules determining a calculus thereby determines the "meaning" of its signs too. Put more strictly: the form and the rules of syntax are equivalent. So if I change the rules—seemingly supplement them, say—I change the form, the "meaning." (*Philosophical Remarks*, p. 178)[12]

Syntactic rules thus account for semantic connections. It is but a short step from this rule-defined account of particular systems of representation (he also sometimes calls them "coordinates of description") *within* language to the idea that language *as a whole*, language in its *essence*, is a rule-governed system of such systems. And thus we reach the image of language that is so much the target of Wittgenstein's self-criticism in the *Philosophical Investigations*: the notion of language as a "calculus" governed by "fixed rules," which account for its power to represent the world in an orderly fashion (sec. 81). In this way, the notion of the constitutive rule of language has become, in Wittgenstein's thinking, the hook on which language-as-representation is hung. The examination of linguistic rules is for Wittgenstein thus the examination of that ancient philosophical idea as well.

III

With these basic hermeneutical reminders in place, and with this sketch of its immediate philosophical background completed, I now turn to the text itself. There is, of course, no question of trying to give a general or summary account of Wittgenstein's "philosophy of language"; as I argued in section 1 of this chapter, nothing could be less in the spirit of the *Philosophical Investigations*. Instead, I will focus on a single but central thread in his discussion there, namely, the remarks on rule following. Not only does that thread directly connect his later thinking with his own first philosophical convictions, it also offers a

---

12. See also Ludwig Wittgenstein, *Philosophical Grammar*, pp. 63, 67.

ready way to think about Wittgenstein in relation to the basic question of this essay: the question of *vorstellendes Denken* and its connection to the threat of philosophical nihilism. The crucial passages to be examined are sections 79–108, especially 80–88, and sections 142–242. (The discussion of "private language" that begins at section 243 can be seen as an extended application of the themes developed in 142–242.) The material can be approached from many different directions; here I will emphasize those considerations that have to do with what Wittgenstein calls "the scene for our language-game" (sec. 179).

The immediate question at issue is: Can language be represented as a "calculus" governed by "fixed rules"? The question is not a trivial one, since it seems that the plausibility of the traditional idea of language-as-representation depends upon a positive answer to it: What other than a determinate and comprehensive system of syntactic rules could account for the (putative) ability of language appropriately to connect to—that is, determinately to represent—the reality that is its object? A proposition has, after all, a determinate sense, does it not? It says just what it says, and not something else. (Otherwise how could it be either true or false? That is, how could it be a *proposition* at all?) And what fixes the definiteness of that sense? It must, it seems, be the internal structure of the proposition itself, a structure that "horizontally" connects that proposition to others in the same "coordinates of description" (e.g., color attributions) and that "vertically" connects it to some particular state of affairs that it depicts (e.g., the red surface of object *O*). And what could such internal linguistic structure *be*, other than a comprehensive calculus of determinate rules of syntax? How else could one simultaneously account for, as apparently one must, both (1) the character of language as a *general system* (or system of systems) and (2) its representational connection to specific states of affairs? Wittgenstein's strategy is not to answer these questions directly. His remarks are, one might say, an investigation of what it might mean to answer them at all.

One of his first tactics is to focus attention on the empirical conditions under which any rules are initially learned and applied. When one thinks philosophically of language as a calculus of rules, there is the powerful temptation—this is common to all philosophical speculation, of course—to be entranced by a certain picture of the matter, to idealize a certain image of language, and thus to forget what it could mean to be able to apply that picture in a concrete instance. The picture conjured up by philosophical thinking seems to contain its own application. It seems to vouch for its own metaphysical obviousness. Thus we are captivated by it. The phrase "language as a calculus of rules," for example, seems to have a clear and specific content: one imagines a linguist of the utopian future being able to write them down in a (long) list and say, "Eureka! This is language." Or one imagines these rules somehow genetically and structurally built into the human brain itself, the innate knowledge afforded by them triggered by hearing others use them in their speech. None of this charming speculation is *false* of course: "The picture is *there*; and I do not dispute its *correctness*. But *what* is its application?" (*Philosophical Investigations*, sec. 424). Part of the application of the calculus picture of language is in how the rules of this calculus could be learned and thus followed. Because language *must* be learned, of course. Babies do not invent the language they first use; they have learned it, in some fashion, from others. If it consists of rules, then, these rules must be learned, or at least one must learn how to follow them. What does one begin to see about the calculus picture when one begins to reflect on how rules are, as a matter of fact, learned?

Consider, first of all, the learning of an apparently simple rule, certainly one much simpler than the alleged syntactic rules of language would have to be: the rule for constructing the series of natural numbers in decimal notation (sec. 143). How does one learn this? Well, one probably starts simply by being directed in a course of imitation. One's hand is held as one grasps a pencil, perhaps, and the numerals are traced out with it, *0* through *9*. This will be done again and again, and in various ways, until, it is hoped, the pupil can form these shapes for herself. (And that process is not likely to follow a smooth upward curve, or to happen once and for all: errors will recur, to be eliminated only gradually and with further instruction.) Then, once the shapes can be formed with relative accuracy and ease, the *order* of the numerals will become the focus of attention. The teacher will write out the series in proper sequence, and will try to get the pupil to follow suit. Here again, the learning is not likely to be instantaneous, and the natural mistakes—transposing the 6 and the 7 in counting, for example—will disappear (if they do) only with time, correction, and practice. Then, perhaps, it will be possible to draw the pupil's attention to the way the same series of numbers recurs in the tens' place, and in the hundreds' place. Once that has been made clear, then one can say that the rule in question has been learned.

But so what?, one might ask. Even if this bit of a priori theorizing about child development is accurate, is it not so simple and familiar as to be philosophically trivial? Wittgenstein thinks not.

> 129. The aspects of things that are most important for us are hidden because of their simplicity and familiarity. (One is unable to notice something—because it is always before one's eyes.) The real foundations of his inquiry do not strike a man at all. Unless *that* fact has at some time struck him.—And that means: we fail to be struck by what, once seen, is most striking and most powerful.

What are we unlikely to have noticed in this everyday example of learning to follow a rule? Well, we might not have been sufficiently struck by the fact that the process of learning proceeds by fits and starts. The pupil may *seem* to have grasped the principle for forming the series of numbers past 9, for example, and then may later begin to make mistakes that indicate that perhaps she hasn't grasped it after all. Some of these mistakes may be random ones, while others may be systematic; some may even be such that we cannot say which sort they belong to (sec. 143). And maybe they're not really mistakes at all, but jokes, or disguised appeals for attention, or expressions of weariness. Has the rule really been learned?

It is important to notice these quite obvious facts because they help to undercut a certain philosophical picture of what it is to "learn a rule," and thus of what a "rule" actually is. It is tempting to think of rule learning as the throwing of a two-position switch: either one has learned the rule or one hasn't (either the current is switched on or it isn't). But this is a picture that is difficult to apply to some of the cases that, as we have just seen, typically occur in a process of rule learning: cases in which, for example, one wants to say that the rule is "partly" learned. (How can a two-position switch be "partly" on?) Under the pressure of the philosophical picture, we forget or ignore such inconvenient cases. Reminded of them (sec. 127), we are less likely to be the picture's captives.

So, learning a rule is not like flipping on a light. Some of the same cases that made us see (that is, remember) that fact, can also help us to see other important things about rules as well. In section 143 and again in section 145 Wittgenstein stresses the fact that the possibility of learning to follow a rule depends upon the pupil's capacity for *appropriate reaction*. In reference to teaching a child the rule for forming the series of numbers, he writes:—"At first perhaps we guide his hand in writing out the series 0 to 9; but then the *possibility of getting him to understand* will depend on his going on to write it down independently" (sec. 143). A great deal turns on our appreciation of this point. When we begin to think philosophically about "learning a rule" (or about "understanding" in general) we are likely to think of it as a "mental event" or a "mental process." At our crudest, we are even likely to picture it literally as something taking place (the switch getting thrown; the light coming on) "in" the "mind" or even in the brain. In one way, of course, there is nothing wrong with calling rule learning a *mental* process. Such a grammatical remark may serve a useful purpose in some circumstances. (We will return to this point.) What is at issue now is what such a mentalistic picture of learning and understanding causes us to forget.

To think of rule learning as mental is to be likely to forget how much it depends on what is not mental at all. Given the philosophical history of the term, to characterize something as *mental* is always to oppose it in some way to the *physical*. In the classic Cartesian account of this distinction, "mind" is one sort of "substance" (nonspatial, nonextended, "private," etc.); the physical "body" is a "substance" of quite another sort (extended in space, "public"). And even if few of us are any longer metaphysical dualists of the hard-nosed Cartesian sort, *conceptually*, at any rate, the assumption remains current that the mental and the physical are conceptually exclusive and independent: A given "mental" occurrence (e.g., learning a rule) may have its necessary "physical" correlate (e.g., the brain process with which it is "contingently identical"), but the *meaning* of "learning a rule" is assumed to be independent of any such "physical" circumstances. The "vocabularies" of the mental and the physical are assumed to be separate and self-contained.

But this is just what Wittgenstein is questioning here. The very *possibility* of the pupil's *understanding* the rule "will depend on his going on to write [the series] down independently" (sec. 143). Not: the possibility of his understanding (conceptually) depends on some prior *understanding*; rather, the possibility (conceptually) depends on a certain *reaction*, in this case an imitative one (sec. 145). If that reaction is not forthcoming, it will make no *sense* for us to say of the pupil, then or later, that she understands (or does *not* understand) the rule in question; the natural scene—as we might call it—of such a claim would be lacking. The "mental" vocabulary of "understanding" itself, its sense and usefulness to us at all, rests squarely upon the *fact* that most pupils will have the proper reaction to a certain sort of training. "What we have to mention in order to explain the significance (*Bedeutung*), I mean importance, of a concept, are often extremely general facts of nature: such facts as are hardly ever mentioned because of their great generality" (p. 56 n).

The unperspicuous grammar of the "mental" and the "physical" blinds us, or can blind us, to these significance-granting facts. We can thus forget that the very possibility, the very sense, of a particular language-game always rests on something other than that language-game and its categories. This dependence of language upon its natural scene is a constant theme of Wittgenstein's later reflections, and I will be giving it much fuller attention as the discussion proceeds. For now, however, note that the immediate danger of thinking of rule learning as a "mental process" is that it obscures the most important ways in which such learning is not distinctively "mental" at all. In that way it encourages us to remain blinkered by an apparently exclusive mental/physical conceptual dualism—a dualism with profound effects on every aspect of Western intellectual and ethical life—that cannot be supported by an *übersichtliche Darstel-*

lung of our grammar. Even more important, perhaps, a mentalistic picture of rule learning can make us think of a rule as *itself* something essentially "mental," as a sort of "mental representation" of the process to be carried out in accordance with it. Thus "understanding a rule" can come to be identified with "grasping" this "mental representation," as if "learning a rule" were the same as "being able to state (or at least call to mind) the formula that describes the actions to be performed." Such an identification is, in Wittgenstein's view, a nest of very deep and important confusions, and tracing them will bring us to the most fundamental levels of his thinking.

IV

Wittgenstein begins to untangle this mare's nest by looking at the connection between *understanding* a rule and *applying* it. Under the spell of construing the rule as a sort of "mental representation" of a process, one is likely to want stringently to separate the two notions:

> —Perhaps you will say here: to have got the system
> (or, again, to understand it) can't consist in continuing
> the series up to *this* or *that* number: *that* is only apply-
> ing one's understanding. The understanding itself is a
> state which is the *source* of the correct use. (Sec. 146)

Part of the problem here is grammatical. Is it appropriate to think of "understanding a rule" as a *state* of the person who understands it—especially as a "mental" state of that person? No.

> 149. If one says that knowing the ABC is a state of the
> mind, one is thinking of a state of a mental apparatus
> (perhaps of the brain) by means of which we explain the
> *manifestations* of that knowledge. Such a state is called
> a disposition. But there are objections to speaking of a
> state of the mind here, inasmuch as there ought to be
> two different criteria for such a state: a knowledge of the
> construction of the apparatus, quite apart from what it
> does.

But we have no such structural criteria for someone's knowing the alphabet, of course, nor for knowing any other rule; thus it is misleading to characterize that knowledge as a "mental state." Nor is the objection averted by substituting 'process' for 'state'.

> 153. We are trying to get hold of the mental process of understanding which seems to be hidden behind those coarser and therefore more readily visible accompaniments. But we do not succeed; or, rather, it does not get as far as a real attempt. For even supposing I had found something that happened in all those cases of understanding,—why should *it* be the understanding? And how can the process of understanding have been hidden when I say "Now I understand" *because* I understood?! And if I say it is hidden—then how do I know what I have to look for. I am in a muddle.

In large part, at least, the muddle here comes from the philosophical vocabulary of the "mental." To think of understanding as something "mental" is to think of it as something "private," as something single and central, as a mysterious reality hidden "behind" its characteristic behavioral "manifestations" like saying "Now I can go on" or "Now I understand." But a closer look at the actual phenomenology of understanding, such as we get in section 151, shows the fruitlessness of such an assumption. There *is* no single, central "mental process" characteristic of someone's understanding something; and even if there were, it would not do the job required (sec. 153). To see "what is common" to cases of understanding we must look *outward*, not inward.

> If there has to be anything 'behind the utterance of the formula' it is *particular circumstances*, which justify me in saying I can go on—when the formula occurs to me.
>
> Try not to think of understanding as a 'mental process' at all.—For *this* is the expression which confuses you. But ask yourself: in what sort of case, in what kind of circumstances, do we say, "Now I know how to go on," when, that is, the formula *has* occurred to me?—

> In the sense in which there are processes (including
> mental processes) which are characteristic of under-
> standing, understanding is not a mental process. (Sec.
> 154)

The very sense of 'understanding' depends on public, inter-
subjective, demonstrable acknowledgments that it has occurred:
Those are the *"particular circumstances,"* in Wittgenstein's
phrase, that justify the use of the term. Thus the actual grammatical distance between *understanding* a rule and actually *applying* it, is not as great as it first appeared to be.

> 150. The grammar of the word "knows" is evidently
> closely related to that of "can", "is able to". But also
> closely related to that of "understands". ('Mastery' of a
> technique.)

Once that grammatical gap between understanding and application begins to close, it becomes increasingly difficult to
think of a rule as a sort of "mental representation" like an algebraic formula. Under pressure of the traditionally "mentalistic"
vocabulary of understanding, as we have seen, one is tempted
to think of "understanding a rule" as a matter of "grasping
a principle," where the latter phrase means something like "becoming conscious of a formula." The rule, thus understood, now
seems to be a complete and unambiguous representation of a future course of events, namely, the events that the rule itself
"prescribes." Indeed, those events, and just those events, seem
to be somehow "contained" in the rule itself, as if it could represent in advance the results of its own correct use. Such a picture
of understanding a rule is sometimes invoked even when it must
be admitted that no such "formula" can actually be stated by
the one who ostensibly understands. Think of a calculating
prodigy, who can almost instantaneously give the correct answers to complicated arithmetical problems but who cannot explain the process of calculation that led to them. In terms of the
"mentalistic" picture of understanding, either she doesn't understand what she is doing at all, in spite of the spectacular results; or she does understand, but the appropriate "rules" she is
using are (as yet) only "unconsciously" grasped. In some cir-

cumstances (e.g., the prodigy has substantial learning disabilities across the board) one may lean to the former description; in others (e.g., the prodigy is highly verbal, is able to grasp the fundamental principles of arithmetic, etc.), the latter.

Wittgenstein wants to call attention to the way in which this picture of the rule as a formula, attractive as it apparently is, actually disguises its own inability to account for understanding as a "mental" process. The picture of a rule as a *formula* or a *principle* seems to do exactly the explanatory work we want, in two ways. First, a formula—not of course its written or spoken *symbol* but the formula itself—seems to be something intrinsically "mental." It belongs wholly to a system of "ideas," from which it gets it significance as the particular formula that it is. Second, a formula seems to fix the understanding of a rule unambiguously, as if the formula mapped out a railway "invisibly laid to infinity" (sec. 218). "The rule, once stamped with a particular meaning, traces the lines along which it is to be followed through the whole of space" (sec. 219). But of course this isn't so; or, rather, the philosophical picture operating here covers over what makes it so, if it is.

> The point is, we can think of more than *one* application of an algebraic formula; and every type of application can be formulated algebraically; but naturally this does not get us any further.—The application is still a criterion of understanding. (Sec. 146)

A formula doesn't apply itself. Even an algebraic symbolization of the simplest sort always requires a particular application before it is working *as* a formula, and there is never only a single such application that can be imagined in a given situation. The formula *is* the formula *that* it is *only in terms of some consistent practice of application*. Thus the "mental" artifact or operation is again seen to be dependent on some "physical" circumstances for its sense. Only the application of a formula determines whether the formula *qua particular formula* has been grasped at all. Thus its application, not merely its appearing before the mind's eye as some set of symbols, remains a criterion of understanding (sec. 146).

It is easy to forget this if one calls to mind only formulas whose application is not a matter of dispute. Some formulas are so familiar in their application that they seem to apply themselves; indeed with them there seems no separable activity of application at all. To one who has learned algebra, the formula '$X^2 + X + 1$' seems to leave no doubt whatsoever as to how it is meant to be carried out for any value of the variable: One does not have to puzzle over what rule it represents. That is true enough, of course; one *doesn't* have to proceed on tenterhooks. But why not? The formula itself, its nature as a perspicuous "mental representation" of a process, seems to provide an answer. The rule seems to apply itself. In reality, of course, it does no such thing.

> 85. The rule stands there like a sign-post.—Does the sign-post leave no doubt open about the way I have to go? Does it show which direction I am to take when I have passed it; whether along the road or the footpath or cross-country. But where is it said which way I am to follow it; whether in the direction of its finger or (e.g.) in the opposite one?—And if there were, not a single sign-post, but a chain of adjacent ones or of chalk marks on the ground—is there only *one* way of interpreting them?—So I can say, the sign-post does after all leave room for doubt. Or rather: it sometimes leaves room for doubt and sometimes not. And now this is no longer a philosophical proposition, but an empirical one.

The way to read a standard signpost is so familiar to us that it is only in unusual cases that we have to ponder our ability to do so. But that is a function of our training and of our innate ability to *be* properly trained (cf. sec. 145), not of the "intrinsic" clarity of a signpost per se. The search for a self-applying formula—one whose intrinsic meaning is independent of a conventional, public practice of training and employment—is a paper chase that leads nowhere. There are no "intrinsically unambiguous" signposts.

The point is driven home in sections 185-92 with the discussion of the '+2' rule. Imagine that a pupil has mastered the series of natural numbers, and has even been taught sufficiently about cardinality so as to be able to follow a rule '+n' by writing down a number series of the form: 0, n, 2n, 3n, etc. So at being given the order '+1' he will write down the series of natural numbers. Suppose his mastery of the '+n' rule has been successfully tested again and again but never with exercises that have run beyond 1000. Now, says Wittgenstein, imagine that we ask him to continue '+2' past 1000, and he writes, 1000, 1004, 1008, 1012, etc. We challenge him, but on repeated trials he does exactly the same thing: 996, 998, 1000, 1004, 1008, ...

What is one to say? That he has not understood the rule? *What* rule? Certainly he has understood the command '+2' *differently from us*: "Such a case would present similarities with one in which a person naturally reacted to a gesture of pointing with the hand by looking in the direction of the line from fingertip to wrist, not from wrist to finger-tip" (sec. 185). The first point to notice here is that the correct application of '+2' is not somehow magically contained in the formula '+2' itself, even when the formula has been carefully taught and explained: "It comes natural to this person to understand our order [viz., '+2'] with our explanations as *we* should understand the order: 'Add 2 up to 1000, 4 up to 2000, 6 up to 3000, and so on' " (sec. 185). So it seems that the formula '+2' must be *meant* by us to be taken in a particular way, one that (in this case) *excludes* the continuation of the series as: 1000, 1004, 1006, 1008, ... Yes, says Wittgenstein, but don't be misled into identifying that meaning of the formula as a particular mental act of yours: "For you don't want to say that you thought of the step from 1000 to 1002 at that time—and even if you did think of this step, still you did not think of other ones" (sec. 187).

Does this mean that when I learn and teach the '+2' rule the step from 1000 to 1004 is *not* excluded? Does the rule or formula leave this somehow *undetermined*? That also would be misleading to say.

> We used the expression: 'The steps are determined by the formula. . . . ' *How* is it used?—We may perhaps refer to the fact that people are brought by their education (training) so to use the formula $y = x^2$, that they will all work out the same value for y when they substitute the same number for x. Or we may say: 'These people

are so trained that they all take the same step at the
same point when they receive the order "add 3".' We
might express this by saying: for these people the order
'add 3' completely determines every step from one
number to the next. (In contrast with other people who
do not know what they are to do on receiving this order,
or who react to it with perfect certainty, but each one in
a different way.) (Sec. 189)

Notice the crucial emphasis on *training*. It is *that*, and not "private" "mental" acts of meaning, that determines the exclusion
of 1004, 1008, etc., in the "correct" (cf. sec. 186) continuation of
the series: "It may now be said: 'The way the formula is meant
determines which steps are to be taken.' But what is the criterion for the way the formula is meant? It is, for example, the
kind of way we always use it, the way we are taught to use it"
(sec. 190).

And what is the basis for that teaching? What makes it possible for us to learn from it? At the bottom of all successful
training is the appropriate *reaction* to training: the brute fact
that most of us are able to master certain physical routines of
appropriate imitation and continuation, like copying the numerals (cf. sec. 143). This does not depend on our *understanding*;
rather, our understanding depends on this. At the bottom is not
thinking but *doing* (Wittgenstein, *On Certainty*, sec. 204), doing
that meets certain public norms of successful performance. Our
ability to learn the '+2' rule, in whatever way it is meant, depends on our being able to respond appropriately to a certain
course of training that leads to a uniformity of practical application of the rule. Without these appropriate responses, we cannot learn any rule at all. And that is not (merely) a remark
about the empirical psychology of human rule learning; it is a
remark about what it *means* to say that a rule has been learned
überhaupt.

So understanding is *not* independent of application, in fact;
and thus the "mental" is not independent of the "physical" in
the way it seemed to be. These are grammatical remarks, of
course, not metaphysical claims. They are remarks about the
way certain of our concepts are connected to one another and to

the world, and a reminder that some familiar features of our grammar may tempt us to overlook or to misconstrue these connections. But the philosopher's attention to the facts that remind us of these important grammatical truths—the fact just recounted about the '+2' rule, for example—may now lead to a comparable misunderstanding in the other direction. The point of the reminders assembled so far is that a rule (or formula, or principle) is not some sort of magical "mental representation" that intrinsically contains all its "correct" applications. Quite the opposite, in fact: the actual course of its application is the criterion for what it "intrinsically" means in the first place. A rule determines its own reading no more (and no less) than a signpost determines how we react to *its* direction. The rule, like the signpost, just stands there, in Wittgenstein's vivid phrase (*Philosophical Investigations*, sec. 85). At this point, therefore, it may begin to seem that a rule per se is impotent and vacuous. Rather than a powerful and unambiguous determiner of meaning and action, the rule may now appear to lack any genuine force of its own: What matters is apparently *what we do* in response to it. That is, what really matters is how we *interpret* the rule in a given case. Isn't an application, after all, an interpretation of a rule in relation to particular circumstances? Don't I follow the signpost by interpreting its pointed side as a directional indicator? Thus a rule without an attached interpretation seems as dead as an automobile battery without fluid: the rule's power to generate or to direct action begins to flow only when the interpretation is added by us.

But Wittgenstein sees that such a picture leads to a very unwelcome implication, namely, that a given rule R rules out *nothing*, since for any course of action C there is some interpretation of R such that C is in accordance with R (cf. sec. 201). Take the '+2' rule, for example. Does it rule out the continuation of the series by 1000, 1004, 1008, and so on? No, because there is a possible way of interpreting that rule ("Add 2 up to 1000, then add 4 up to 2000, then add 6 up to 3000, . . .") that would allow, indeed would *require*, its continuation in that unexpected way. And the point here is a general one: For *any* course of action, no matter how weird, an interpretation of R can be produced that would allow it. And this will be true no matter how rigorously R

is stated, even if it is rendered mathematically, for example (cf. section 146). So it seems that our recognition of the necessity of rule interpretation, a recognition apparently generated by Wittgenstein's reflections on the '+2' rule, has the paradoxical effect of destroying the notion of a rule altogether. If a given rule rules out *nothing*, if *anything* can be interpreted so as to be in accordance with it, then in what sense is it a rule at all? In another way, then, our philosophical thinking about rules seems to have landed us in a muddle.

There are several (related) confusions here, according to Wittgenstein. First, we have not looked carefully enough at the notion of interpretation itself. In the picture sketched just above, it appears that the interpretation of a rule possesses an intrinsic power, like the acid added to an automobile battery. The interpretation seems to be the source of energy that turns the mute rule, the dumb signpost, into a determiner of our thought and action. It converts the general formula into a specific order to be followed (or not) by us. But this cannot be so, of course, for cannot an interpretation *itself* be variously interpreted? Unless one imagines an interpretation as a kind of magical mental act whose "meaning" is absolutely and intrinsically transparent from the first, one must realize that merely adding an interpretation to a rule gets one no further in answering the question of how rules actually do their work. It merely poses the question yet again. Think of Wittgenstein's example of adding chalk marks on the ground to aid the traveler in the use of a crossroads signpost (sec. 85). Are such marks any less in need of interpretation than the signpost itself? Sometimes they *may be* clearer in meaning, of course, as when the signpost has sunk over to hang at a crazy angle; but this illustrates just the point that needs to be appreciated: only *in certain circumstances* is an "interpretive" chalk mark clearer in meaning than the signpost it is intended to interpret. (In some cases the interpretation may even muddy the waters more, not clarify them.) Certainly there is nothing in the nature of an interpretation per se (for example, the added chalk mark per se) that makes its meaning any clearer than the rule it is supposed to interpret. So, *if* one thinks about rule interpretation independent of its particular public circumstances, that is, *if* one thinks of an interpretation as another "mental representation" added like battery acid to the original "mental representation" of the rule in order to charge it with specific meaning, then "any interpretation still hangs in the air along with what it interprets, and cannot give it any support. Interpretations by themselves do not determine meaning" (sec. 198). It seems, then, that we have only replaced the mystery of the meaningful rule with the enigma of the meaningful rule interpretation, and that is no philosophical advance.

This brings one to a second problem with the "rule + interpretation" picture of what it is to follow a rule, namely, as a matter of fact we *do* on occasion follow a rule (or obey an order [cf. sec. 206]) *without* going through some intervening interpretation of it. There are times that we respond directly, confidently, and "without thinking," as when, for example, we pull the car onto the roadside in order to let the speeding ambulance pass. There we were following a rule, and there was no question in this case about what the blinking lights and the wailing siren "meant" in relation to it. We did not have to puzzle over how to "interpret" them and what they required of us. There would be, for example, no point in trying to justify in traffic court our delay in yielding the right-of-way by appealing to our necessity to "interpret" the rule in question. Such a claim would—*in this case*—be patently concocted to avoid punishment. It would lack sense *as a justification* (or even an excuse). "What this shows is that there is a way of grasping a rule which is *not* an *interpretation*, but which is exhibited in what we call 'obeying the rule' and 'going against it' in actual cases" (sec. 201). So the "rule + interpretation" picture is not only philosophically useless, it is also inconsistent with our experience.

None of these reminders is intended to deny that we sometimes find the meaning of a rule obscure to us and may need an interpretation. (Think of trying to figure one's income tax with nothing but the government's furnished instructions.) But successful interpretations are in effect nothing more than illuminating restatements of the original rule itself, "the substitution of one expression of the rule for another" (sec. 201); there is nothing magic *in them*, so to speak, that was intrinsically lacking in the first statement. As with the rule itself, the power of an interpretation appropriately to guide one's behavior does not reside in the interpretive formula per se, but in the particular circumstances in which the formula is learned and used.

The fundamental problem with the "rule + interpretation" picture is not just that it gets extended far past its proper boundaries, however; it is that it makes the idea of interpretation itself seem personal and individual, something like a "private," "mental" act or process. We sometimes say things like, "Well, that's just *your* interpretation of the situation," or "Let me try out on you a rather peculiar interpretation of the *cogito*." The grammar of such locutions makes us think of interpretation as something that takes place primarily in our individual heads or in our individual studies. It originates *with us*, like Kekulé's serpent in the dream. Then we may decide to share it with others, to "go public" with it, as we say. None of this is false, exactly. (Grammatical pictures are never false, nor indeed true; they are only liable to mislead us in the course of their use in philosophical reflection.) A given interpretation *may* of course originate in the thought of a particular person and may never be shared with anyone else, may never even be written down or uttered aloud; in that sense it is perfectly appropriate to think of it as "personal," "private," even "mental." But by focusing overmuch on such (unusual) cases, and by too easily misconstruing the actual uses of the terms we are inclined to apply to them, we can be distracted from the wider social scene of all rule following and thus of all interpretation of rules.

> 204. As things are I can, for example, invent a game
> that is never played by anyone.—But would the follow-
> ing be possible too: mankind has never played any
> games; once, however, someone invented a game—which
> no one ever played?

We tend to forget that the instances of "private" interpretation, whether of rules or of poems, make sense only against a public, institutional background of such interpretations: a background consisting of their formulation, their acknowledgment, and their use.

> It is not possible that there should have been only one
> occasion when someone obeyed a rule. It is not possible

that there should have been only one occasion on which a report was made, an order given or understood; and so on.—To obey a rule, to make a report, to give an order, to play a game of chess, are *customs* (uses, institutions). (Sec. 199)

Once it is recognized that an interpretation is no more magical than the rule it is designed to interpret, because *both* rules and interpretations are dependent for their power—their point, their sense—upon a background of *customary response* finally grounded not in intellectual "understanding" but in brute similarity of *natural reaction*, then the "rule + interpretation" picture (along with its attendant paradoxes) loses its grip on our thinking. We can let go of conceiving either of rules or of their interpretations as self-contained, intrinsically motivating "mental representations" of a course of events. And that means we are finally ready to let go of the intellectual fetish of "the rule" itself. Not, of course, that we will give up the notion of rules altogether; rules of language, rules of etiquette, rules of calculation, moral rules: all of these will continue to have their places in our grammar of self-reflection. Rather, we will be able to scale down our expectations of what the notion of a rule can do for us in a "philosophical" or "theoretical" account of our lives. It will no longer seem the key for unlocking the secrets of rational thought and action.

V

The intellectual fetish of "the rule" is the result of the way rules seem to play an essential role in the description and explanation of distinctively human behavior. To see this, consider the case Wittgenstein recounts in section 206:

Suppose you came as an explorer into an unknown country with a language quite strange to you. In what circumstances would you say that the people there gave orders, understood them, obeyed them, rebelled against them, and so on?

This question is essentially the same as: in what circumstances would you say that these people were (capable of) *following rules*? (After all, "Following a rule is analogous to obeying an order," as he says in section 206). That this is a profoundly important question, not a trivial one, seems to be borne out by what follows:

> 207. Let us imagine that the people in that country carried on the usual human activities and in the course of them employed, apparently, an articulate language. If we watch their behavior we find it intelligible; it seems 'logical.' But when we try to learn their language we find it impossible to do so. For there is no regular connection between what they say, the sounds they make, and their actions; but still these sounds are not superfluous, for if we gag one of the people, it has the same consequences as with us; without the sounds their actions fall into confusion—as I feel like putting it.
>
> Are we to say these people have a language: orders, reports, and the rest?
>
> There is not enough regularity to call it "language."

This is a very puzzling set of circumstances that Wittgenstein has described. What exactly is it supposed to show? Clearly this much at least: there is a conceptual necessity linking language to the appropriate regularity (*Regelmäßigkeit*) of our vocalization and our molar behavior. If the appropriately regular connections between what we say and what we do are absent, as is hypothesized here, then genuine *language* is absent as well. But that seems a claim hardly worth making: who has recently doubted it? We must push deeper than this truism in order to engage Wittgenstein's real point here. The truly puzzling feature of the case he describes is the question of *what is involved* in our postulated recognition that "there is no regular connection" between the sounds these people make and their actions (sec. 207). How could we know that? What does it *mean* for us to be able to deny "regularity" here? If we recognize and define *language* in terms of some *regular* patterns of connection between vocalization and behavior, as is clearly being done in section 207, then in terms of what do we recognize and define *regularity itself*? It is *that* puzzlement Wittgenstein wants us to feel. To avoid emptiness and circularity, are we not forced back to defining regularity (*Regelmäßigkeit*), and thus of course ultimately language, in terms of the prior presence of a *rule* (*Regel*), a "mental" form that cannot be reduced to the merely "physical" pattern of regularity that it produces? Isn't the notion of such a rule therefore essential to account for the regularity of language, in spite of Wittgenstein's earlier criticisms of it? That is part of what is at issue in these sections, and I shall return to it.

But the curious case at section 207 is supposed to provoke a further level of reflection, I believe. For what now would be our intellectual and moral relationship to the strange citizens of this "unknown country"? They do not speak a language, apparently, although their behavior—we are told—seems "logical." Are they genuinely rational creatures like us, or are they a strain of hairless apes? (After all, the social behavior of an ape is "logical" too.) Are these strangers retarded, because they cannot speak a language, or are we retarded, because we cannot recognize that they do? Should we try to establish solidarity with them, or treat them (respectfully, one hopes) as a part of the exotic fauna of the planet? The point is not to try to answer these questions here and now. The point is that these are the sorts of questions that must naturally arise from such a case as Wittgenstein describes. The notion of language is not one among many; it is deeply and closely connected to the idea of rationality, and thus to the idea of personhood itself. And since our most fundamental ethical and political ideals and institutions are typically person-referenced, the question of whether these strangers can speak (if only to one another) inevitably raises matters of the most morally sensitive kind.

This connection to rationality and personhood indicates a deeper level to the notion of linguistic regularity, a level being hinted at in section 207, I believe. When we say that the presence of language requires a certain regular connection between vocalization and behavior, we mean more than just the sort of regularity that a cat shows when, for example, it cries every evening to be fed. The linguistic regularity missing among the strangers described in section 207 is not, apparently, just their failure to make a series of recognizable sounds at standard times, sounds that would be the equivalent of gestures like rubbing one's stomach when one is hungry. (If their behavior is "logical" at all, as is claimed, that sort of gestural regularity—vocal and otherwise—is presumably a part of it.)

So what do they lack? The regularity essential to full-fledged language is in a fundamental way *open-ended* regularity. The concepts we are taught by appeal to a small number of examples are not restricted to those examples. Genuinely to learn these concepts is at the same time to learn how appropriately to extend them past the immediate contexts of their learning. "Teaching which is not meant to apply to anything but the examples given is different from that which '*points beyond*' them" (sec. 208), and language is learned and taught by the latter kind of instruction. It is this open-ended aspect of language that connects it so closely with our notion of rationality, with its Enlightenment overtones of freedom and autonomy. To be rational is not just to engage in "logical" (sec. 207) behavior; even a cat can do that, in the sense of adopting "regular" patterns of vocalization and activity that are to the animal's benefit. To be rational is to be able to "go on in the same way." It is to be able to extend one's understanding into new situations, to be "creative" in one's use of a word. It is to be, at the same time, both constrained and free.

So it is not just that language requires regularity and that regularity apparently requires rules as its explanation. It is the particular *kind* of regularity—the open-ended, "creative" regularity of language—that seems to demand the presence of rules to account for it. What else other than the learning of rules could explain our ability to move from the particular examples we are shown to the general concept of which they are examples? And what other than rules could account for the typical *agreement* of our extensions? Because most of the time we *do* agree, of course: we do learn "how to go on" *together.* That is what it means to be a full part of a rational community: to (mostly) agree with one's fellows about what is to be said about such-and-such; to be able to speak the same language as they do (or at least to be able to get them to speak your own). And that is why the encounter with the strangers of section 207 is so disturbing. We don't know how to "go on in the same way" with them; neither we nor they can extend our knowledge of one another past a fairly limited point. A certain kind of trust, along with the ethical and political institutions that sort of trust supports, is not possible in such circumstances. We cannot be sure, to adapt an image from section 218, that our lives and theirs run on the same rails.

Thus the notion of a rule, by virtue of being an apparently noncircular explanation of the peculiarly open-ended regularity necessary to genuine language, seems to be an essential part of our philosophical self-description as distinctively rational beings, and thus essential to the sort of ethical and political life we live. To give up the rule as our fundamental explanatory concept for rational action would seem to make unintelligible how our common, that is, reasonable, life *as distinctively human beings* is possible.

At this point Wittgenstein seems to have put himself into a bind. In the sections between 142 and 207 he has undermined, in various ways and from different directions, our philosophical confidence in the *rule* as an explanation for how language is taught, learned, and used. Our attention has been directed instead to the public circumstances of language acquisition and employment, the "scene for our language-game." We have been encouraged to see how these often-overlooked social surroundings play an essential, perhaps even decisive, role in accounting for behavior we have usually thought of as rule following. In this way the traditional philosophical picture of the rule as a mysterious Platonic "something" behind our various practices of regular behavior has begun to fade. We are apparently being eased into a sort of transcendental behaviorism.

Yet the case he describes in section 207 seems to return one, on a careful examination of it, to needing the very notion of the rule that we have been trying to jettison. In his comments on this case he seems to be admitting, however cryptically, to the problems of circularity and emptiness that afflict all "behaviorist" accounts of language (see sections 208–10). What, if not the presence of a rule to be followed, could be an adequate explanation of our creative regularity of action and response in speech?

So the bind is a nasty one: we need to account in a nonbehaviorist way for the possibility of language; yet the only apparent explanatory alternative—the efficacy of the rule—is bankrupt.

As I have emphasized, the difficulty here arises in the context of *explanation*. The crucial linguistic phenomenon at issue is clear enough. The use of a word is learned on the basis of a very limited number of examples, descriptions, ostensive definitions, and the like; yet we are usually able to move from acquaintance with those few cases to grasp the use of the word "as a whole": that is, to apply the word appropriately, "regularly," in contexts unrehearsed and unforeseen in the process of learning it. And this is not only *sometimes* the case. *All* words are learned in this way. It is a fundamental characteristic of language learning that it proceeds by this kind of regular extension from the seen to the unforeseen. *Investigations*, section 209: " 'But then doesn't our understanding reach beyond all the examples?'—A very queer expression, and quite a natural one!—." So the question before us is: how is this "creative regularity" in the use of words—*all* words—possible? It does not seem appropriate simply to let the phenomenon stand without comment: "But is that *all*? Isn't there a deeper explanation; or mustn't at least the *understanding* of the explanation be deeper?" (sec. 209). It is here that something like the mysterious efficacy of the rule seems a necessity: " 'But do you really explain to the other person what you yourself understand? Don't you get him to *guess* the essential thing? You give him examples,—but he has to guess their drift, to guess your intention' " (sec. 210). That is, he must guess—or *intuit*, as he puts it in section 213—the *rule* you are operating on and that you intend indirectly to communicate through the examples you've presented.

Wittgenstein does not attack our impulse to, and need for, an explanation of this very basic and very puzzling phenomenon of language. He just wants to make sure that the explanation we finally give is a *real* one, not an illusory philosophical substitute. The problem with the notion of rule following as the explanation of the "creative regularity" of language is that it doesn't really do the job; as we have seen, it simply pushes the mystery back to another level. He summarizes this objection for us at section 213:

> 213. 'But this initial segment of a series obviously admitted of various interpretations (e.g. by means of algebraic expressions) and so you must have chosen *one* such interpretation.'—Not at all. A doubt was possible in certain circumstances. But that is not to say that I did doubt, or even could doubt. . . .
>
> So it must have been intuition that removed this doubt?—If intuition is an inner voice—how do I know *how* I am to obey it? And how do I know that it doesn't mislead me? For if it can guide me right, it can also guide me wrong.
>
> ((Intuition an unnecessary shuffle.))

Here the animadversions on intuition recapitulate all the earlier deflationary remarks about rules, interpretations, intentions, and the like. They are *all* an unnecessary shuffle; they all leave unexplained the phenomenon that called them forth.

The problem, as I have said, is not our desire for it to be explained. (Wittgenstein is not some sort of intellectual Luddite, determined to smash the soulless machinery of explanation per se.) The problem is our insistence that this explanation be of a specific philosophical form. We want an explanation of language (and hence of rationality) that is *itself rational* all the way down. In this case in particular, we want to be able to believe that there is some *reason* behind our typical agreement in extending the use of a word into an unforeseen context. That is what the mysterious rule (or interpretation, or intention, or intuition) is supposed to be: a *reason* for doing what we are doing, and a *reason* for our general agreement in the way we do it. And it is just that that Wittgenstein attacks:

> 211. How can he *know* that he is to continue a pattern by himself—whatever instruction you give him?—Well, how do I know?—If that means 'Have I reasons?' the answer is: my reasons will soon give out. And then I shall act, without reasons.

To insist on the grounding presence of a rule is to insist on a reason, to insist that what we are doing is reasonable, even if we do not (yet) fully understand the reason that supports it.

The magical power of the self-applying rule invoked to explain our linguistic practices is therefore no mere slip or accident. Granted that we do not understand how such application-directions can be built into the rule itself. Such mystery is just the point; that is, it is essential to preserving the myth that the rule is a reason after all. That mystery allows us to believe that, at a deeper level we don't yet fathom, there is some explanation of what we are doing—namely, "going on in the same way" in our use of a word—that reveals us to be following orders, to be acting under rational authority, so to speak.

We want, perhaps even need, to believe that we are fundamentally rational in our lives and constitutive social practices. We want to insist that there are no intrinsic limits beyond which the rationalization of our lives cannot extend. The view of human life *sub specie aeternitatis* should show it as a thoroughly rational structure in its potential if not in concrete actuality. Rational practices must ultimately rest on self-sufficient grounding reasons. The reasons postulated by this metaphysical picture of our lives do not even have to be "good" ones. What matters most is the idea that we are following *some* direction in what we do, not what the direction in fact is. To be rational, in the philosophically crucial sense, is not necessarily to be intelligent or decent or wise. After all, one might unfortunately be acting on principles that make one's behavior stupid or vicious. The important thing is that one is finally acting on some principle or other: *that* is what makes one rational *tout court*.

What is ultimately at issue here, of course, is an entire ethical/political/philosophical—call it *metaphysical*—self-conception, which is very close to the Western bone: are we at bottom the thoroughly rational, potentially autonomous self-determiners described by Enlightenment philosophical propaganda? Are our lives open to the possibility of unfettered self-direction through complete self-knowledge? Can we hope to make conscious the principles that our actions exemplify, and thereby bring those principles—and thus the actions and practices erected upon them—within the scope of our conscious scrutiny and choice?

Obviously, the matter of language is fundamental to such questions, since language is the practice fundamental to so many more, especially those that seem distinctively human. If language itself is not "rational," if it is not a comprehensible structure of reasons all the way down, then it is difficult to imagine that *any* significant human practice could be so. And this, of course, is the real agenda for Wittgenstein's examination of the claim that language can be represented as a system of rules to be followed by those who speak it. A rule is, in the philosophically crucial sense, a *reason*. It directs and determines one's behavior, if one follows it; thus it is, as a reason must be, a ground-level explanation for why one is doing what one is doing. More, a rule can—in theory at least—be scrutinized, be recognized for what it is, and then be either accepted or rejected as a determiner of one's behavior. Once articulated, a rule can be obeyed or disobeyed, followed or ignored. Thus, to understand rules as reasons (and reasons as rules) gives substance to the traditional identification of rationality with moral freedom. Since the efficacy of rules demands one's conscious or unconscious assent to them, then to be a rational human being, whose actions are defined and determined by the rules one is following, is to be a creature potentially free to discover and therefore to choose for oneself the direction of one's conduct. To be able to represent oneself metaphysically as a rule follower is thus to be able to conceive oneself as potentially and ultimately one's *own*: one recognizes oneself as one who can autonomously determine the principles on which one acts.

In respect of language, first of all, Wittgenstein is presenting a different view. We cannot make our own the ground on which our language rests. Our representation of our language as a system of rules encounters a limit beyond which it cannot, on pain of nonsense, travel. Language—at least any language rich enough to contain the sorts of practices we think of as most characteristically human—always involves the creative yet regular extension of its terms into unforeseen contexts; and that is a phenomenon that, as we have seen, *cannot* be sensibly accounted for in terms of rules. This is not the claim that there are no "rules of language"; it is only the reminder that, even if there were, their presence would still leave unexplained the phenomenon finally at issue. There would still be the question of how I am to understand and to obey these rules in such a way as to produce the appropriate (i.e., "creative yet regular") agreement with any fellow language users.

> 217. 'How am I able to obey a rule?'—if this is not a question about causes, then it is about the justification for my following the rule in the way I do.
> If I have exhausted the justifications I have reached bedrock, and my spade is turned. Then I am inclined to say: 'This is simply what I do.'
> (Remember that we sometimes demand explanations [*Erklärungen*] not for the sake of their content, but of their form. Our requirement is an architectural one; the explanation a kind of ornamental coping that supports nothing.)[13]

Wittgenstein is exactly right here. What we want to locate is not the cause of our agreement but a justification of it; we want an explanation of our linguistic rule following that portrays the rule as a *reason* for what we do, and thus represents us as rational agents while we do it. We want to be able to see our agreement in the use of words, and thus our whole common life together, as demonstrating an essential presence in human beings of clear sight and free choice: at bottom we can see, articulate, choose, and thus own, the foundations of our lives.

But do our linguistic justifications reach all the way down? No: "If that means 'Have I reasons?' the answer is: my reasons will soon give out. And then I shall act, without reasons" (sec. 211). At some point, fairly soon in fact, I (we) can no longer explain (i.e., give a reason for) what I (we) do in using a word in the way that I (we) do.

> If I have exhausted the justifications I have reached bedrock, and my spade is turned. Then I am inclined to say: 'This is simply what I do.'

And the hypothetical presence of linguistic rules to be obeyed does not alter this barrier to our digging, since there too my justifications come to an end.

13. Note the change in translation.

> When I obey a rule, I do not choose. I obey the rule
> *blindly*. (Sec. 219)

That is, the effective power of a rule, once it is seen as no more and no less than the conventionally useful signpost that it is, does not support, in the way it is reported to do, the metaphysical picture of the autonomous rational self. "Following a rule is analogous to obeying an order. We are trained to do so; we react to an order in a particular way" (sec. 206). At the bottom of our rule-governed behavior is *obedience*, not choice; *blindness*, not whole sight.

This is not to say, of course, that no one ever examines a given rule, linguistic or otherwise, and then decides whether or not to follow it. Certainly we do, and often should, engage in such a process of deliberation. Wittgenstein's aim is just to point out that such deliberation necessarily has an end, that it cannot extend its scrutiny and choice all the way down to the ground of our lives. It cannot encompass the whole of it, in the way that the rationalist metaphysical picture claims and requires. The possibility of our conscious self-direction in accordance with some rule finally rests not on our capacity to see the rule clearly and then to opt for it; rather, it depends on our capacity *to be moved* by the rule in a particular way, to *respond*, not to act "on our own." At the foundation of our lives together is a community of sensibility and reaction, not an identity of potentially rational apperception conjoined with radically free choice. And that grounding sensibility is not itself representable as *yet more* rules to be made conscious; that gets us no farther. At some point in such representation we hit bedrock, impervious to further penetration with the tools at hand.

At that point we must admit that the sort of explanation we are seeking is simply not to be had. Language is not sensibly to be represented—all the way down, at any rate—as a system of rules to be followed by the (potentially) autonomous self. We cannot justify in that way the general agreement (the creative regularity) on which all linguistic communication, and thus all human life, depends. It is just here that the parenthetical last paragraph of section 217 is so helpful, since it forces us to ask *why* we wanted the rule-following explanation in the first place.

To suggest, as Wittgenstein does here, that our requirement in that direction "is an architectural one," that such explanations are essentially "ornamental," is to direct our attention to the large-scale metaphysical picture that ultimately funds our interest in these matters.

The architectural image of ornamentation should not be taken to imply superficiality or triviality, of course. In a baroque church, for example, the golden sunbursts above the altar are strictly ornamental—i.e., they do not support the ceiling or strengthen the walls—but they are by no means negligible in a just account of the building. Their presence indicates the influence of a complex set of theological and aesthetic ideas, whose power to compel belief and action must be appreciated before any full understanding of such a church is possible. The church, ornaments and all, reflects a certain style of life, one might say; and the meaning, the significance, of the ornamentation can be grasped only in reference to that style and to its roots in belief and sensibility.

So it is with the philosophical "ornamentation" of rules and rule following. Our insistence that such an explanation be given for our linguistic abilities is a requirement that derives from the hidden agenda of Enlightenment rationalism *cum* voluntarism. It is because we think we must augment and defend that metaphysical picture of the self—along with all its ethical and political corollaries—that we insist that our explanations of the creative regularity of language meet these particular "architectural" canons, that they must be of this specific style. And to recognize this is useful in two ways. First, by seeing that the rationalist requirement on explanations is imparted rather than intrinsic, that it is more conventional than it announces itself to be, we can more easily acknowledge that it often does not square with the facts it is supposed to accommodate. Thus the rule-following account begins to lose its hold on our imaginations; our intelligence is less "bewitched" (sec. 109) by that particular picture of our grammar. We can begin to look around for explanations of other sorts. Second, the collapse of the rule-following account can then provoke questions about the rationalist picture now seen to be so deeply connected to it. Once the architectural ornaments begin to look a bit flashy, or a bit dated by circumstance, then it becomes possible to inquire about the style of life that produced them. We can begin to see the metaphysical picture *as a picture*, just as we can begin to see the baroque as a particular style; and that means we are no longer captive to it. This is—in part, at least—why Wittgenstein says, "The problems arising through the misinterpretation of our forms of language have the character of *depth*" (sec. 111). Philosophical puzzles are rooted, through language, in our deepest assumptions about who and what we are. Through an examination of those puzzles, therefore, we can encounter those assumptions per se and can perhaps begin to discover a new relationship to them.

To summarize, in this section I have been trying to indicate how the notion of rule following can so easily become a fetish in philosophical explanations of language. At the foundation of our ability to speak with one another is a very puzzling phenomenon, namely, what I have been calling our creative regularity in extending the uses of words into unrehearsed, unforeseen circumstances. How is that phenomenon to be explained? Since behavioristic accounts of such regularity seem to be circular and therefore empty, one seems forced into postulating some avatar of the self-applying rule as the explanation. But that notion, upon close examination, collapses utterly: no rule (or principle, or law, or interpretation, or intention) per se can predict or constrain the vicissitudes of its future employment. Thus the bind: only the self-applying rule could explain the creative regularity of language, but no such rule can actually be found in our experience. So the rule—the hidden Rule—becomes a fetish of linguistic explanation: a magical object assumed to account for our general agreement about what to say when. Wittgenstein sees that what produces both the bind and the fetish is the requirement that our explanations of language take a particular form, specifically, the requirement that they preserve our metaphysical picture of ourselves as rational (and therefore free) all the way down. Without *that* assumption, we would be free to try to explain the fact of basic linguistic agreement in more promising ways: biologically, physiologically, genetically, and so forth. We would, that is, be able to return explanation to its proper province: to move it out of philosophy and back into natural science, where it belongs.

VI

It is time to raise our heads a bit, to look about and see where we have come so far. We can see, first of all, that the linguistic rule as traditionally conceived by philosophers—the rule as the rational engine of language: the intelligent power that guarantees and justifies our general agreement in what we say about the world—is a myth. There are plenty of genuine "rules of language," of course: rules of grammar, orthography, usage, and the like. And it may even be important at some point for one to learn these rules and to follow them as one speaks. But these rules of language, real as they are, do not reach all the way down, as I have put it. They do not, that is, provide some genuine *explanation* for the creative regularity in word use on which our linguistic community with one another ultimately depends. They are at best descriptions of what we (typically) do, not explanations of how and why we are able to do it.

The central difficulty with the agency of the rule as an explanation of language is that such an explanation leaves the efficacy of the rule itself utterly unexplained. Any rule—along with its associated interpretations, intentions, "mean-ings," etc.— simply hangs in the air, unable on its own to account for its apparent power to direct action in a determinate and regular fashion. Furthermore, in the absence of any public pattern of application, the very idea of *"the* rule we are following" becomes questionable, empty. *Which* rule? Any symbolic expression, anything that brings forth "the rule" that directs one, is open to an indefinite range of interpretations and specifications: which of these is "the rule" that grounds one's linguistic insights and practices?

Such considerations indicate that it is what Wittgenstein calls "the scene for our language-game" (sec. 179) that is the true power behind language and its rules. It is a particular set of circumstances, which themselves depend on certain "extremely general facts of nature" (*Philosophical Investigations*, p. 56n), that makes it possible for us to follow a given rule *as* a given rule in the first place. It is a particular context of *training* that gives the rule, the signpost (section 85), its power to govern us. At the root of that training is an *obedient imitation* that does not itself depend on our prior understanding of what is demanded of us. It is that capacity for obedience—that sensibility to command as such, along with the ability to respond to it appropriately— that is finally "the scene" for *any* of our language-games. The grammar of 'rule' is closely connected to that of 'training' and 'reaction'.

This grammatical insight leads to a second important recognition: the traditional philosophical rift between the vocabularies of "the mental" and "the physical" cannot be sustained, at least not in this instance. In spite of misleading grammatical appearances, the notion of conscious rule following (and thus of the rule per se) is not essentially "mental" at all. Insofar as one can be said to be following a rule in a particular case, that description of one's behavior is rooted *for its sense* in the manifestly "physical" circumstances of training and application just discussed. These circumstances are not just *evidence* for one's rule following (as if there were other, more direct, indications potentially available); they are *criterial* for that description *überhaupt*. That is, without them it would make no sense at all to characterize one's behavior in that paradigmatically "mental" way. The grammar of the "mental," that is, of the rule, is here not independent of the grammar of the "physical."

The grammatical connection just established is of wide import. In our philosophical tradition the disjunctions *mental/ physical* (or *mind/body*) and *rational/nonrational* have long taken in one another's dirty laundry. We have, for instance, used the former disjunctions as a kind of metaphysical explanation of the latter one, trying to account for the gap between rational and nonrational beings or abilities by reference to possession or lack of a particular "substance" or "quality." Thus to see, as we do now, that paradigmatically "mental" descriptions (like conscious rule following) cannot in fact be separated from those paradigmatically "physical" circumstances that give them their sense, is also to see that the "rational" cannot be cleanly separated from the "nonrational." Both disjunctions begin to lose their apparent exclusivity at the same time. To be rational, to be capable of recognizing and following the rule as such, *itself* ultimately depends not on some "mental" sort of insight but on our animal capacity for imitative obedience. Mind thus returns to its proper embodiment, to its proper earthiness. The "mental" and the "rational" begin to lose their aura of metaphysical privilege.

A third thing to be noted at this point concerns the representationalist account of language. My sketch in section 2 of the background to the *Philosophical Investigations* made clear that Wittgenstein's close attention there to rules of language was provoked by his own earlier reliance on them to save some form of the Tractarian picture theory. The syntactic rules that constitute the various "systems of propositions" in language—this is the view of the *Philosophical Remarks*—are also what make it possible for those propositions to refer to, that is, to represent, a determinate reality: "form" generates "meaning." Thus the collapse of the rule as the rational engine of language is also for Wittgenstein the collapse of the representationalist myth.

The philosophical connections between rules and representations are complex, and I will touch on only one by way of illustration. We have seen Wittgenstein insisting that the rule (or principle, or interpretation) is itself powerless to determine one's behavior, that the signpost points a specific way (that is, is a signpost at all) only in the context of a "scene" set by training and appropriate reaction. This recognition forces one to rethink the nature of semantic connections themselves. If what gives a linguistic rule its sense is "the scene for our language-game," then the real engine of language—what makes it go, what "connects" it to "reality"—is our practical *activity* in relation to one another, not our spectatorial contemplation of the facts as such. That is, the spectatorial attitude itself, the sense of the language-game of coolly noting and reporting "This is how things are" (sec. 134ff.), is not fundamental and self-given; that attitude is possible, that language-game has its sense, only because it is rooted in a "scene" that is *not* contemplative. Pure sight ("This is how things are") is grounded in blind obedience and a capacity for appropriate imitation; at bottom, then, "understanding" is not "insight."

The collapse of the "visual" or "contemplative" image of basic human "understanding"—that is, the recognition that our fundamental relationship to language (and thus to reality) is not one of "seeing how things are" but one of blind, imitative obedience to training—saps the philosophical strength of language-as-representation. The representationalist account was interesting to philosophers only insofar as it could claim to be fundamental, only insofar as it could claim that the representation of reality was the foundation on which all other uses of language (joke-telling, singing, cursing, giving orders, asking questions, etc.) must finally rest. The recognition that saying "This is how things are" is only one language-game among many, and that like every other language-game its sense is granted only by its practical "scene," turns a philosophical thesis ("Language depicts reality") into a truism. *Certainly* "language depicts reality." Only don't forget to pay attention to the particular circumstances—the "extremely general facts of nature"—that give sense to such a claim. The representing mind is not an autonomous "transparent eyeball" that floats free of earth; the representation of reality is not a practice liberated from the animal conditions that constrain and empower the other forms of human life. Once that is seen, once these Wittgensteinian grammatical reminders are perspicuously in place, then the representationalist account of language will have lost its power to charm. So the remarks on rule following are, as claimed in section 2 of this chapter, an essential moment in Wittgenstein's criticism of the metaphysical conception of language (and self) that dominates the *Tractatus* and the typescripts of the early 1930s.

So where are we left by these three points—the powerlessness of the rule per se; the emptiness of the mental/physical disjunction; the triviality of linguistic representationalism—that have emerged from Wittgenstein's discussion? What do we now say about our question of whether language can be represented as a set of rules to be followed by speakers? It would be misleading, I believe, to present Wittgenstein as entering a flat *no* to this query. He is not floating, in the bits and pieces of the *Philosophical Investigations*, some sort of transcendental argument against the possibility of such representation. After all, he is concerned in that book, as I pointed out in section 1, to show the *nonsense*, not the falsity, of traditional philosophical programs and positions. So he does not claim that, as a matter of fact or logic, one *cannot* represent language as a structure of rules; rather, he tries to indicate the *pointlessness* of trying to do so.

Whether or not such an abstract representation of language is actually possible to produce (it may or may not be: who can predict the limits of human ingenuity?), it is nevertheless *misleading* to try. It is misleading because such a representation must omit the conditions that would make it possible for those "rules" actually to *be* effective rules at all. The philosophical program of trying to represent language as a system of rules to be followed by speakers therefore leaves the real questions about language (and thus self) untouched. Those are questions about what it would take to turn an abstract representational recipe of that sort into a functioning language for recognizably human beings. They are, that is, questions about "the scene for our language-game" (sec. 179).

Thus the Wittgensteinian objection to such representations of language should not be seen as an attempt to set a transcendental limit to certain philosophical-*cum*-linguistic research programs (a program like AI, for instance, or "cognitive science"). There may be limits to such endeavors, but if there are, they will be the familiar empirical ones: at some point the material may finally prove recalcitrant, or "the pupil's capacity to learn may come to an end." The Wittgensteinian point is not to predict (or idly to hope for) such failures of science; the point is to try to get the philosopher to see that such programs, however successful, will not answer to the *philosophical* interests that helped to bring them forth. (Other sorts of interests, for example economic or military, may be perfectly satisfied by their success, of course.) That is because the philosophical interests at issue are always deeper than they appear and always less straightforwardly empirical.

In this case, as I have already mentioned, the deepest philosophical interest in the matter of language is the traditional query: Who are we really? Given our intellectual history, the philosophical scrutiny of language cannot fail to lead to questions about the nature of logic, of truth, and of rationality, and through the last to questions about what it means to be a distinctively human being at all. Philosophical questions about language thus always connect us, at whatever distance, back to the ethical and spiritual interests that led Socrates to abandon the cosmological speculations of the Ionians in favor of his search for rational and public self-knowledge. In the Western philosophical context, language is always an avatar of the self; and a particular philosophical conception of language always intimates, willy-nilly, a particular image of that self whose language it is supposed to be.

That is certainly true in the instance we have just been examining. The representation of language as a system of rules to be followed by speakers is not simply the founding assumption of a particular scientific research program; rather, it is a way of reinforcing the traditional Enlightenment picture of the self as an intrinsically free and rational being. Rules, as Wittgenstein realizes, are reasons. In our philosophical context a rule is understood to be a sort of "mental representation," complete in itself, of a determinate future course of actions, namely, the actions that "follow from" that rule. Further, to follow a rule is consciously and deliberately to let one's own actions be determined by it, to make (so far as possible) one's own behavior identical to the behavior that the rule by its nature specifies. Understood in this way, rules function as one's *reasons for acting.* Not only do they explain why one's pattern of behavior is what it is, but they explain it in such a way that the self's autonomy and power of sight are preserved all the way down.

How so? The rule, on this account, somehow contains within itself all the behavioral steps that are to be taken in accord with it; it is supposed to be, in Wittgenstein's image, a set of rails already laid to infinity (sec. 218). Thus, to "grasp" the meaning of the rule is at once to see all these steps, mentally to travel the whole length of the railroad. To be acting fully in accordance with some rule, therefore, is to be in a position to oversee completely the nature of the actions one is thereby undertaking to perform. One is not, so to speak, taking a leap into the dark, risking the possibility of a nasty surprise; rather, one is moving down a corridor of events well-lighted by the rule one is following.

In this way one's oversight of one's action seems assured. One knows just what one is doing (or trying to do). Insofar as one is a rule follower, there is no intrinsic limit to the self-knowledge of the nature of one's intended actions. The self's power of self-oversight in action thus seems to be indefinitely extendable. There is, of course, no guarantee that accidents will not happen. The train may be derailed by an earthquake or a flood. In various ways one's intentions may be shaken off their established tracks by a recalcitrant reality. But such happenstances, however terrible, do not indicate a necessary limit to one's self-transparency. They only show that the world is not correspondingly pellucid, and that sad truth is not a threat to the Enlightenment conception. All *that* requires is that the self can oversee its own projects all the way down: There are no *intrinsic* limitations on the knowledge of what one is doing (or trying to do). One's capacity for rational self-oversight extends throughout the whole of one's essential being.

So this philosophical conception of the rule buttresses the Enlightenment conception of the self as philosophically rational, that is, as fully self-transparent in regard to the nature of its intended actions. It does more than that as well, because it also strengthens the Enlightenment identification of self-knowledge with moral freedom and responsibility. If my reasons are rules, and if I can become fully aware of what those rules are and thus can "grasp" what actions they in themselves "contain," then— and *only* then—I can fully exercise my moral freedom in respect of those actions. I can, that is, fully and responsibly choose whether or not to undertake them; I can act autonomously rather than heteronomously.

If I don't really know what I am doing, then I am not fully doing it, according to the Enlightenment account. I am not fully free, fully responsible—i.e., fully autonomous—insofar as I am the prisoner of ignorance, especially ignorance of the true nature of my own undertakings. So autonomy, full self-determination, requires the kind of complete self-transparency furnished by this philosophical conception of the rule as reason. The rule, because its full "meaning" can become completely clear to me, can be in the fullest sense chosen or rejected, obeyed or disobeyed. In fact, it is only if I can see my actions *as* instances of some rule or other that I can recognize them for what they really are. Their "significance" as actions is generated by the rule that defines them. Insofar as I do consciously obey such a rule, then I am acting autonomously: I fully grasp the law (principle, rule) that my actions exemplify, thus fully understanding the significance of those actions, and I am therefore fully responsible for them. This philosophical conception of the rule thus simultaneously supports both pillars of the Enlightenment conception of the self: rational self-transparency and moral autonomy. And it is from this support, I believe, that our deepest philosophical interest in the rule-referenced conception of language derives.

The point here is a general one. Like Wittgenstein, we have been focusing our attention on language, and on whether or not it can be sensibly represented as a system of rules; but language is only one case—perhaps the clearest and most important case, to be sure—of a human practice claimed by philosophers to be so representable. The fundamental philosophical issue here is about that sort of representation. Can our lives sensibly be represented as sets of relatively self-contained epistemic and ethical practices, practices constituted by the rules (principles, laws) we follow (or try to follow) by engaging in them? Wittgenstein's attempt to undermine the plausibility of the rule-referenced conception of language is the thin end of the wedge: If it is successfully inserted, then grammatical reminders may be able to split the whole stone of rationality-as-representation.

As with his remarks on rules of language, Wittgenstein's aim is not to provide a knockdown transcendental argument against the philosophical idea in question. He does not want to claim that our behavior in epistemic and/or ethical contexts *cannot* be described in terms of some postulated rules that it aims to exemplify, that is, that such a form of self-description is either conceptually or empirically *closed* to us. (How could he claim *that*, after all? He knows neither the limits of human artifice nor the bounds of conceptual evolution.) Rather, it is a *misleading* sort of description, even if it could someday be carried through to our satisfaction. To represent our lives as composed of various practices constituted by rules to be followed is to overlook—perhaps quite deliberately—just what would make that sort of description sensible in the first place, namely, the brute, animal capacity for appropriately imitative reaction that grounds all rule following. The philosophical ideal of rationality-as-representation thus is, as Wittgenstein would put it, a paradigm case of philosophical nonsense, not falsity.

I stressed in the first section of this chapter that such a criticism is a very particular one. The Wittgensteinian charge of nonsense is the criticism of a certain form of intellectual practice from the standpoint of another form of such practice; in the final analysis it is the criticism of a certain kind of *character*, of a certain kind of *life*, that Wittgenstein has come to abhor: the kind of life and character that he associates with the practice of metaphysical philosophy itself. An important facet of the philosophical nonsense of rationality-as-representation is its peculiar form of self-forgetfulness: one might even say self-*denial* or self-*deception*. This characteristic self-deception, which shows itself clearly in the philosopher's systematic neglect of the empirical conditions for rule following, is a denial of the animal in favor of the godlike; it is an attempt to construe the human world on the grammatical models exploited by our traditional religious and metaphysical myths rather than on the images furnished by the more mundane parts of our grammar of self-knowledge.

Let me illustrate. I have been arguing that the final philosophical payoff of the rule-constituted conception of language is its support for the Enlightenment account of the self as being both wholly self-transparent and wholly self-determining. Since rules are (assumed to be) reasons, a thoroughly rule-constituted language is thoroughly rational as well: I have *reasons* for what I say when, reasons that (*qua* rules) are potentially subject to my scrutiny and my choice. Thus as an inhabitant of "the house of language," to use Heidegger's image, I am not (*pace* Nietzsche) a prisoner who cannot even trace the dimensions of his cell; on the contrary, by discovering and then either accepting or rejecting the various rules that constitute it, I can rebuild the structure along lines of my own liking, if I wish.

Clearly, the general philosophical ideal of rationality-as-representation is an even stronger support for this Enlightenment self-image of autonomous power. If the whole of my life can be represented as practices constituted by rules (principles, laws) that can—in principle—be scrutinized and chosen by me, then my whole life is (potentially) "rational." That is to say, my whole life is subject to my control through my self-knowledge. I can plumb my life's constitutive practices all the way down, seeing exactly which principles my actions exemplify; thereby I can make those actions wholly my *own*, through my subsequent acceptance or rejection of the principles (rules, laws) that generate them. I thus take possession of myself, of my life. I become, in principle at least, the self-possessed, free and equal rational being of philosophical myth.

This is to construe human life as constituted by a potentially godlike freedom. One's world, one's life, now is—in principle—one's own to create. At bottom, like a god, one is essentially *the will to self-creation*. (Strictly speaking, this last claim is the Romantic efflorescence of the self, building on the Enlightenment foundation of its rational autonomy.) Philosophical self-knowledge awakens the god within one, making possible its (i.e., one's) autonomous self-direction. It is no accident, of course, that these Enlightenment and Romantic conceptions grew up in a culture founded so deeply in the Jewish and Christian scriptures, scriptures in which a single divine will is pictured as the basis of all reality.

The nonsense of rationality-as-representation is the nonsense of the godlike self. It is, in the final analysis, the nonsense of the narcissistic identification of oneself with an independent, self-sustaining, world-representing center of will: the "godhead of the independent I," as Wittgenstein calls it in the *Notebooks 1914–1916* (p. 74). In this way, as in so many, the *Philosophical Investigations* can be understood only against the background of the thinking (and life) that produced the *Tractatus*, since the philosophical discovery (one might almost say philosophical *invention*) of the godlike self is the ethical point of the earlier book.[14] The Tractarian account of the nature of the proposition as world-representation, as a picture of reality, leads in that book to the discovery of the metaphysical self, the "limit of the world" (5.632) that is the necessary condition of any such representation. From there it is an easy path to the idea that this "godhead," this self-conscious will to world-representation that originally makes linguistic meaning by connecting names to simple objects, also makes, through its own self-created "attitude" (*Notebooks*, p. 87), the ethical meaning that the world as a whole has for the happy or unhappy human being (*Tractatus*,

14. See Edwards, *Ethics without Philosophy*.

6.43). The Tractarian metaphysical self is the ultimate narcis-
sist: utterly independent of the body and the world, both of
which it secretly fears and despises; safe from danger or destruction at the hands of another self; the maker of all meaning,
linguistic and ethical, by reference to itself. Such a self floats
free from the world it surveys and whose meaning it creates; it
is no longer subject to the animal requirements and vulnerabili-
ties that afflict those without proper self-knowledge. It has become a god.

One can characterize Wittgenstein's thinking (and life) as a
long struggle to take the measure of such narcissism, to discover its roots in our grammar, and then to set aside its claims
to philosophical and ethical hegemony. The remarks in the
Philosophical Investigations on rules must be seen as a part of
that effort. To undermine the rule-constituted conception of language (and thus to begin to call into question the ideal of rationality-as-representation itself) by reminding us of the brute
animal capacities, the earthy and bodily facts, which it systematically neglects but on which it utterly depends, is to begin to
return the self from its narcissistic self-forgetfulness. It is to
force us to remember those aspects of our grammar that put the
lie to any of our claims to be "the limit of the world." It is to remind us that whatever sense we make in language, and therefore whatever sense anything finally makes to us, cannot be
abstracted from the fact that we definitively and vulnerably
"belong to the world" (*Tractatus*, 5.632), that is, that we are
sensitive and fragile bodily creatures placed among other sensitive and fragile bodily creatures that we imitate both in love
and in fear for their power over us.

VII

In particular, a perspicuous presentation of our grammar, which
is just what Wittgenstein is trying to provide in his remarks
(*Philosophical Investigations*, sec. 122), will show us that the
godlike self of the philosophical tradition achieves its plausibility only through its systematic neglect of the empirical conditions of our grammar of selfhood per se. The recognition that no

rule is a self-contained, self-applying rational engine, that is, that no language-game floats free of those general facts of nature that give the game its identity and its grip on reality, forces us to recognize that the self is likewise neither a self-contained nor self-directing center of pure consciousness that floats free of the brute reality it surveys and orders. Just as the identity and the efficacy of the rules of our language-games are rooted in such facts of nature, so is the self rooted in material circumstances that it cannot control and perhaps cannot even see. This is not just to point out that the self's chosen projects may come to grief on the rocks of happenstance; even the most blissful Romantics knew that, of course. Rather, it is to recognize that the self *itself*—its identity as a single, self-identical center of consciousness and will—is not self-given; it depends on the cooperation of a world independent of and (initially at least) unknown to the self that it authorizes.

Wittgenstein's attempt to give a perspicuous presentation of our grammar of selfhood begins at section 243, and comprises what has come to be called the "private language argument," running at least through section 428. As its placement indicates, it should be seen as a continuation and development of the discussion of rule-following that concludes in sections 240–42. Here it will not be necessary to canvass all the twists and turns of his discussion; a single instance will be able to represent the whole. A central feature of the godlike self is the essential "privacy" of its experiences. Such privacy is much more than an epistemological claim ("Only I know exactly what I mean by 'pain' "); it is ultimately a claim about the autonomy of self-consciousness itself. It is the claim that the self's awareness of itself *as* a self is self-given; that self-consciousness is thoroughly and originally self-transparent, so that I—the self—can immediately know myself to *be* a self, and can therefore know (and personally name: hence epistemological privacy) the contents of the consciousness that I recognize myself to be. My access to myself qua self is thus independent of anything other than myself qua self. I am (qua self) not essentially a part of "the world" that lies "outside."

Many of the remarks of the "private language argument" attempt to show how such a view distorts the actual grammar of our self-consciousness. Look, for example, at the famous "diary case" of section 258. It is crucial to see that the statement of the case there presupposes the godlike autonomy of self-consciousness that Wittgenstein is aiming to undermine. Following the lead of section 256, in section 258 he presupposes the independence of any of the "contents" of self-consciousness (sensations, e.g.) from their natural expression in characteristic bodily movements or facial grimaces. The "diary case" assumes that such expressions are, from a first-person point of view, mere accidents of human physiology and socialization, that is, that they are inessential both to the existence and to the particular identity of the sensations themselves. Here is the way he puts it: "—But suppose I didn't have any natural expression for the sensation, but only had the sensation" (sec. 256). This is to suppose that the reality and the identity of the particular sensation qua particular sensation is dependent upon nothing outside the self-consciousness whose sensation it is; it is to suppose that pure self-consciousness unhooked from any natural physical expression—the essentially disembodied "I" postulated in section 256— is capable of recognizing its constitutive "contents" without any essential reference beyond that self-consciousness alone. Even more, it is to suppose that such a self-consciousness could immediately know *itself as such*, could recognize itself as an "I" having such sensations in the first place.

This is to picture the self as if it were a being capable of knowing itself as such, immediately and in complete independence from everything else: a god who thus creates itself *as* itself through such unmediated self-awareness. All this, then, is the philosophical backdrop to the case described in section 258. The question immediately arises: What would our grammar of sensation-language have to be like in order to accommodate itself to this metaphysical picture of the self? How, for example, would a given sensation get its name in such a case? Well, the self would simply assign a name—a purely conventional verbal designation—to the sensation immediately present to its view: "And now I simply *associate* names with sensations and use these names in descriptions.—" (sec. 256).

Does such a sensation-grammar make sense? Imagine, as in section 258, that I—the godlike self of immediately given self-consciousness—want to keep a diary noting the recurrence of a certain sensation. When the sensation first occurs I write down 'S' in my diary, intending 'S' to be the sign, the name, of the sensation whose frequency I wish to track. 'S' is a purely personal and conventional designation, of course; whatever meaning it has as a sensation-name will have to be given it by me— the essentially disembodied I—as the result of an act of individual will within my self-consciousness alone. "But I speak, or write the sign down, and at the same time I concentrate my attention on the sensation—and so, as it were, point to it inwardly" (sec. 258). Thus I give myself a kind of private ostensive definition of 'S'. I attach a meaning to the sign through the willful direction of my self-consciousness, simultaneously focusing on 'S' and its "object," thus linking the two together in my memory. So that after that initial act of association, I can use 'S' in my diary as the name of a particular sensation.

Notice that such a procedure of private definition is an absolute necessity, given the philosophical picture of the godlike self assumed here. Not only would some such method of association be the only way to establish the meanings of the sensation-names to be used in one's everyday communication with others (presuming, as seems doubtful, that there *could be* such communication between such selves); but also, and much more important, some procedure of this sort would be necessary to the possibility of self-consciousness itself. The point of the "diary case" is not just to point out the peculiar (and, as it turns out, epistemologically disastrous) grammar of sensation-language, given this picture of the self; it is to raise questions about the coherence of that picture per se. Since the Wittgensteinian moves are fairly subtle, I will need to go slowly in tracing them.

To be a self at all is to be able to recognize oneself as, and to be recognized by others as, continuous with oneself over a certain stretch of time. I don't exist just as, or just in, the present moment; I am, for example, conscious of myself as the one who had such-and-such a pain (or hope, or belief, or intention, or fear) at such-and-such a time in the past. Or I know myself to be the one who (*ceteris paribus*) will be in South Carolina next fall. The self is extended beyond the "here" and "now" in both memory and expectation, my own and others. (These are, it should be noted, neither remarks on the phenomenology of human experience nor controversial philosophical claims about the criteria for personal identity; they are merely reminders of a part of our everyday grammar of selfhood, of how we use words like 'I' and 'she' in our ordinary descriptions: as when we say "I hurt like the devil last weekend," or "I'll see you there in October," or "She will be there too.")

So, self-identity requires consciousness of one's identity through time. Now, how is such identity to be established in the purely first-person case? (Remember: because of the godlike self-givenness of the self-consciousness that is being presupposed and criticized here, such identity would *have* to be able to be established in the first person, by the pure "I." That is just what the claim of self-givenness comes to: the power of the self to know itself *as* a self wholly *through* itself.) To establish such identity, that is, such self-continuity, in the purely first-person case would require at least a continuity of individual memory about what "I" have felt, thought, seen, hoped for, feared, and the like. After all, if self-consciousness is somehow self-given, as claimed here, then one can't be forced to establish a proper self-continuity through appeal to something *outside* pure self-consciousness, like the continuity of my body or the continuity of the memories of others.

Therefore, in this account one can be conscious of being a self only because one can remember, for example, that one had this same sort of headache yesterday, or (more to the point) because one can remember that there was pain "here" two minutes, or two seconds, ago. Only the connections of memory could provide, in the pure first-person case, the temporal self-continuity that minimal self-identity demands. To be a self-given self at all, one needs to be able to recall *something* about what was happening "here" in the past (even if just the very recent past) and then to be able to connect that in memory, by way of sameness or of difference, with what is happening "here" now. Since this is so, then the recognition of certain (for example) sensations as *the same as*, or *not*, the sensations felt "here" earlier, is necessary to one's recognition of oneself *as a self*. Indeed, only if one can constantly keep the sort of internal "diary" hypothesized in section 258 can one sensibly be said to be a self at all in this case. The self-given "I" must establish its continuous self-identity through its recall of the identity (or difference) of the "objects" (like S) that appear to it.

So, establishing the meaning of 'S', and thus establishing the possibility of, for example, remembering having had S yesterday, is a necessary condition of self-given selfhood. Could the godlike "I" postulated for section 258 establish for itself the meaning of 'S'? No, says Wittgenstein. The meaning of 'S' would be established only if the sign is hooked to the "object" in such a way that it really becomes the sign of *that* "object." This means that there must be some difference between its *correct* use (viz., 'S' as the sign for S) and its *incorrect* use (e.g., 'S' as the sign for R, where $R \neq S$). Could that difference be established in the present case, when the meaning of 'S' is supposed to be fixed solely by a willful act of focusing one's attention? No.

> A definition surely serves to establish the meaning of
> a sign.—Well, that is done precisely by the concentration
> of my attention; for in this way I impress on myself the
> connection between the sign and the sensation.—But "I
> impress it on myself" can only mean: this process brings
> it about that I remember the connection *right* in the fu-
> ture. But in the present case I have no criterion of cor-
> rectness. One would like to say: whatever is going to
> seem right to me is right. And that only means that here
> we can't talk about 'right'. (Sec. 258)

Unless memory is supposed a priori to be infallible, which means that one has stopped talking about human *memory* altogether, the difference between correct and incorrect uses of 'S' collapses. There is no way for such a first-person procedure to reidentify S as the same as (or as different from) what was "here" before. And therefore, because in the purely first-person case self-identity could *only* be established through the recall of the identity (or difference) of the "private objects" of consciousness, there is no sense here in the claim of self-identity at all.

Like the discussion of rule following that precedes it, Wittgenstein's remarks on "private language" are intended to remind one of the "scene for our language-game" (sec. 179). Just as the possibility of following a given rule of arithmetic depends on, for example, one's brute capacity for successfully imitating one's teachers in forming the numerals, so too the possibility of attaching names to sensations depends on the fact that those sensations have "natural expressions" (*naturliche Äußerungen*) in movement and physiognomy. It is that "natural" connection—our "natural" incarnation, one might say—that allows for the possibility of checking and correcting first-person memories against something outside pure self-consciousness, thus allowing us to make a distinction between correct and incorrect uses of a name like 'S'. No language-games, therefore, not even those that involve the most intimate forms of self-awareness, float free of those "extremely general facts of nature" (*Philosophical Investigations*, p. 56) that grant them their sense.

And that means that the self, the self that I in fact am, does not float free of those facts either. My self-consciousness is not immediately self-given; rather, it depends for its very possibility on the satisfaction of certain empirical conditions utterly beyond my control. One of these conditions is my embodiment, of course. Another is the immediate, unlearned presence of the "natural expressions" of sensations. And a third has to do with the fact that I am, early on, surrounded by *other* such bodily creatures as I am, with a certain set of attitudes (*Philosophical Investigations*, p. 178) toward the feelings naturally manifested in my *Äußerungen*. All these features of "the scene for our language-game" help me to see that I am not "the limit of the world," but inescapably a *part* of it. I am not the self-given "godhead of the independent I."

The self-given self is a nonsensical notion, then. Not only would it lead to terrible epistemological consequences (namely, all the familiar theoretical and practical difficulties of solipsism), it also undercuts its own ordinary empirical conditions of possibility. Wittgenstein's remarks in section 258 show one the full cost of the philosophical picture of such self-givenness, namely, that one must suppose one's memory to be (in certain respects, at least) infallible, so that one's self-identity can be founded on it. And that is a *nonsensical* supposition for us, not just a false one. True, the claim of such infallibility does not square with our ordinary grammar of memory, and in that sense it is false to us, false to the lives we ordinarily live. And this falsity shows that, in the ordinary run of things, self-identity cannot be self-given through first-person recall alone. But does this show that self-given selfhood is a flatly incoherent notion? Is this some sort of transcendental argument against the very possibility of the godlike self?

To answer *yes* would be to misunderstand the force of *nonsense* in Wittgenstein's vocabulary of self-criticism.

> 499. To say 'This combination of words makes no sense' excludes it from the sphere of language and thereby bounds the domain of language. But when one draws a boundary it may be for various kinds of reason. If I surround an area with a fence or a line or otherwise, the purpose may be to prevent someone from getting in or out; but it may also be part of a game and the players are supposed, say, to jump over the boundary; or it may show where the property of one man ends and that of another begins; and so on. So if I draw a boundary line that is not yet to say what I am drawing it for.
> 500. When a sentence is called senseless, it is not as it were its sense that is senseless. But a combination of words is being excluded from the language, withdrawn from circulation.

To speak of a philosophical view as nonsense is not to claim it to be somehow literally inconceivable ("its sense that is senseless"); rather it is to claim it to be out of bounds *for us*. 'Nonsense' is, as I have said, a term used for the criticism of a form of life, from the perspective of another form of life. The limits of sense are set by a grammar, and a grammar is not written in the stars: it reflects a way of life. *Our* way of life, in the case described in section 258, is such that "here we can't talk about 'right'." Our grammar, our life, is such that it makes no sense for us to say right or wrong only by reference to uncheckable first-person memory.

Could there be, then, *another* form of life: one in which the self approached true self-givenness; in which someone's memory was increasingly assumed by him or her to be infallible; in which one's own perfectly "remembered," perfectly self-constituted history of sensation and desire becomes more and more the standard by reference to which the world's whole present and future are imagined? We should not be too quick to say *no*, especially when we reflect on the ways our own lives are already beset by temptations to such grandiose narcissism.

The philosopher is the one who must cure himself of many sicknesses of the understanding before he can arrive at the notion of the sound human understanding.

If in the midst of life we are in death, so in sanity we are surrounded by madness.[15]

The hope of pointing out the nonsense of such narcissism is to recall to us the very different grammar of our common life, a grammar as yet only incompletely obscured by the fantasies of metaphysical philosophy. Wittgenstein is trying to get us to see exactly what form of life is here being exalted by this philosophical picture of the self-given, self-transparent, autonomous self. Once that form of life is fully seen, and once a perspicuous presentation of our grammar has shown what support it does or doesn't have there, then the *philosopher's* job in respect of that life is over. Or at least it radically changes character, for now comes a kind of ethical or spiritual criticism of that way of living and thinking. Nonsense is not *impossible* to think and to live, of course; the necessity to reject it is not, in the final instance, an *intellectual* necessity. The sound human understanding after which Wittgenstein hungers, and in terms of which all his thinking is referenced, is not a prize guaranteed to those who spend their lives thinking about it, no matter how patient and acute their thinking is. That insight—coming at the right time, which can never be guaranteed, of course—can be another reminder of the limits of philosophy and of the self it encourages us to love.

VIII

In this chapter I have looked at two prominent themes of the *Philosophical Investigations*, the discussion of rule following and the "private language argument." Their deepest common

15. Ludwig Wittgenstein, *Remarks on the Foundations of Mathematics*, p. 157.

thread is an attempt to mitigate the charms of a particular metaphysical picture of the self. That picture, which came into flower in the European Enlightenment and which still provides the basis for a good deal of our self-reflection (including in its ambit books as different as *Being and Nothingness* and the *Tractatus Logico-Philosophicus*), emphasizes the essential independence of the self from the material and social world it inhabits: the metaphysical self is self-given, self-transparent, autonomous in action, essentially self-creating. It thus approaches the traditional status of a god, gazing *sub specie aeternitatis* at the world that stands over against it. Nothing can touch it, unless it allows; it sustains itself only by appeal to its own will, which appears in various disguises: infallible memory, omnipotent intention, limitless rationalization, the self-applying rule—all the avatars of the self-interpreting self. And with this picture of the self comes a form of life, a certain kind of narcissistic privacy in intellectual and moral activity: the collapse of the common world into a hypothetical contractual agreement on first principles, epistemological and ethical; the slide of language into various discrete "vocabularies"; the analytical disintegration of all wholes into constituencies of atoms, on the assumption that whatever wholes there are—intellectual or social—exist as such only through the will of some self or other.

We have seen Wittgenstein trying to undermine this picture of the self, and therefore its correlative form of life as well, by reminding us of the ways in which they systematically ignore the material and social conditions they actually presuppose. The rationalist conception of rules and rule following, for example, conveniently forgets the ways in which the very possibilities of identifying and following any particular rule depend on certain "extremely general facts of nature," like our capacity and desire for imitating another's behavior. And in the "private language argument" we see Wittgenstein trying to illustrate the nonsense involved in any claim that the self-given "I" originates those regularities of usage that are the bedrock of any of our language-games. So the "I" cannot, without such nonsense as he has identified, be the hoped-for center of "sufficient reason" at the bottom of our language and life.

These grammatical reminders, even granting their efficacy,

certainly do not add up to a Wittgensteinian "philosophy of language," much less to a full-fledged Weltanschauung. (Either would be, in this day and age, the "trick of a cheat.")[16] Nevertheless, they are not devoid of significant implication. In particular, they seem to have interesting and important things to say about the source of linguistic authority, about the basis for our typical agreement about what to say when, and thus about the nature and source of authority *tout court*. By way of conclusion, it is time to return to these matters. Specifically it is time to return to the philosophical fantasy of the wholesale collapse of authority—what I have called the threat of philosophical nihilism—in order to see what Wittgenstein's response to it would be. This will return us as well to some important matters left hanging fire at the end of chapter 2, matters having to do with the moral and political dangers attendant on abandoning the metaphysical self of the Enlightenment tradition. We must see, that is, whether Wittgenstein's appeal to the sound human understanding lacks the whiff of incipient totalitarianism that arises from Heidegger's rhetorical obeisance to the primordially speaking *Logos*.

16. See the preface to *Philosophical Remarks*.

4

Language and Its Authority

I began this essay by sketching the philosophical fantasy of a wholesale collapse of epistemic and ethical authority. Building upon the familiar experience of objective self-correction, the Socratic recognition that some of our habitual actions and beliefs may exemplify principles of conduct and of evidence that would not survive our full self-consciousness of them, I tried to imagine a situation that extended such self-inflicted disenchantment to its limit: a situation in which iterated philosophical reflection caused *all* one's most basic epistemic and ethical principles to appear objectionable in some way or other, thus leaving one condemned either to intellectual and moral paralysis or to galloping bad faith. Such a collapse, were it ever to occur, could properly by called *philosophical nihilism*, since by its origin in pure reflection it could be distinguished from the more common kinds of pervasive despair or unscrupulousness, also often called 'nihilism', that are produced by disease, injury, or vice. Philosophical nihilism would be, apparently, a nihilism intrinsic to the unimpeded course of reflection itself: the irony of the self-consuming intellect. Modern philosophical rationality is haunted by fantasies of self-destruction.

But of course this potential collapse *is* just a fantasy, and philosophical nihilism is therefore just a threat to us, not a reality. The question is: Is it a threat worth taking seriously? Is there something incoherent about the nihilist fantasy in the first place, so that we can dismiss it out of hand? And if not, what is it in the practice of contemporary philosophical reflection—in our contemporary philosophical lives—that makes us vulnerable to such fears? Can we take the measure of philosophical nihilism in such a way as to both locate the source of our fascination with it and then pass judgment on its sense? These are the questions that have set the background for my discussion of Heidegger and Wittgenstein. It is now time to see what, if anything, I can say in answer to them.

I

In chapter 1, I argued that a crucial ingredient in the fantasy of philosophical nihilism is a characteristic way of representing human activities when those activities are taken as the matter for sustained philosophical reflection. Modern philosophy has typically assumed that a given form of human life—later twentieth-century bourgeois liberalism, for example—should be seen as a set of various ethical and epistemic *social practices*, that is, definite (though not of course mechanically rigid) routines of thought and behavior that are taken more or less for granted by those who live according to them. Such philosophy has further assumed that these practices are given their specific configuration and identity by the particular *rules* (laws, principles) of thought and/or action that they exemplify. The identity of an individual action per se is always to be characterized by reference to its belonging to some relatively well defined social practice, in this view. A social practice is to be analyzed in terms of the rules governing the actions that properly belong to it.

Thus the nature and significance of an individual human action can always be determined by its relation to some normative practical rule. Whether exemplified or defied, the *rule* becomes the touchstone of an action's meaning and value *qua* action. The rule thus becomes the fundamental explanatory concept used in characterizing distinctively human, that is, *rational*, action itself; hence it becomes the mark of rationality *tout court*. To put it summarily, in this view a human social practice can be represented as a *pattern of normative rules for action*, and the (relatively rare) individual who is reflectively and self-consciously attempting to participate in a given practice—the ethical practice of democratic social justice, say—is thereby trying to conform his or her behavior to the rules that have been discovered ideally to constitute that practice.

This characterization is, of course, very rough-and-ready, leaving all sorts of interesting theoretical questions unanswered, like what exactly a rule is, or how specific social practices are to be individuated; but such vagueness is no real objection, since the original idea did not need to be very rigorously formulated in order to exercise tremendous philosophical influence. It was never much more than a *picture*, to use the apt Wittgensteinian term, but it was a picture that seemed to confirm itself everywhere the post-Cartesian philosopher looked. It was a picture that seemed to incorporate simultaneously a concrete research program, a recovery of philosophical tradition, and a moral and political advance. It seemed to offer a new and "scientific" way of making sense of the traditional critical task of reflective intellect—namely, to discover the rules that constitute a given epistemic or ethical practice, thereby furnishing an objective matter for Socratic scrutiny and criticism—while at the same time this form of representation secured the philosopher's rational freedom from the practice in question, thus making possible its deliberate reform or replacement. The picture seemed, indeed, to offer an unprecedentedly clear image of what philosophical rationality (and thus philosophical freedom) *is*: it is to achieve an objective view of a form of life (perhaps even one's own) by representing it as a structure of rules (laws, principles) to be followed by those whose form of life it is.

The philosophical view *sub specie aeternitatis*, the distinctively metaphysical gaze, has now come to be understood as this rule-constituted representation of human thought and behavior. For modern philosophy, philosophical rationality *is* representation-as-rule; and such representation *is* freedom, since once a form of life has been so represented, then it is possible either to accept or reject it. A rule once recognized may be either followed or ignored, and a law once revealed may be either obeyed or disobeyed; so this sort of representation gives the self the freedom to choose the life it wants to have. To represent a practice as a pattern of rules is thus a way of giving sense both to the Socratic idea that objective philosophical reflection on human life is possible and to the Kantian idea that such reflection, such self-consciousness, is true moral freedom in respect of that life.

Thus we can see that this sort of representation goes hand-in-glove with a particular conception of the self, one that I have been calling (loosely, to be sure, but traditionally) the *Enlightenment* conception. The phrase abbreviates a number of philosophical convictions, but chief among them is the idea of the self as a center of *autonomous yet rational will.* There is a powerful internal tension in this idea, of course. With respect to the fundamental ethical and intellectual character of its life, the Enlightenment self is assumed to be essentially *responsible,* and therefore essentially *free,* not a leaf blown helplessly before the wind; only such metaphysical freedom could guarantee full moral responsibility. At the same time, I am aware of myself as a (potentially) *rational* being. My freedom to act and to judge is not chaotic; it is not pure spontaneity: at its best it shows an orderliness that approaches the order of nature itself. So how are both freedom of will and rational determination to be metaphysically represented as belonging to the same being? In what way can I make coherent sense of my felt power of orderly moral and intellectual self-direction?

At this point, the rule-constituted representation of human life seems to hold the key. If my life can be represented by me as a set of social practices analyzable as rules to be followed in thought and action, then my life is subject both to objective orderly characterization and to my undetermined choice. Philosophical rationality and philosophical freedom coincide on this account, since the analytical and objective representation of myself as a rule follower at the same time gives me the freedom to refuse the rules thus revealed. I am, apparently, provided with a form of self-description that does justice both to my sense of myself as rationally ordered (namely, I am following some determinate rule of thought or action, rather than simply bouncing from movement to movement, or from judgment to judgment) and to my sense of myself as morally free (namely, I am, once I recognize myself to be a rule follower, also free *not* to follow the rules hitherto in operation). Like the rest of nature, I am subject to laws governing my actions; unlike the bricks and the brutes, however, I am free to choose these laws for myself. The vocabulary of rules and rule following is an attempt to do justice both to the objective and to the subjective qualities of human self-awareness. This vocabulary seems to offer the possibility of thorough and objective self-scrutiny, thus creating a field for the genuine "human sciences"; but it does so with no corresponding diminution of individual moral responsibility, thus preserving ethical life against any scientific reduction. No wonder the appeal of this characteristically modern account has been so strong.

So, rationality-as-representation strengthens the Enlightenment conception of the self. The apparent successes philosophers have had in representing some important ethical and epistemic practices as constituted by rules to be followed (as principles to be exemplified, as laws to be obeyed)—think of Descartes and Rawls, touched on in chapter 1—have encouraged them to accept the picture of the self as a center of fully autonomous will, rationally deliberating on all its courses of action and judgment. This is not to suggest, of course, that either rationality-as-representation or the Enlightenment conception is *foundational* for the other. Rather, they offer mutual support; they belong together as important parts of the whole form of life that shapes so much of our contemporary civilization. The apparent plausibility of some rule-constituted representations of our social practices (for example, Rawls's theory of justice) buttresses our moral and political ideal of rational autonomy, while at the same time our deep conviction of our rational autonomy assures us—often in the teeth of the evidence—that more such rule-based representations of our lives are on the way. The two views do one another's dirty laundry quite well. Moreover, they set the stage for the nihilist fantasy.

In its most radical (and therefore its most interesting) forms, philosophical nihilism requires one to occupy both the philosophical standpoint of objective scrutiny of one's life and the more usual standpoint of subjective engagement within it. The classical nihilist fantasy intends a situation in which repeated philosophical reflection reveals apparently irremediable difficulties with all the epistemic and ethical practices open to one. Thus it requires that one stand apart from those practices, that one view them as so many *possibilities* for a human life, possibilities apparently open to crushing philosophical objection. That is the objective moment of nihilism. Its subjective moment is the recognition that one must nevertheless act in relation to those practices, that one must choose either to accept them, to reform them somehow, or to reject them. One must either live, or lie down to die; and in either case one will—it seems—be exercising one's individual choice in relation to the only options open to one, namely, those social practices revealed by one's objective reflection.

Thus, in trying to take the measure of philosophical nihilism it is important to examine more closely the sort of objectivity it requires; to examine it not only for its own sake, but also because, as we have seen, that postulated objectivity plays directly into the sort of subjectivity associated with Enlightenment conceptions of individual autonomy. Neither idea stands alone: each needs the other to define it by way of contrast; and philosophical qualms about objectivity are sure eventually to extend to doubts about subjectivity as well.

So, what is the key to achieving the philosophical objectivity required by the nihilist fantasy? What is the nature of the "*vorstellendes Denken*" that could objectively reveal to me my life's rational strengths and weaknesses? It is just here that rationality-as-representation commends itself to us so strongly, since the representation of the forms of human life as social practices constituted by rules to be followed, offers just the sort of objectifying distance and clarity that is wanted by the philosophical critic. Such representation seems a particularly perspicuous way of defining our practices so as to make their essential features available for straightforward identification and evaluation. Perhaps there are other forms of philosophical objectivity, other ways of instantiating the metaphysical gaze *sub specie aeternitatis*; but in respect to Western philosophy after Descartes and Kant, rationality-as-representation has fair claim, I believe, to be first among equals in this regard. It is certainly the metaphysical picture of objectivity that lurks beneath so many of our modern philosophical texts and techniques.

The question about philosophical nihilism thus becomes for us, at least at first, the question about such representation. Does it make sense? Can it be done? And such questions must focus on language, because the epistemic and ethical practices of human beings are all essentially linguistic ones. Language is not an adjunct to a distinctively human life, a handy tool we might have had to do without. At bottom all our games are language-games. Language is not a *medium* for our lives and practices; rather, it is the stuff of human life itself, the thread out of which all our patterns of thought and action are woven. Unless language can itself be represented as a social practice constituted by rules to be followed, then it seems extremely unlikely, if not impossible, that the philosophical program of rationality-as-representation can be carried through. If language cannot be represented as rules "all the way down," then neither can a distinctively human life.

And can language be so represented? That is the question I have put to both later Heidegger and later Wittgenstein, as a way of trying to engage them in conversation on the threat of philosophical nihilism. Curiously, neither is inclined to answer with a direct *no*, though both are clearly antipathetic to rationality-as-representation as a philosophical program. Both certainly distrust—indeed, despise—the idea that human beings can objectify language, and can thus falsify their own relationship to language, in this fashion; both want to demonstrate the "subjection" of the self to language, rather than the reverse. Yet neither tries to do this by engaging *"vorstellendes Denken"* head on, trying somehow to demonstrate its inadequacy to its programmatic claims; to do so would be to fight the battle on the enemy's own field: to try to use philosophy to transcend philosophy, which is hopeless.

Heidegger's response, as we have seen, is to attack rationality-as-representation by attacking the relationship of language and self that it presupposes. To be able to represent language as a system of rules "all the way down," as this program aims to do, is to be able to make language an "object" for a human being; it is to put the human being in an external and superior position in relation to language, to make language completely subject to the scrutiny (and presumably thus the *control*) of the reflective human being whose "object" it is. Language thus becomes understood as a verbal tool of human beings: as a technique of representation (Locke, Descartes) or as a "means of expression" (Nietzsche). According to this view, human beings speak their various natural languages in order to define, to communicate, and to accomplish their own human purposes.

In stark contrast, Heidegger asserts that *die Sprache spricht.*

Language is not *ours* to define and to use: on the contrary, we belong to language. Human beings do not first speak, and do so in service of their ends; rather, *language* speaks, and we speak only in response to that primordial speaking. Since language is, in Heidegger's image, the house of Being, and therefore the house of our being as well, we cannot step outside language to represent it as an object, as a system of rules, for example. Language—now recognized to be the all-encompassing *Logos* to which the pre-Socratics testified—creates and sustains us, not vice versa. For Heraclitus, '*Logos*' was the word that revealed the Being of beings itself. So understood, language can never be truly "represented." We are not the kind of beings who could ever make language—that is, the Being of beings—our object. A human being cannot be the independent, self-sustaining metaphysical "subject" (*hypokeimenon*) such "objectivity" would require. Indeed, *no* mere being could be such a subject; one cannot objectify the condition of all objectivity.

To recognize that *die Sprache spricht* is to have an experience of language (and thus of world, thing, and self) that makes the philosophical program of rationality-as-representation seem ludicrous, because it is an experience that destroys the plausibility and charm of the metaphysical "humanism" that goes with that program hand-in-glove. Heidegger's reflections on language are an attempt to recall to us an earlier and (in his view) deeper form of self-consciousness, one in which the differing, appropriating *Logos*—not the human being—is at the originating center of things. In this view, all our "representations," however "correct," are "sendings" of the *Logos*, and as such cannot be identified with the truth of the *Logos* that "sent" them. To construe a natural language as a formal structure of rules to be followed by speakers is not technologically impossible, perhaps, but it is the height of absurdity to take such a "representation" as the essential truth of language itself. That would be strictly analogous to the absurdity of identifying a particular being, no matter how powerful and magnificent, with the Being of beings per se.

Rationality-as-representation properly belongs, according to Heidegger, to the age of ego-subjectivity, reaching from Descartes through Kant and beyond; its "humanism" locates final authority in the individual human being, whether understood as the epistemologically secure but bare self-consciousness revealed by the *cogito* or as the more substantial noumenal self required by one's dual experience of the starry heavens without and the moral law within. To acknowledge that *die Sprache spricht*, however, is to recognize that all authority is located in the *Logos*; *it* speaks, even in our responsive speaking, and thus in all our speaking we obey it, blindly. We speak only because we are spoken to, and the words we have to speak are only the words we have been given. Thus Heidegger's experience of language as the pre-Socratic *Logos* runs fundamentally counter to the Enlightenment ideal of the autonomous self: that free and rational human being who defines and determines for himself or herself the principles that his or her thought and action will follow. In Heidegger's account, such an ideal of fundamental self-determination, that is, self-obedience, could at best be self-deception; at worst it is an erroneous and prideful defiance of one's true condition as the essentially passive interlocutor of the *Logos*.

As will be clear on a moment's reflection, this experience of language utterly removes the threat of philosophical nihilism. Not only could there be no objective representation of the language/*Logos* that is one's original place of being, but there is also no possibility that one could find rational fault with all one's practices in the way the nihilist fantasy requires. To acknowledge oneself as the creature of *Logos* is, quite clearly, to surrender to its authority; better, it is to recognize that one's own authority as an individual directly descends from the prior authority of *Logos* itself, so there is simply no possibility that one could on one's own, so to speak, find *that* authority to be objectively compromised. One has, as it were, no independent place to stand to make such a judgment. There is no place outside the house of Being from which the details of its architecture can be criticized. There is, to put it most sharply, no *self* for one to be other than the one that *Logos* "sends." At some point, one has no recourse but to accept that self—i.e., that set of epistemic and ethical practices, that language—and live it to the fullest.

As I pointed out at the end of chapter 2, however, this sort of deconstruction of the Enlightenment self in favor of the Heraclitean *Logos* may have ethical and political consequences of the most unappealing kind. It flirts not just with historicism but with a kind of historical totalitarianism. The autonomous individual threatens to disappear completely into the *Logos* revealed in the various ethical and epistemic "sendings" of a particular time and place. There is apparently no secure vantage, no "original position," from which radical criticism of those "sendings" can be mounted. And this in turn threatens, not philosophical nihilism exactly, but another kind of despair—or another kind of boundless enthusiasm. It risks either an apathetic or a rabid *submission* to one's present arrangements and convictions: a total identification of oneself with them and their progeny, for good or for ill; an identification that may be either *resigned*, because one recognizes the futility of resistance (Nietzsche's "pessimism of weakness"), or *wholehearted*, because one sees the silliness of crying over eternally spilt milk (the "pessimism of strength"). Either way, the result is disturbing. Heidegger's experience of language seems to have laid to rest the ghost of philosophical nihilism, all right, but only at the cost of raising another sort of spook in its place.

II

At first glance, Wittgenstein seems to do no better. He too attacks rationality-as-representation and its correlative, the Enlightenment self; and like Heidegger's, his attacks are indirect, and his arguments nontranscendental. As we have seen, his basic claim is not that language *cannot* be represented as a rule-constituted social practice, but that any such representation, however comprehensive, must omit from its view those empirical conditions—those "extremely general facts of nature"— that are necessary to give any rule the sense that it has. Such a rule-based representation of language is not *false*, only *partial*, and thus perhaps misleading.

Language may be no more than rules, he thinks, but rules are more than their representations. No rule interprets or applies itself; it is only in terms of a certain "background," so to speak— a background that ultimately is not another rule (for what would then interpret or apply *it*?) but a "fact"—that the rule can be followed at all, that is, that it can have a definite sense. Only against a given "background" is a rule a *particular* rule, that is, is it a *rule* at all. Rationality-as-representation ignores this essential "background" to our social practices; or, rather, it surreptitiously identifies that background as the *self*. It assumes that the application or the interpretation—that is, the sense—of a particular rule is given it by the individual self in whose consciousness it originates: that this sense is essentially "private" (as is, therefore, the practice that the rule defines). In this way, one can see again the deep connection of rationality-as-representation to the Enlightenment self. If social practices are to be construed as patterns of rules to be followed, then the autonomous individual self is apparently necessary as the source, through interpretation and application, of what those rules actually mean. It is on the self-given, "private" authority of that self that all social, "public" meaning ultimately rests, since it is the self that creates ("gives meaning to") the social practices that constitute the world. "The world is *my* world: this is manifest in the fact that the limits of language (of that language which alone I understand) mean the limits of *my* world" (*Tractatus* 5.62).

The point of the so-called private language argument is, as we have seen, to show that the self, understood as an individual center of autonomous consciousness and will, cannot be the essential "background" for the rules of language, and thus cannot be—*pace* the *Tractatus*—the source of the world's meaning. In the *Investigations* the world is not *my* world, either linguistically or ethically. That is because I am not (by nature) the self-given self—the "limit of the world"—that I would have to be in order to make it mine in that way. I am not, according to Wittgenstein, forced by the ordinary grammar of my self-knowledge to conceive myself as the transcendental subject, that is, as an autonomous atom of will and consciousness that constructs for itself a language and a life. On the contrary, a perspicuous presentation of that grammar indicates a "background" for our social practices, and especially language, that is not such an atomistic, transcendental self at all. In Wittgenstein's presentation the individual self shows itself to be the grammatical precipitate of a particular form of language and of life, not the other way round.

In this way, Wittgenstein, like Heidegger, is attacking the Enlightenment picture of the self, and in particular is attacking what in chapter 1 I called *moral rationality*: the philosophical and ethical ideal that identifies the moral life as action undertaken in accordance with rules (laws, principles) that one has chosen entirely on one's own. If that attack is successful, then Wittgenstein too has shown the threat of philosophical nihilism to be an empty one. If the Enlightenment self is a grammatical fiction, as he seems to be claiming, then there is no possibility that one (*who?*) could stand outside all one's language-games in order to pass judgment on them. The objectifying distance between oneself and one's life, an estrangement absolutely necessary to the classical nihilist fantasy, would now be seen to be illusory. One *is* one's life, in a very real way; one's self-consciousness is given one *by* that life and cannot be wholly detached from it. Just as the language-game cannot be separated from the factual "scene" that gives it its sense and power, so too the self—a particular self-consciousness—cannot be separated from its "scene" of particular language-games, of particular social practices. I *am* those social practices "all the way down"; I *am*, no more and no less, the one who plays those language-games. Thus there is no possibility that I could radically fault them all; to think that I could is a transcendental illusion of the worst sort.

So it seems that the later Wittgenstein has scotched the threat of philosophical nihilism by undermining rationality-as-representation and the Enlightenment picture of the self; but it also seems that, like Heidegger, he has done it at a very high price. His attention to the actual grammar of our rules and of our self-consciousness has made us aware of our inescapable immersion in the "scene" of our language-games, and thus has shown us the folly of imagining some sort of wholesale philosophical alienation from them, but the cost of that intimacy is apparently the loss of any basis for radical moral and intellectual criticism of the form of life we actually live. Specifically, we seem to lose *ourselves* as such potentially radical critics. Criticism of one's life seems to lose not so much its standards as its source. There seems to be no fixed point, no substantial entity, from which it now could issue. Who is left to be the prophetic voice proclaiming the vanity of all we are? No one, apparently: that voice is a transcendental illusion.

The danger in this, of course, is the loss of those human excellences that, since the seventeenth century, at least, have been tied to metaphysical ego-subjectivity. If the autonomous Enlightenment self disappears into its constitutive language-games, which it neither creates nor authorizes (rather, they create and authorize the self who plays them), then will not the Enlightenment ethical and political ideals of individual self-determination, of individual privacy ("rights") held against the power of the crowd, and of personal freedom of thought and conscience, disappear as well? Will not the *ethical* reality of the autonomous individual self vanish in favor of a linguistic/moral/political (and perhaps ultimately *metaphysical*) holism—and historicism—that runs the risk of totalitarian identification with some transpersonal authority, a risk just mentioned in connection with Heidegger? If so, then later Heidegger and later Wittgenstein, for all their very real differences of rhetoric and philosophical background, look very much of a piece on essential matters. They stand or fall together, or so it seems.

But perhaps that is too simple. It is true, I believe, that both later Heidegger and later Wittgenstein ought to be seen as anti-Enlightenment thinkers. Through their attentions to language, both are trying to wean us away from Cartesian metaphysical ego-subjectivity and in particular away from the Kantian refinement of Cartesianism that pictures the human being as a self-given center of potentially autonomous will: the Enlightenment self, the transcendental subject. Both Heidegger and Wittgenstein are, therefore, trying to uncover a source of linguistic authority—authority for what to say when—outside individual consciousness altogether. That means that for both there must be a radical rethinking of what *any* substantive claim of authority—epistemic, ethical, political—comes to. If language, which one might call the ultimate and essential human social practice, is not—whether through rules, intentions, interpretations, or feelings—authorized by the individual self who speaks it, then *no* social practice is finally so authorized. If *linguistic* authority doesn't reside originally in the individual, if I cannot in the first instance make my words mean what I want them to mean (and I *cannot*), then *no* real authority resides there. And that is so because any claim to epistemic or ethical authority in a particular instance must itself be a claim made *in language*, and must therefore trade upon some prior linguistic authorization. *All* authority is finally linguistic authority: that is why a perspicuous presentation of language is the key to the question of philosophical nihilism. The Heideggerian and Wittgensteinian attacks on what we might call *individual speaking*, as opposed to the speaking of language per se, are at bottom attacks on the metaphysical ego, on the transcendental subject, and are therefore attacks on that ego-subject as the source of all legitimate epistemic and ethical authority.

So both Heidegger and Wittgenstein may correctly be said to stand aside from the ego-referenced metaphysics of language and human culture that has nourished some of our most central ethical and political ideals. Were their alienation to become general, it might work to put those ideals themselves in jeopardy. We must admit in all fairness, I believe, that it is not clear to what extent these ideals can survive—much less flourish—without their wonted philosophical foundation. Certainly, because they are so inconvenient for all the forms of tyranny we are heir to, these ideals are fragile and have proved in the past to need all the intellectual support we could muster. Even those of us who have no illusions as to the degree to which abstract philosophical ideas today directly make a political difference in the Western democracies may nevertheless begin to be fearful about the long-term effects of the Heideggerian and Wittgensteinian critiques, especially when we consider that whatever alternatives these thinkers offer are so hazy by comparison to what they demolish. Poetry may make nothing happen, as Auden says, but philosophical ideas have at least *helped* some things happen in our history; and the manifest *absence* of philosophical ideas, their removal without corresponding replacement, may be an even more effective agent of change. One thinks here of the story with which Tolstoy opens *A Confession.*

S., a clever and truthful man, once told me the story of how he ceased to believe. On a hunting expedition, when he was already twenty-six, he once, at the place where they had put up for the night, knelt down in the evening to pray—a habit retained from childhood. His elder brother, who was at the hunt with him, was lying on some hay and watching him. When S. had finished, and was settling down for the night, his brother said to him: "So you still do that?"

They said nothing more to one another. But from that day S. ceased to say his prayers or go to church. And now he has not prayed, received communion, or gone to church, for thirty years. And this not because he knows his brother's convictions and has joined in them, nor because he has decided anything in his own soul, but simply because the word spoken by his brother was like the push of a finger on a wall that was ready to fall of its own weight. The word only showed that where he thought there was faith, in reality there had long been an empty space, and that therefore the utterance of words and the makings of signs of the cross and genuflections while praying were quite senseless actions. Becoming conscious of their senselessness he could not continue them.[1]

In light of Wittgenstein's and Heidegger's very powerful ridicule of our habitual philosophical prayers to the ego-subject, one wonders whether our own walls of liberal democratic faith will continue to stand.

Of course, that way of putting the matter makes it sound as if such collapse were clearly a bad thing, and perhaps one shouldn't assume that either of our philosophers would see it that way. Heidegger in particular is no democrat, as I have already noted, and Wittgenstein's politics are notoriously difficult to make out. Maybe both would welcome apocalyptic change of this sort: the end of a civilization that has played itself out. Nonetheless, it is likely that most of *us* would not welcome it, or would welcome it only with very strict conditions attached. So perhaps it is worth

1. Leo Tolstoy, *A Confession, The Gospel in Brief, What I Believe*, p. 5.

trying to draw the distinction between Heidegger and Wittgenstein a bit more firmly and deeply. Although both are antipathetic to the metaphysical faith of the Enlightenment, I do not believe that their critiques of it leave them in the same place. If the work of both philosophers suggests the need for a basic change in our typical ethical and political conceptions and arrangements, and I believe that it does, then it is certainly not clear that in both cases the anticipated change is in the same direction. This difference, if it exists, may *make* a great deal of difference to us in the long run. A great deal may turn on just how one responds to, or just how one characterizes the implications of, the eclipse of Enlightenment faith in the autonomous self. To plot such headings is in any case very difficult, and especially when, as with both Heidegger and Wittgenstein, the thinker in question explicitly tries to avoid large-scale philosophical "views." Certainly a good measure of speculation will be necessary, and I might get some things wrong. But the potential importance of the matter encourages me to try.

III

The fundamental matter at issue here is *authority*. Linguistic authority first of all is challenged to answer what reason, what right, have I for saying *this* at *that* point, for using *this* vocabulary rather than *that*, for choosing *this* particular word, for following *this* rule of grammar? Consequent upon the primacy of linguistic authority all the other forms of authority, including the epistemic, the ethical, and the political, are challenged as well. Taken together, all these queries constitute the basic question pushed to (or perhaps past) its sensible limit by the fantasy of philosophical nihilism: by what authority do I live my life— speak my language, assert my truths, inculcate my values, love my friends, war against my enemies—in good faith? For there is no question that I *do* these things, and there is equally no question that I feel I need the *right* to do them. The general question of authority, of right, of justification, of ground, is for us sensible and inescapable. We understand it, and we recognize that, in some way or other, it must be answered—even if that answer doesn't look like what we have been taught to expect as an answer.

Both later Heidegger and later Wittgenstein address the general philosophical question of my life's authority by addressing the question's essential appearance in my authoritative use of language to characterize and to account for that life. Their attacks on rationality-as-representation and the Enlightenment self, particularly as these correlative conceptions surface in connection with such traditional philosophical accounts of language as representationalism and expressionism, are attempts to displace ego-subjectivity as the ground of all intelligent critical reflection and practice. For Heidegger, as we have seen, the autonomous ego is shoved aside in favor of primordially speaking *Logos*. It is not I, the individual human being, who first of all and essentially speaks, but language itself. Thus the ultimate authority—an authority I may on occasion borrow in its service, just as my own individual self-consciousness is borrowed in *its* exercise from something beyond it—is the authority of *Logos* itself, and that is to say, an authority located in nothing that I, the individual, can philosophically represent or personally identify with.

In later Heidegger, therefore, the question of authority, linguistic and otherwise, does not disappear, nor does its form essentially alter; it is only that the sole truthful answer to that question becomes a mystification, in traditional philosophical terms. That the question does not change its essential form—and this is, as we will see, a crucial point—is best shown by the way in which Heidegger's answer to it remains rhetorically *theological*, as it were: the condition of all our knowing and meaning—namely, the *Logos*—is, like a god, precisely that which itself can never be metaphysically known or named. The condition of our control and self-control through language is just that which itself can never be controlled, and certainly not by us. Thus *Logos*, in Heidegger's account the fundamental condition of the world (that is, the world of *things* which to us only appear by being named in our language), lies completely outside the world that it creates and sustains through its words; it is, in that respect, holding the place (the grammatical place, Wittgenstein might say) formerly occupied by a god. The theological metaphor can be pushed even farther, since the Heideggerian *Logos* appears in his language for it as *single* and *centralized* and *numinous*, just as a god is. Even if the truthful answer to the question of authority cannot be metaphysically represented, as Heidegger insists, it must still be named and textually placed. Both the pretentious names he gives it (for example, *Logos*, the One, the All) and the ways he locates its occurrence in other texts (for example, in the dark sayings of Heraclitus) are calculated to indicate and to strengthen our sense of its self-identity and its numinosity.[2] In Heidegger's rhetoric, and in the rhetoric of those from whom he borrows the name, *Logos* appears as *mysterium tremendum et fascinans*, as the holy center of our life.

So, the Heideggerian grammar and rhetoric of authority remain essentially theological; or, putting it less figuratively perhaps, they are still inherently *patriarchal*. Authority comes to the human being from without, from *above*, from a place properly unoccupiable by those that are finally governed by it. *Die Sprache spricht*, and one must in stillness first listen to and then obey "*the* law"—however allegedly "gentle"—that comes with that speaking (*On the Way to Language*, pp. 128–29). Given such a patriarchal image of authority, obedience is the key to my good faith. My authority, the authority of the life I actually speak and live, derives solely from the quality of obedience that my life shows. I am responsible only for attentively listening to *Logos* as it speaks and then for conscientiously doing what it says. There is, after all, no conceivable authority outside my relation to *Logos*, and that relation is one that puts all authority on the *Logos* side. I can speak (think, act) only in the language I have been taught, and am always being taught, by the speaking of language itself; I am not my own creature to make, nor do I make the words that make me. Obedience to those words, that world, is ethically required of me only because it is all that is possible for me anyway. Language does not speak by *my* consent, after all. All that remains to me is to *hear* it speak, to still the chatter with which I am tempted to drown it out, and by do-

2. See, for example, the essay on Heraclitus in Martin Heidegger, *Early Greek Thinking*, pp. 59ff.

ing so to release myself into the possibility of full response to what I hear.

Heidegger's later work is full of references to listening, to keeping quiet, to the patient stillness required for the kind of thinking he asks of us. As has often been remarked, he seems to be trying to substitute, as the basic image of human sentience, the metaphor of *hearing* for the more familiar Platonic one of *vision*. And all this is directly connected to what one might call the most obviously ethical theme of his later work, namely, his critique of technology and of the form of life it shapes. Technology, by its apparent power of converting all of what there is into *Bestand*—into "standing reserve" to be used at the will of, and for the good of, human beings—strengthens us in the temptation to see ourselves as self-given, self-directing centers of purposeful action. Surrounded by the paraphernalia of technology, and by its sedative first-fruits, we can easily forget that we always answer to something beyond ourselves. As technocrats we seem to be fully in control, to be shaping reality to fit our own chosen ends: to be giving the orders, not following them. In contrast to this sort of *hubris* and systematic self-deception, Heidegger promotes *Gelassenheit*, a "letting-be" that is a mode of sensitive and discreet receptivity, not bumptious "activity." Thinking comes to be understood, not as a pragmatic attempt to cope with or to control reality for human purposes, but as "openness to the mystery"; action is not our technological manipulation of "raw material" into consumer "goods," but is "releasement toward things" (Heidegger, *Discourse on Thinking*, pp. 54–55).

There is much here that is attractive, of course, especially to a civilization perhaps losing its zest for the long race and beginning also to be aware of the environmental and social costs of its comforts, but it is too easy to overlook the total economy within which Heidegger's exaltation of *Gelassenheit* is presumed to have its place. To "release" in this way, to "let be," is not just to *spare*, as one might let a harmless insect be, or even just to *let go of*, as one might gratefully let slip the heavy levers of power. It is also to *release oneself into*. It is to put oneself into the keeping of something else. To listen to the speaking of *Logos* is always preparatory to doing what it says. Obedience to *"the law"* becomes the fundamental ground of justification and authority. It is therefore finally *oneself*—oneself understood as something fixed and essential, as "subject"—that one "releases," since to listen silently to *Logos* is to be furnished the language within which any and all of one's self-understanding will henceforth take place. One thus will come to know oneself only as one is known, known by the other who speaks and tells one who one is. One will know oneself only as the creature created by that Word that sounds in the voices of the fathers.

That may seem to some philosophical readers to put it too fancifully, but the point here is to see that there *is* a fancy, a fantasy, behind Heidegger's language. The critique of technology, the references to the lost integrity of peasant life, the attention to the pre-Socratics, the veneration of Hölderlin, the quasi-religious rhetoric of silence and *Gelassenheit*—all these hang together, and the key to this unity is the fantasy of original human soundness—now, alas, lost. It is the fantasy of a former Eden, spoiled by human self-assertion against our proper place within it, but recoverable only if we will listen, recall (*Andenken*), and return.

The connections of this fantasy to Heidegger's work could be developed in many directions, of course, but perhaps the most important for us here is the way in which such dreams of innocence lost and regained seem to include, if not even to require, social structures of the most authoritarian sort. Any Garden must, it seems, have its patriarch to walk there in the cool of the evening. What is demanded of its other inhabitants as the condition of their living there is absolute obedience to his commands. The integrity of human life, thus construed, turns on our willingness to find ourselves in an order—a vocabulary, a set of institutions—given to us from without, one might even say from *above*, and then to borrow our own authority to speak and act only from that. It means to surrender any claims to individual autonomy, to see them as instances of a prideful and false "humanism": to find *"the* law" only in what is spoken to one, not in what—*per impossibile*—one would, if one could, say for oneself. And this "law" is the fugitive god for whom we are now enjoined to wait, the one who alone can save us (as Heidegger told *Der Spiegel*): the patriarchal Word that will enjoy and compel our wholehearted assent to its "gentle" direction.[3]

It does not matter, of course, whether or not Heidegger himself was aware of, or happy about, this decidedly authoritarian strain at the heart of his later thinking; still less does it matter whether he had any clear ideas about how the primordial authority of *Logos*, upon the acknowledgment of which our salvation as a culture depends, could be exemplified in actual political terms. What matters is that the strain is undoubtedly and profoundly there. Heidegger's rhetoric, the fundamental economy of his later thinking, leaves one utterly submissive before language and history. Indeed, it makes a positive virtue of such a dire necessity; one must first of all listen to *Logos*, he says, and then speak only in obedient response. That is what is so worrying: humble, attentive silence, submission, and *Gelassenheit* are too easily and too often the virtues proclaimed as such for the oppressed, so that they will continue to assent to their oppression. They are qualities typically commended for those— like women and children, say, or "the people," idealized and thus patronized—over whom the patriarchal lords are wont to rule, and upon whose convenient backs the whole order of oppression rests. To honor such qualities, as later Heidegger so notably does, to make them the central marks of enlightened human being, is to open one's thinking to a certain kind of objection, or at least to license a certain kind of fear in respect of it.

For Heidegger, then, the god of the fathers remains at the center of his thinking, and this in spite of his vigorous critique of ontotheology. I do not mean, of course, that an explicitly divine (and male) metaphysical entity is still a part of his intellectual furniture; he has, I admit, apparently avoided that old-fashioned sort of *vorstellendes Denken*. But the grammatical *place* of a patriarchal god remains, nevertheless; and that is what gives rise to the threat of totalitarian oppression by the primordial Word. That grammatical place of a god is marked most clearly by Heidegger's continuing rhetorical assumption

3. The interview took place on September 23, 1966, and was published in *Der Spiegel*, May 31, 1976.

of a centralized source of sense for our particular epistemic and ethical practices. His vigorous and insightful critiques of representationalism and, especially, of expressionism effectively displaced the self as that original center of sense, but they did not touch the more deeply philosophical assumption of centrality itself—or at least they did not eradicate it, since it remains in play in the quasi-religious rhetoric of *Logos*, of primordially speaking Language.

In spite of Heidegger's own acute protests against metaphysics and ontotheology, *Logos* retains *rhetorically* the force of a god; it continues to have the status of a patriarchal *subiectum* from which all human sense and authority unilaterally descends. In his mouth 'language' becomes 'Language'; it is grammatically deified. It does not avail that Heidegger himself would certainly disavow any concrete representation of *Logos* in theological terms; the force, the reality, of the notion is given by the grammar, the rhetoric, the religious drama of Fall and Salvation, one might almost say, within which it is embedded in his work. And that grammar continues ontotheology, in the sense that it continues to refer us beyond ourselves to some single, authoritarian, patriarchal, godlike center of sense and authority: *die Sprache spricht.*

It does Heidegger no good to struggle, as he does, against the literalization of *Logos* into a name, divine or otherwise, when the whole of his rhetoric bends us in that direction. He is a prisoner, not (as he thinks) of certain philosophically corrupted *words* that must be replaced or refurbished, but of his unconscious acceptance of a particular picture of the grammar, of language and of life, within which the words must function. It is that grammatical picture which is authoritarian and patriarchal—which is, one might say, "metaphysical" or "ontotheological"—and not the words themselves. Thus if there is a substantial difference between later Heidegger and later Wittgenstein, one that would somehow remove or mitigate the threat of the kind of totalitarian architecture of authority, linguistic and otherwise, we have just noted, then it is a difference that will have to show itself in their grammar, not just in their words. Let us see what that difference is.

IV

I have just been calling attention to the fact that later Heidegger's critique of the self as the center of linguistic authority is not an attack, or not sufficiently an attack, on the idea of centralized authority itself. It does not sufficiently challenge the standard philosophical picture of the source of authority as something single, rationally coherent, and numinous, a *subiectum* that grants effective power to beings and their world. I have claimed that in his work the laws of authority simply get transferred from the godlike autonomous self to primordial *Logos*, a god of another sort; indeed, a god at least as fearful as the runaway self that threatens to bring on philosophical nihilism. Heidegger's apparent intention in his later work—at least this is his rhetorical *result*—is to return authority to its proper place, to restore the true center of things outside and above the human: to Language itself, the house of all Being.

It is important to see that Wittgenstein's critique runs in a very different direction. True, he wants to show the nonsense in our giving to the self the status of final and central authority, linguistic and otherwise. But—and here is the crucial difference from later Heidegger—that demonstration is not in service of locating *another* such center, not even a fundamentally mysterious and nonhuman one like the Heraclitean/Heideggerian *Logos*. It is, one might say, a demonstration in service of the grammatical *dispersal* of authority, not its centralization. Wittgenstein, one might say, is a thoroughly polytheistic thinker. His point is to show that there *is* no center of authority of the sort we have been taught to expect: not God; not the self; and not anything else—like Language—that could serve as a postphilosophical double for these rottenly metaphysical and monotheistic notions.

This is not to say, exactly, that there is *no* authority for what we say and do; it is not to say that authority is a myth that we must, with either exhilaration or despair, resign to oblivion. Rather, it is to suggest that our typically metaphysical grammar òf authority, our expectations of what it would have to look like in order to be authority at all (namely, some sort of single, central, granting source of effective power for life: a god, in other words), is faulty. What makes it possible for us to speak as we do, says Wittgenstein, is "the scene for our language-game," no more and no less. That "scene" is in no way a single, centralized entity that could double for the divine presence. It is quite the opposite: namely, a wide and indeterminate range of general facts of nature, different for the different games being played.

This is the point summarized in sections 240-42 of the *Philosophical Investigations*, remarks that conclude a major part of the discussion of rules and rule following.

> 240. Disputes do not break out (among mathematicians, say) over the question whether a rule has been obeyed or not. People don't come to blows over it, for example. That is part of the framework on which the working of our language is based (for example, in giving descriptions).
>
> 241. "So you are saying that human agreement decides what is true and what is false?"—It is what human beings *say* that is true and false; and they agree in the *language* they use. That is not agreement in opinions but in form of life.
>
> 242. If language is to be a means of communication there must be agreement not only in definitions but also (queer as this may sound) in judgments. This may seem to abolish logic, but does not do so.—It is one thing to describe methods of measurement, and another to obtain and state results of measurement. But what we call 'measuring' is partly determined by a certain constancy in results of measurement.

How is one to account for the agreement among mathematicians referred to here? This is, after all, just the sort of case in which some appeal to metaphysical authority has its ancestral home. That the mathematicians agree about the rules in question is a *fact*, of course; but it is not, it seems, *just* a fact, like the fact that most of us get thirty-two teeth. It is a fact that apparently needs to be accounted for, that needs to be buttressed by some sufficient reason. The agreement in this case, since it involves general considerations of truth and falsity, seems to us to require some special warrant to back it up; it must be more than an accident. Mathematicians must agree about the rules *because* . . . , where the ellipsis is to be completed with some such phrase as "they are in perfect touch with mathematical reality" or "they jointly hear *die Sprache spricht*" or whatever.

In his remarks, Wittgenstein does not disparage our natural inclination to try to account for this typical unanimity among mathematicians, nor does he find ridiculous our desire that any account of it should recognize it as something special and worthy of note. Our lives do turn, after all, on considerations of what is true and what is false, in a way they don't turn on the usual number of our teeth. Our general agreement in the latter fact is (at present, anyway) trivial; our general agreement in matters of truth and falsity is not. And since it is just those latter considerations that are at issue here, it is perfectly appropriate that we should wonder how such considerations are possible for us at all. If our ability to make sensible judgments about truth and falsity ultimately depends on our ability to agree on, for example, whether a certain rule has actually been obeyed—and that seems to be one of the points to emerge from Wittgenstein's discussion prior to section 240—then it is no surprise that we want to know how such agreement can take place.

The question is: What sort of explanation of agreement do we expect? What sort of answer to the question of authority will count *as* an answer? It is here that Wittgenstein's originality begins to make itself felt, for he is resisting both the standard sort of philosophical answer *and* the idea that the question cannot be answered at all. He has, he thinks, the truthful answer to it, thus disappointing both the pragmatist who wants to dismiss the question as transcendental nonsense and the pessimist (whether "weak" or "strong") who thinks it real but unanswerable. But Wittgenstein's is an answer of a very peculiar sort, and will not please the traditional philosopher either; so everyone is frustrated: skeptic, pragmatist, and metaphysician.

His answer is peculiar more because of its form than its content. This is clear in section 241, which opens with a quoted question tempting Wittgenstein to assume a standard sort of philosophical position, one that tries to use the fact of human agreement *itself* as the "ground" of truth and falsity. This would be not only to accept the philosophical question of authority as legitimate, but also to answer it by construing authoritative distinctions between truth and falsity as a kind of convention, arrived at by human beings to facilitate their relations to their own desires and to one another. On this account, deliberate human agreement grants authority; truth and falsity are finally and appropriately distinguished from one another only by what human beings have explicitly agreed to. This is, whatever its merits or faults, at least a recognizably philosophical answer to our wonderment at how truth and falsity are possible at all. It, like other such answers, assumes that whatever authority there is must be *singular* and *centralized*; authority must still be granted monotheistically, so to speak, and in this case is granted by the divinized self, individual or collective, in agreeing to its conventional discriminations.

In the second half of section 241, Wittgenstein clearly rejects this as an account of what he is saying, but not because as an account it has the wrong elements in play. It just has them arranged wrongly, presented unperspicuously, so that a misleading impression of our grammar of authority is created. It has these elements arranged around a metaphysical center, as it were, rather than as scattered in a range. It is perfectly correct that human agreement—agreement in judgments, not just in definitions (sec. 242)—is fundamental to authoritative discrimination between truth and falsity, but we forget that such agreement, understood as voluntary human action, is not itself centralized and primordial. It too depends upon something else, what Wittgenstein calls here agreement in "form of life." Our agreement with one another is not finally voluntary, or self-given; it is the natural result of a whole range of facts over which we have no control, those "extremely general facts of nature" that constitute the "scene for our language-game." It is agreement understood as a brute *congruence*, not as deliberate identity of affirmation. Agreement there is, to be sure, and that agreement is, as the conventionalist maintains, fundamental to any of our claims of authority; but *pace* the conventionalist, that agreement is ultimately not to be explained by anything that can be represented, pictured, as a metaphysical center from which everything else flows, like a god or a self or a constitutional convention of selves. Congruence has no center from which it springs; it is coincidence of outline, nothing more.

The reference to a way of *picturing* our agreement and my use of the image of congruence, of coincidence of outline, in that respect are not inessential, because I am claiming that Wittgenstein's originality here consists in—as he himself affirms—his illuminating *arrangement* of our ideas, a rearrangement that radically alters their customary physiognomy. His point is not to offer us a radically new answer to our philosophical questions about truth, agreement, and authority, or even to disabuse us of the questions; it is to get us to see that an answer—an answer that is not a philosophical theory—can be found in the elements already given, if only they are looked at from another perspective.

It is the *picture*, the grammatical image of authority in play here, that is the key. Is it an image of centrality, of a single and central source of power? Or is it an image that cannot be construed in that way? Wittgenstein is trying for the latter, of course. If we can come to see our agreement in form of life, that is, our brute congruence in reactions and response, as the *background* for all authoritative affirmations, for all the specific overt agreements we make with one another, then we can account for the possibility of those agreements in a way that preserves their wonderfulness, their *Pathos* (to use a powerful word of Wittgenstein's own), but at the same time refuses to become ontotheological.

A background, *qua* background, cannot become a figure; and that is what "the scene for our language-game," our "agreement in form of life," must be for Wittgenstein: the background to *all* thinking, including *this* thinking about the background, and any of its extensions. If the background cannot become a figure, then it cannot become a double for the divine; and the centralized, patriarchal, incipiently totalitarian architecture of authority is therefore displaced. But it is displaced without leaving a void where a figure should go, since the background is now to be seen there, and a background, while certainly not a figure, is not a void either.

So for Wittgenstein our general agreement with one another—the agreement in form of life that originally makes possible all our discriminations between truth and falsity, right and wrong, beauty and ugliness, and so on—can also be seen to be our final *authority* for those discriminations, and thus for all the social practices in which they figure; but it is an authority that resists being construed as a single organizing principle of the life it constitutes. Human agreement, understood now as a background of natural congruence in "how to go on," cannot easily be hypostatized as a quasi-divine entity or "explanation," any more than the background necessary to a Gestalt figure can sensibly be considered another figure simultaneously alongside or behind the first, "causing" or "explaining" its appearance. Our general agreement with one another is not *one big fact*, so to speak, one that somehow "causes" or "explains" all the others, but simply the happy concurrence of an indefinite number of little facts, facts of physiology, psychology, social organization, and so on.

This agreement is therefore just another name for *nature*, but nature de-divinized, as it were, nature always written with a lower case 'n'. Wittgenstein's later thought thus can be seen as a part of an ethical and intellectual tradition that firmly sets human life within the natural world, a nature to which it finally answers for the authority of its practices; but it is a nature not conceived as organized on some single, rational principle. It is not nature understood as part of the Great Chain of Being, not nature that is an emanation of something "higher." It is not nature in any way "idealized," or seen as the expression of some controlling idea or form. Rather, it is nature *dispersed*, nature *proliferated*: a topography with no central feature.

Yet is it, as I have said, a nature that still possesses its *Pathos*, its impressiveness. Our human lives together, resting as they do upon an agreement—an aggregation of individual correspondences—that is beyond our capacities to explain or to control, can now be seen as the fragile webs they are. The natural world that fosters such delicacy can thus be seen as a kind of miracle, a proper object of wonder. It cannot be *worshipped*, since it is not one thing, or even an organized pattern; but it can still be respected. It can still call us to a certain kind of *atten-*

tion (*Achtung*) in regard to the natural and social relationships we necessarily inhabit.

The background of our natural agreement, because it exemplifies no particular idea, because it cannot be pictured as some central source of meaning, cannot present itself as something to be *obeyed*; but, seen in the right light, the appeal to nature can still have that *Pathos* that can quiet our anxious fears of rootlessness, our fears that our lives have floated free from anything real. It will be a reminder sufficient to remind us that our ethical and intellectual lives do answer to something beyond themselves, something that sets limits—however distant or flexible—to what we can think true, good, and beautiful. Yet this understanding of the natural rootedness of our lives will resist any totalitarian architecture, since the nature being appealed to as a limit is not a figure, not a trope, for any particular order or idea. It is not nature understood as any sort of organized Garden, to which we must obediently return for our well-being. It is, rather, a nature we have never strayed from, except when we have forgotten it in our philosophical flights of fancy. Because it is not idealized, it is not a nature that can at a stroke solve our ethical and intellectual problems; it will not tell us what to think or what to do. But it can assure us that as we try to decide these things, our efforts, successful or unsuccessful, are nourished by the common world—the "scene for our language-game"— that we share with others. That is, perhaps, enough to answer the threat of philosophical nihilism but not enough to threaten one with an equally frightful totalitarianism of the Word.

V

To recognize this difference beween Heidegger and Wittgenstein does not, however, banish all our ethical qualms. Wittgenstein's reflections on the sense of our language and its roots in our natural congruence, while less obviously open than Heidegger's to reactionary ethical and political implications, nevertheless alter the familiar conventions of post-Enlightenment moralizing. It is no longer so simple to ground our typically individual-

istic and democratic ethical and political convictions by reference to a metaphysics that privileges the self as the autonomous
atom out of which all linguistic and social reality is constructed.
No longer can we claim that our attribution of inviolable moral
and political rights to individuals is justified by the epistemological and metaphysical priority of the 'I'. On the contrary,
Wittgenstein's reflections show the patent nonsense of treating
the 'I' as a self-given *primum mobile*; one learns to use the first
person—one becomes an 'I'—just as one learns everything else
basic to one's language, namely, by being taught it in language
by a community of others, not by creating it on one's own. As
the one who can say 'I', one is not "the limit of the world"; one
is not a metaphysical self, a transcendental subject, causally
and epistemologically independent of the world one surveys.
Rather, one is a part of that world, a world understood as a holistic community of agents and speakers, a world made possible
by our natural agreement—i.e., our normal coincidence—with
one another in what we are inclined to do and say.

This is not to say, of course, that our comfortable and cherished beliefs about the supreme worth of the individual and
about the wickedness of totalitarian political structures will have
to go in order to be consistent with Wittgenstein's thinking.
That would be simply to reverse the Enlightenment thinkers:
whereas they assumed that the truth of their ethical conception
had to be referred to a prior metaphysical ground, we would
now be assuming that the loss of the wonted metaphysical
ground they claimed must mean the falsity (or at least the objectionable "relativity") of the ethical conception formerly erected
upon it. We would thus be continuing to think within the philosophical frame of metaphysics itself: we would still be assuming
the necessity to link truth to some metaphysical ground for it.

But the point of Wittgenstein's later work is to question just
that assumption. His aim is to point out the nonsense involved
in always requiring a *reason* construed philosophically sufficient
for what one says and does. This does not mean that there *are*
no good reasons for honoring individual rights against state
power, say, or that such reasons, even if they exist, don't really
matter; it simply means that what reasons there are, and what
reasons we have for paying attention to them, are not indepen-

dent of those "extremely general facts of nature" that we are inclined to forget or to despise in our philosophical thinking. It is those facts, those wonderful accidents of natural congruence, that account for—that make possible—our (typical) agreement "in judgments" (sec. 242), or our (untypical) lack of it.

And these facts are not, and truly cannot become, a philosophical *ground* in the old sense. As the brute and independent facts they are, they represent no "idea." They are bound together by no necessity. They cannot go proxy for some centralized god or Reason that accounts for their being what they are. They are just those things themselves, with nothing more "behind" them. They are the bedrock upon which the spade of philosophical intellect is turned—or, rather, they are lots of individual stones, dispersed in a stratum, not a single megalith that could achieve numinosity in our gaze. This is what is most difficult to characterize in Wittgenstein's work: the way it is dispersive without being reductive; the way it breaks up and scatters all the false centers and sources of meaning—self, rules, language, gods— that metaphysical philosophy postulates, while never becoming a familiar sort of iconoclasm. His point is not to smash the idols in order to make straight the way for the True God to come; rather, his is an attempt to preserve our capacity for awe, for appreciating the *Pathos* of things, against our desire to find something to worship.

That, of course, is a very difficult distinction for us to draw, much less to feel and live. To be able to honor it would give one's life and world a very different physiognomy, one we don't have easy words for. God-ridden as we are, our temptation is always to trade *Pathos* for worship, to translate our childlike wonder at the contingency of things into double-minded self-abasement before an intelligible power—double-minded because that prostration is, as we surely believe, our only chance to get our own way, to survive and to flourish, in the long run. Gods and fathers, even jealous and capricious ones, are in the end great comforts, because there's always the chance of getting on their good side. And it is now a cliché, of course, that we don't scruple to invent these figures when need be.

What is most remarkable, and least remarked, about Wittgenstein's work is its capacity for exhibiting a kind of spirituality

without worship—or, to put it a bit more concretely, its capacity
to allow for meaning (in all its senses) without presupposing
some hidden, central source of it. "Meaning is a physiognomy,"
he says at section 568: a wonderful image, since the meaning of
a face, its boredom or its wrath, is not given to it by some one of
its features, but by the whole range of them working together.
The meaning is dispersed throughout the whole, is in its total
"aspect," not centered in a particular part. It is not just the eyes
or the mouth that make up a human countenance; a laughing or
a scowling face has no true center. And even a dead face, or one
of the flower-countenances painted by Archimboldo, is still a
face, for all its lack of animation. The presence of a (hidden)
soul does not create a face out of brute facts. It is more like this:
the facts, arranged as they happen to be, let us see (sometimes)
the presence of a soul. Just so, any meaning, any significant
physiognomy, emerges from a fortuitous constellation of particular contingencies; not from some metaphysical center like a
god or a rule or an autonomous self.

This emergence of meaning from a range of coincidences is
what I have tried to gesture at in speaking of Wittgenstein's attempt at dispersal of the conditions of sense-making, and in trying to connect that dispersal to the *Pathos* that attaches to
grammatical illusions and philosophical problems.

> 110. "Language (or thought) is something unique"—
> this proves to be a superstition (*not* a mistake!), itself
> produced by grammatical illusions.
> And now the impressiveness [*das Pathos*] retreats to
> these illusions, to the problems.

In the next section he claims that philosophical problems have
the character of *depth*: "They are deep disquietudes; their roots
are as deep in us as the forms of our language and their significance is as great as the importance of our language" (sec. 111).
But then comes a surprise, for this depth is, he says, the same
as the depth of a grammatical *joke*. Such a joke is founded on a
pure linguistic contingency, such as the fact that in English the
word 'bank' can mean both the land at the edge of a river and a
depository for money. The depth of the joke, the way it touches
us so deeply, depends upon the consequences, comic or horrify-

ing, that flow from this happenstance. The joke is an anxious acknowledgment that much can come from very little: that from such "meaningless" accidents, grammatical and otherwise, wonderful or terrible trains of consequence can run. The power of the joke to move us, then, turns on its recognition—and perhaps its simultaneous camouflage or mitigation—of the *Pathos* of such contingency at the bottom of our lives. The depth of such a joke is that it *isn't* "deep"; we laugh because the reason at work here isn't a "reason" at all. It is just a brute *fact* that 'bank', for example, has more than a single sense.

The standard Western philosophical or religious response to this *Pathos* is, as I have said, to convert it into worship by postulating a metaphysically sufficient reason for the fact or facts at issue, that is, to discover some sort of god behind the appearances of the fortuitous yet decisive happenstances that grant sense. Heidegger's *die Sprache*, understood and employed by him as the latest name for the Heraclitean *Logos*, is such a double-god; so, of course, is the Enlightenment (or the Romantic) conception of the self-given self. One might say, following Wittgenstein's lead in section 110, that such responses are fundamentally *superstitious* ones. We need to believe that, for example, "Language (or thought) is something unique" (put into Heidegger's vocabulary, that *die Sprache spricht*) or that the self is an autonomous atom of agency, because otherwise we would have to admit that we are essentially out of our own control, that there is perhaps nothing we can do to get what we want (and think we deserve). Language *must* be unique, because there must be—we think—evidence of some spiritual center there, of something more than "mere fact," that grants sense to sounds, to marks, to events, to lives. For philosophy, language has become the last stronghold of "spirit." But Wittgenstein calls this superstition. Superstition is a way of imposing oneself on accident, of insisting that there are rules (spilled salt, broken mirrors, rabbits' feet) that govern and explain one's good and bad fortune. It is a denial of the *Pathos* of pure contingency, of meaning as a physiognomy constellated out of happenstance.

As I read him, Wittgenstein's great distinction in his later work is his power to resist superstition of this sort, and to foster such resistance in others. He is always showing us the nonsense involved in asserting metaphysical centers and sources of meaning, whether these be self-interpreting rules, self-given selves, or self-creating divine beings. All these devices, so attractive to us, are revealed as "the trick of a cheat" (*Philosophical Remarks*, p. 7). All are attempts to deny the true depth of philosophy, which is the true depth of life itself, namely, the pure contingency and independence of the conditions of all meaning. The deep *Pathos* of philosophy and life is just that acknowledgment: that there is no single, central source and ground for the sense we happen to make to ourselves and one another; that sense appears as a face does, constellated out of elements fortuitously dispersed in a field, with no-thing as its source and center and guarantor.

I have termed Wittgenstein's attention to this dispersion of the conditions of sense, his attention to the *Pathos* of the contingency and independence of the elements of our jointly constellated physiognomies of meaning, a kind of *spirituality*. It is, I want to say, a spirituality without the "spirit," a life without any ghosts. The words are vague but (so far) indispensable. One needs them to remind one that for Wittgenstein philosophy was a struggle, against great odds, to attain the sound human understanding and life, not a cool attempt to paint reality's portrait: "It was true to say that *our* considerations could not be scientific ones" (sec. 109; my emphasis). In his hands, the technique of dispersal is in service of deepening one's sensibility; it is a way of heightening one's capacity for lively yet humble response to things.

In the *Phaedo* (64A) Socrates says that to do philosophy is to practice dying.[4] One can hear the crucial phrase in at least two ways. Practice can be understood as a *prior rehearsal*, as when one says that the actor practices his lines, or it can be understood to refer to a *consistent course of action*, as when one says that the physician practices medicine. Taken in the second of these ways, Wittgenstein's philosophical work is truly the practice of dying, in the sense that it is the consistent attempt to disabuse one of one's philosophical intimations of immortality. It assembles reminders that all the "centers of meaning" in life

4. I am indebted here to Roy Holland. See his essay "Suicide," pp. 72–85.

have no center, that nothing—and certainly not the individual self—has an existence or a "sense" independent of a happenstance (those "extremely general facts of nature": "the scene for our language-game") that cannot be "idealized" into a god or a reason.

Stated so flatly, of course, the idea may seem trite. (Aren't we all—except for the lunatic fringe—already completely convinced "naturalists"?) What is remarkable, however, is the force it actually has in Wittgenstein's hands. He *shows* us, over and over again, both how we all, even the most tough-minded, are tempted to deny such contingency (through the fetish of the Rule, for example) and also how such denials cannot withstand the light of day. Fleshed out with his remarks and reminders, the idea is no longer just an idea; it is an experience. We *feel* the *Pathos*, the wonder, that there is something (that is, something meaningful) rather than nothing. We wonder at the existence of the world.[5]

And this *Pathos* takes us very far away from deadness and apathy. We do not lose interest in things once we appreciate their utter contingency, or at least we *need* not do so; it can be instead a spur to deeper care for them. One does not love a child the less once one realizes the astronomical odds against the existence of just this particular person; on the contrary, that precarious individuality adds to, perhaps in some moods almost constitutes, the child's extraordinary preciousness. Or it *can* do so, in certain circumstances, circumstances themselves equally contingent and precarious of course. And so it can begin to seem wonderful that anything, including this, can seem wonderful, can become an object of our wonder. How lucky we are, how wonderful it is, that it does; if it does. And sometimes, at least, it does.

Does this Wittgensteinian cultivation of wonder at the existence of the world furnish us with an ethical conception? Does it fill out the notion of the sound human life in such a way that it can serve as a coherent, comprehensive, and refreshing alternative to the ethical and metaphysical "humanism" characteristic of the modern West? At this stage of the appropriation of Wittgenstein's work, it would be impudent to try to say one way or

5. Rush Rhees, "Wittgenstein's Lecture on Ethics."

the other. To this point we philosophers have mostly concentrated on finding our way about in that work itself; it has not yet very much stimulated us to "thoughts of [our] own" (preface, p. x). There are signs that this professional captivity is slowly coming to an end, almost forty years after the publication of the *Philosophical Investigations*; but it is still too early to see what, if anything, will be the permanent result.

One tempting sort of misunderstanding may be anticipated and set aside, however. There is certainly no hope of, so to speak, starting over from the *null-punkt*, of trying to generate a new form of ethical life *ex nihilo*. If Wittgenstein's work is to have any fruitful influence, that influence will show itself in how we face the ethical and political lives we are given *now* to live in: in how we will approach, characterize, seek to account for, seek to resolve or to surrender to, the various agreements and disagreements we now find with one another. The point is not, *per impossibile*, to wipe the slate clean and begin again, with *Pathos* as our master concept; the point is our *attitude*, to use a hopeless word, toward what is already written there. What shall we say about these agreements and disagreements? Are they to be objects of fear, of curiosity, of condescension, of scorn? Shall we take them for granted and try to make the best of them? Shall we see them—the disagreements in particular—as dire threats to be overcome, by main force if necessary? Or shall we treat them, more complacently, as examples of the infancy of the race, inevitably to be left behind if we are lucky enough to have a long future on the planet? What would be the ethical result of our wondering at, and thus paying a certain kind of attention to, the range of brute contingencies that let such agreements and disagreements be in the first place?

The questions are not to be answered here; it is enough to raise them, and thus to set the terms for a course of reflection that doesn't so much take for granted the ordinary frame of philosophical inquiry. But at least this much is immediately clear: ethical agreement and disagreement cannot be assumed to be peculiar. How we ultimately know (or don't know) what to say about good and evil is, for Wittgenstein, not a different matter from how we ultimately know (or don't know) that the '+2' rule has been followed or that Granchester is over *that* way.

Our ability to make sense, and thus to speak the truth and to tell lies, to ourselves or to one another, is finally to be accounted for only by appropriate reference to "the scene for our language-game." What can make this reference an *end* to our traditional philosophical, religious and ethical questions without yet being an *answer* to them, is just the difference between wonder and worship, a difference finally to be appreciated only by encountering it in the work, like Wittgenstein's, it makes possible. Not, of course, that our philosophical and religious and ethical sensibilities are extirpated or even blunted by such reference to the "extremely general facts of nature" that our lives so radically depend on; instead, those sensibilities are deepened, and preserved against an always premature dessication, by an acknowledgment of their own—and our—contingency, and thus of the fragile and pathetic mortality of all that we most love.

Bibliography

Baier, Annette. *Postures of the Mind*. Minneapolis: University of Minnesota Press, 1985.

Baker, Andrew W. "Nestroy and Wittgenstein: Some Thoughts on the Motto to the *Philosophical Investigations*." *German Life and Letters* 39:2 (January 1986): 161-67.

Chomsky, Noam. "A Review of B. F. Skinner's *Verbal Behavior*." *Language*, vol. 35, no. 1 (1959): 26-58.

Descartes, René. *Meditations on First Philosophy*. Translated by Laurence J. Lafleur. Indianapolis: Bobbs-Merrill, 1960.

Edwards, James C. *Ethics without Philosophy: Wittgenstein and the Moral Life*. Tampa: University of South Florida Press, 1982.

Farias, Victor. *Heidegger et le nazisme*. Lagrasse, 1987.

Frankfurt, Harry G. *Demons, Dreamers, and Madmen: The Defense of Reason in Descartes's "Meditations."* Indianapolis: Bobbs-Merrill, 1970.

Heidegger, Martin. "The Age of the World Picture." In *The Question concerning Technology and Other Essays*, translated by William Lovitt. New York: Harper and Row, 1977.

———. *Being and Time*. Translated by John Macquarrie and Edward Robinson. New York: Harper and Row, 1962.

———. *Discourse on Thinking*. Translated by John M. Anderson and E. Hans Freund. New York: Harper and Row, 1966.

———. *Early Greek Thinking*. Translated by David Farrell Krell and Frank A. Capuzzi. New York: Harper and Row, 1975.

———. "The End of Philosophy and the Task of Thinking." Translated by Joan Stambaugh. In *Basic Writings*, edited by David F. Krell. London: Routledge and Kegan Paul, 1978.

———. "Letter on Humanism." Translated by F. A. Capuzzi and J. Glenn Gray. In *Basic Writings*, edited by David Farrell Krell. London: Routledge and Kegan Paul, 1978.

———. *Nietzsche*. Pfullingen: Verlag Gunther Neske, 1961.

———. *Nietzsche*. Vol. 4: *Nihilism*. Edited by David F. Krell. Translated by Frank A. Capuzzi. New York: Harper and Row, 1982.

———. "On the Essence of Truth." Translated by John Sallis. In *Basic*

Writings, edited by David Farrell Krell. London: Routledge and
Kegan Paul, 1978.

———. *On the Way to Language*. Translated by Peter D. Hertz. New
York: Harper and Row, 1971.

———. *Poetry, Language, Thought*. Translated by Albert Hofstadter.
New York: Harper and Row, 1971.

———. "The Question concerning Technology." In *The Question concerning Technology and Other Essays*, translated by William
Lovitt. New York: Harper and Row, 1977.

———. "The Word of Nietzsche: 'God is Dead.' " In *The Question concerning Technology and Other Essays*, translated by William
Lovitt. New York: Harper and Row, 1977.

Holland, Roy. "Suicide." In *Talk of God*, edited by G.N.A. Vesey. London: Macmillan, 1969.

Holtzman, Steven H., and Christopher M. Leich, eds. *Wittgenstein: To
Follow a Rule*. London: Routledge and Kegan Paul, 1981.

Kenny, Anthony. *Wittgenstein*. London: Allen Lane, 1973.

Malcolm, Norman. *Ludwig Wittgenstein: A Memoir*. London: Oxford
University Press, 1958.

Nagel, Thomas. *The View from Nowhere*. New York: Oxford University Press, 1986.

Nehamas, Alexander. *Nietzsche: Life as Literature*. Cambridge, Mass.:
Harvard University Press, 1985.

Nietzsche, Friedrich. *The Gay Science*. In *The Portable Nietzsche*,
edited and translated by Walter Kaufmann. New York: Viking,
1968.

———. "How the True World Became a Fable." In *The Twilight of the
Idols*. Reprinted in *The Portable Nietzsche*, edited by Walter
Kaufmann. New York: Viking Press, 1968.

———. *The Will to Power*. Edited by Walter Kaufmann. Translated by
Walter Kaufmann and R. J. Hollingdale. New York: Random
House, 1967.

Ott, Hugo. *Martin Heidegger: Unterwegs zu seiner Biographie*. Cam-
pus Verlag, 1988.

Rawls, John. *A Theory of Justice*. Cambridge, Mass.: Harvard University Press, Belknap Press, 1971.

Rhees, Rush. "Wittgenstein's Lecture on Ethics." *Philosophical Review*
74 (January 1965).

Rorty, Richard. *Philosophy and the Mirror of Nature*. Princeton: Princeton University Press, 1980.

Taylor, Charles. *Human Agency and Language: Philosophical Papers
I*. Cambridge: Cambridge University Press, 1985.

———. "Overcoming Epistemology." In *After Philosophy*, edited by
K. Baynes, J. Bohman, and T. MacCarthy. Cambridge, Mass.:
MIT Press, 1987.

Tolstoy, Leo. *A Confession, The Gospel in Brief, What I Believe.* Translated by A. Maude. London: Oxford University Press, 1974.

Williams, Bernard. *Ethics and the Limits of Philosophy.* Cambridge, Mass.: Harvard University Press, 1985.

Wittgenstein, Ludwig. *Nachlass.* vol. 50. Cornell edition.

_____. *Notebooks 1914-1916.* Translated by G.E.M. Anscombe. Oxford: Basil Blackwell, 1961.

_____. *On Certainty.* Translated by Denis Paul and G.E.M. Anscombe. Oxford: Basil Blackwell, 1969.

_____. *Philosophical Grammar.* Translated by A. Kenny. Oxford: Basil Blackwell, 1977.

_____. *Philosophical Investigations.* Translated by G.E.M. Anscombe. Oxford: Basil Blackwell, 1953.

_____. *Philosophical Remarks.* Translated by R. Hargreaves and R. White. Oxford: Basil Blackwell, 1975.

_____. *Remarks on the Foundations of Mathematics.* Translated by G.E.M. Anscombe. Oxford: Basil Blackwell, 1956.

_____. *Zettel.* Translated by G.E.M. Anscombe. Oxford: Basil Blackwell, 1967.

Index

DATE DUE